A Compilation of Rug A Weaving Techniques

A RUG WEAVER'S SOURCE BOOK

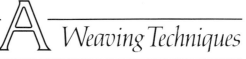
Linda C. Ligon, editor
with chapters by
Marilyn Dillard
Lynne Giles
Inga Krook
Hector Jaeger & Halcyon Schomp
Bryn Pinchin
Martha Stanley
Carol Thilenius

photography by Joe Coca   illustrations by Susan Strawn

INTERWEAVE PRESS, INC.
1984

Acknowledgements

Each author who contributed to this book had the help of friends and relatives who read, critiqued, and gave support; the book is much the stronger for that generous assistance. As editor, I'd like to give special thanks to those who worked so hard to make the book a physical reality: Marc Owens, production manager; Chris Hausman, typesetter; Kay Marquardt, pasteup; and Elizabeth Ligon, drawdown-inker.

Library of Congress Catalog Number 84-082358
ISBN #934026-16-5

Copyright ©1984

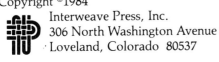 Interweave Press, Inc.
306 North Washington Avenue
Loveland, Colorado 80537

Preface

I remember my first day of classes, years ago, at the university. Walking down the long hall of the Arts and Sciences building, bits and snatches of lectures, murmurs of discussion, strident questions wafted me along as I passed each door. That so many different ideas were being expounded, so many different thoughts being thought, that it was all happening under one roof and engaging so many different people at once, seemed quite wonderful to me then.

That same feeling of excitement has carried me along as I have read and reread the chapters of this book. It speaks with many voices; you will not find final answers here. Our authors don't necessarily agree on what kind of loom to use, or what materials; all have their own techniques for controlling edges, covering warp, keeping their weaving square. What they do have in common is a thoughtful, deliberate approach to rug weaving, and the ability to make good rugs—functional, handsome rugs. They share a commitment to excellent craftsmanship, and a willingness to share; all are skillful teachers and fluent writers.

The way to use this book, I think, is to read it through, and through again before you go to your loom. If your interest is only in plain weave rugs, read all the other chapters nevertheless; you'll find ideas in them that you can make your own, that will deepen your understanding, that will confirm your own experience. You will find some repetition, some conflicting advice; weigh it carefully, and find your own path. What strikes me is that all of these different ways of weaving a rug *work!* I know it is so because I saw and handled all the rugs that are pictured here, and they are good. So may yours be, too.

Linda C. Ligon, editor

About the authors

Martha Stanley

My mother was a weaver for eight or ten years of my early childhood. Mom's loom was a strong 32" Gallinger with a sectional warp beam— she always warped sectionally. I have always admired her work, her taste, her patience and workmanship. But for an inkle band or two in high school, my own weaving did not begin for more than 20 years. It was on a funny old table loom I had bought. I wanted to weave some placemats for her, to match her dining room chairs. My notions of how to go about this first project were from casual memories of her procedures and motions. I overturned two coffee tables and wound the warp around their combined circumference. That first warp was a struggle to get on the loom, but determination prevailed and the project was a success. (Months later I bought Nell Znamierowski's book *Step by Step Weaving* and discovered that most elegant warping aid: the cross!)

I've always wanted to weave rugs. Perhaps because I love floors. Perhaps because of all the small and wonderful old Oriental rugs in her house I grew up taking for granted. We didn't have wall-to-wall carpeting, which I thought would be luxurious. But the legacy of those old Orientals I am now more and more grateful for. My models in weaving are two: the middle Eastern nomadic tribeswomen whose rugs are so strong visually, structurally and emotionally; and the pre-Columbian Peruvian weavers whose structural mastery and inventiveness will probably always remain unsurpassed.

Halcyon Schomp & Hector Jaeger

I first started weaving when I took a private class in California in 1969; Hector started by knowing me. We opened a weaving shop in Denver in the spring of 1972, and have been deeply involved ever since. We now have a mail order yarn business in Bath, Maine, where we live with our daughter, Gretchen.

Though our business keeps us busy full time, we always make time to weave—because we like it so much, because it's an important extension of the business, because we like to keep involved and moving ahead.

Hector has had art training, and is especially interested in using areas of color; my business and math background draw me more toward the intricacies of pattern. We feel this contrast is effective, and makes working together very satisfying.

Marilyn Dillard

The first rug I ever made was crocheted from curtain selvedges; I was 12 years old and the rug was a gift for my grandmother. Thirty-four years have since gone by quickly. Attending Western Michigan University, then Pasadena City College and Mt. San Antonio Junior College in southern California where I lived most of those years, plus marriage and raising two children have all taken up a good portion of time during those years.

I first learned to weave in 1972, just after our move to Colorado. Clotilde Barrett was the teacher, and she asked each of us what we intended to weave. I immediately responded "rugs", without knowing one thing about weaving them. Soon after, I was weaving rugs and discovered that rug weaving is a continual challenge, suggesting new explorations of weaving techniques as well as studies in design and color. I'm now sharing that accumulation of knowledge with other weavers through classes, lectures and workshops.

Inga Krook

I was born in Stokholm, Sweden, and grew up in the country outside the city. After high school I started to study weaving and graduated as a weaving teacher after three years of schooling.

Why I am here now, in the United States, is primarily thanks to Miss Lucy. Miss Lucy Morgan is the founder—and at the time I met her, was the director—of Penland School of Handicrafts in Penland, North Carolina. She came to Sweden visiting my weaving school, bought a piece of drawloom damask I had designed and woven, and later invited me to Penland to teach drawloom damask at her school. I was there for two summers and worked in Mary Pendleton's weaving studio and shop in Dayton, Ohio, the winter in between.

Miss Lucy was the one who found Mary Pendleton for me. Through the years, back in Sweden, I infrequently kept the contact with Mary. She often invited me to come back to the States. Finally in 1977 we started seriously discussing plans for my return.

I returned in 1979 and have since then been a teacher at the Pendleton Fabric Craft School in Sedona, Arizona. I also teach workshops and give seminars throughout the country. In my spare time—if any—I weave in my own studio, for fun and for part of my support. I specialize in rag weaving, which I love wholeheartedly.

Lynne Giles

My weaving life began 11 years ago when I had the good fortune to move to Santa Cruz. The local guild has been a steady source of instruction and inspiration. Serendipity also brought me an invaluable period of study with Lillian Elliott.

For eight years I have been teaching in a weaving studio established by Ann Thimann at the Cabrillo Stroke Center. It has been exciting to discover the broad appeal that weaving has: most of the men and women who try our looms find immediate and lasting satisfaction in the process. And the teachers—there are now five of us—learn from the work of our students.

I have four children, a garden, and a husband who has been unfailingly helpful with loom repairs and the countless quandries that weavers encounter on what one friend calls our "quest".

Carol Thilenius

I grew up in LaGrande, a small town in eastern Oregon. My interest in clothing and textiles led me to the Oregon State Home Economics School. Midway through I switched to Science Education with a special interest in marine biology. Eventually, after teaching for a few years, I got a master's degree in that field. By this time my husband, John, had his doctorate and we went where the job was, to South Dakota and Wyoming. Living in the interior and raising a family made a career in marine biology rather impractical, so I returned to my interest in textiles. A few adult education classes and workshops in spinning, weaving and dyeing, plus a lot of books have kept me intrigued ever since.

Currently, I live on the beach in Juneau, Alaska, with my husband and teenage sons, Jim and Dave. The marine biology is just outside and the weaving seems to fill all available space inside. I teach weaving at the University of Alaska-Juneau, beginning classes in the fall and intermediate classes in the spring. The intermediate class is on a different topic each year (tapestry, clothing, rugs, household textiles), so students can come back again and again. As a teacher I feel it is important to be familiar with a variety of techniques, rather than a specialist in only one. The field of weaving is so rich and varied, I know there will always be new things to try as well as old friends to return to.

Bryn Pinchin

I live and work on a mountain in Bragg Creek, Alberta. A teacher by training, I've been weaving for 12 years. I taught myself initially, but later studied with Marion Brockmann in California, and at the Banff School of Fine Arts and the Alberta College of Art. Five years ago I decided to combine vocation and avocation and teach weaving; I started Erewhon Weaving, which offers a wide range of workshops and classes for weavers at all levels. I find special satisfaction in presenting technical information in a clear and inviting way in order to encourage students to relax and explore new techniques.

I'm most comfortable weaving for a purpose within a technical framework, and so find rug weaving a joy. Lately my work has shifted to designing yardage using fine and luxurious materials such as linen and silk.

I'm married and have two daughters; our family enjoys riding and white-water canoeing. My family is most supportive of my activities, and for that I love them dearly.

Contents

Introduction

Martha Stanley

hat is a rug? That seems the place to begin. Each of us in this book has a slightly different notion of what a rug is, how it should be used, how long it should last, etc. We may not articulate that notion explicitly but it is nonetheless inherent in each approach, as inherent as the warps are in our rugs. Our assumptions, our procedures are as much guided by how we define a rug, how it fits into our lives, as by our own tastes.

You will find here different and sometimes contradictory solutions. It is not really so much that one is right, another wrong, as that there are so many different possible ways of developing things, of understanding the choreography of the weaving process. Rather than find this confusing, you, if you are like me, will become the more fascinated at the possibilities of even the most mundane, presumed part of the process and how it can function. You will have new and challenging questions arise to provoke and stimulate you. For rug weaving is somehow not a set of recipes or guidelines to make floor coverings, but a process of discovery and variety, improvement and growth, with tangible results which reflect the weaver's progress.

Equipment

Let's begin with a discussion of looms and detailing ideal features of a rug loom. Many general purpose looms can adequately handle numerous rugs, though you may want to make some modifications if you plan to weave many. Some looms are better for rugs than others. There is no perfect rug loom.

Three major features of looms for weaving rugs need to be evaluated: capacity of the loom to handle high tension warp, shedding mechanism, and beating effectiveness. You need to think of your warp threads as the strings on a musical instrument; they are taut enough that they twang when plucked.

High tension

For the loom to manage such tension as will be desirable, there must be no give or sway when one pushes it from back to front. It can tolerate a minor amount of give laterally. *All* beams which the warp and cloth move around should be of great strength, so that they do not bow when tension is increased. On wider looms, when the braking system is only at one side of the loom, the combination of tension and hard beating can twist the warp and/or cloth beams, causing slackness in the warp at the unbraked side of the loom. Ideally you should have a braking system at each side. Some looms are built with the braking system at the *opposite* side of the loom on the warp beam from where it is on the cloth beam, neutralizing the effect on the warp. While you wouldn't have tension problems, the beams might still be twisting, however.

In discussing the loom's beams we must look particularly at the warp beam. Its properties can greatly influence evenness of warp tension. The larger the circumference of the warp beam, the more expeditiously the warp will beam on. More importantly, the more of that perimeter that the warp actually floats (rather than pressing on solid beam), the more even the warp will be.

To explain, in weft-faced rugs the warp is relatively sparse in its sett. There is much space between warp threads. Regardless of how much tension is applied during winding on, as the threads build up on a solid beam it is relatively easy for some to slip down into the previously beamed-on layers of warp. Thus individual warp threads travel for different distances around the beam and will cause tension disparity later. Sticks can be inserted as necessary to keep the warp seeking its own level; however, they have a tendency to shift unless the warp is beamed on under more tension than it will be woven off under. Paper and cardboard are practically useless because of high tension and heavy beat.

Not all warp beams have solid perimeters. Here I want to point out those called "sectional beams", a term denoting the manner in which one could warp them. Sectional beams usually have two features: 1) they have lines of pegs, nails or large staples across the beam. The lines are spaced at even 90° intervals around the beam, and the pegs, etc. in each line are usually 2″ apart; 2) the beam's perimeter is not solid but has only a small percentage of wood on which the warp lies in its passage around the circumference of the beam. It is the second characteristic of a sectional beam which need concern us here. (Unless one may want to warp sectionally, there is little need for the nails or pegs; they could even be removed.)

By winding my warp on a sectional beam, I have practically eliminated tension irregularities. That is because, for most of the perimeter of the warp beam, the warp is floating. It is only where the warp covers solid wood that irregularities seem to occur; where it floats things seem to equalize. The illustration shows two schemes for modifying a solid back beam to provide this feature. Timbers should be of equal width for their entire length, so the beam will have the same circumference at all points across its width. They should be bolted through the beam and braced between each other. Countersink exposed bolts and nuts to prevent snagging warp threads.

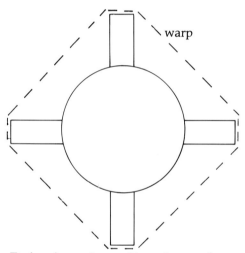

Timbers fastened around beam in cross shape.

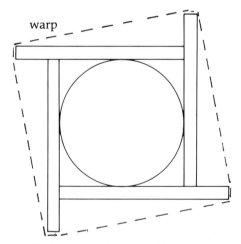

Timbers wrapping around beam.

A temporary "pseudo sectional beam" can be used for looms you are unable or unwilling to modify. Take four dowels of about 1½" diameter and no longer than the warp beam's length and lay them out on a table. Using moderately firm cord, knot two parallel sets of double cords which hold the dowels firmly and at a distance from each other equal to a quarter of the solid beam's perimeter. Push these knotted cords out beyond the width of the warp. The result you are striving for is to have the four dowels parallel and at such a distance apart that when they are wrapped around the warp beam they will be about evenly spaced from each other. Large diameter dowels would produce a larger circumference beam, a plus.

Once the cords are tied on these four dowels and the warp is raddled with its end loops* on the warp-beam's tie-rod (C), crank the warp beam until the tie-rod is between back and warp beams. Stick the string of four dowels inside the loom, i.e., so the warp is between you and the dowels, and tie the end of each of the two sets of cords to the tie-rod. Beam on one revolution of warp. The dowels will lie on the beam just beneath the warps, covering any unevenness caused by loom cords. After this first revolution of warp is beamed on, tie the beginning (A) and finishing ends (B) of the dowel cords to each other firmly so that the dowels cannot move with respect to each other under the warp. You will still have to beam on under heavy tension or else pull at narrow increments of the warp after each revolution of warp (see Collingwood, pp. 63-64). You should not need to use sticks between layers of warp with either a sectional or a pseudo-sectional beam. But you still need to realign the raddle as needed so that you are not getting uneven build-up of warps in some areas across the warp beam.

Shedding mechanism

The loom must be able to change sheds easily while the warp is highly tensioned. Greater distance from breast to back beam reduces stress on a taut warp because there is a greater span of exposed warp to absorb the strain of shed changing.

---

*That old controversy rises up again: Warp front to back or back to front. For rug weaving I find it safest back to front. Then the loops of warp at one end of the warp chain are just slipped on the tie-rod, spaced in a raddle, and beamed on. If you beam front to back, you have to tie the cut warps to the back tie-rod. And heavy beating can disturb the adjustment on some knots near warp's end, ruining tension.

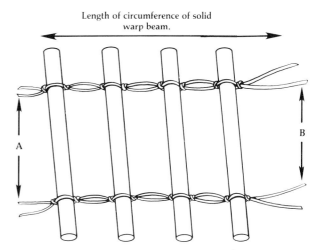

Length of circumference of solid warp beam.

Preparing dowels for pseudo-sectional beam.

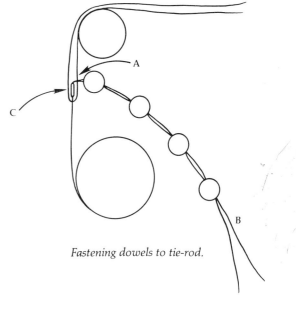

Fastening dowels to tie-rod.

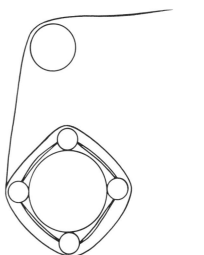

Warp on pseudo-sectional beam.

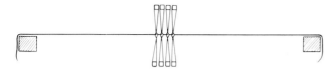

Counterbalance loom at rest.

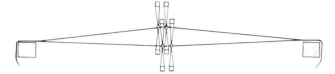

Counterbalance loom in action.

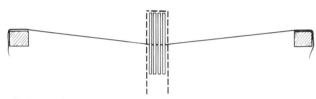

Jack type loom at rest.

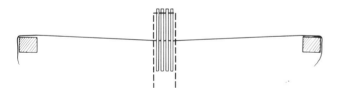

Jack type loom with the warp very taut.

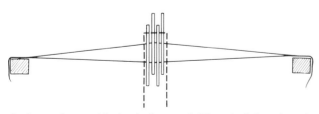

Jack type loom with the shed opened. The raised threads make a larger angle than the threads that remain down.

The sheds must be of adequate depth for the shuttle to pass. A shed larger than necessary for the shuttle puts unnecessary stress on the taut warp.

Looms are classified by the way the shafts and treadles operate to produce the open shed. The classifications counterbalance, countermarch and jack really refer only to the shed changing operation and the way the treadles and harnesses are arranged to achieve it. Let us look abstractly for a moment at the possible ways in which the warps can move to provide an open shed.

On the *counterbalance* loom the warps lie at rest in the neutral position, a theoretical straight line between front and back beams. When the shed is opened the bottom layer threads are pulled down; the top threads up. If the shed is 2½" deep, then each set of threads is stretched 1¼" from this line. When the shed is closed, the threads relax somewhat in the shorter span of the straight distance again. (This is also true on the countermarch loom, except that the shaft-to-treadle tie-up is different.) On a counterbalance the word *balance* is fundamental to understanding its functions and limitations. When one set of shafts is pulled down by treadling, the untreadled shafts automatically go up, rather like a balance scale. Tabby, 2/2 twills, and other weaves where the same number of shafts rise as sink, are easy to weave on a counterbalance loom. But if one undertakes weaves where three shafts must oppose one, the sheds are less well defined; the basic principle governing the shaft mechanism has been compromised. John Tovey in *The Technique of Weaving*, page 21, describes adaptations which can be made to the loom to weave unbalanced sheds more easily.

The *countermarch* loom does not have this structural limitation. Two sets of lams connect the shafts to the treadles. One set allows the shaft to rise, the other to drop. Every shaft is tied to each treadle by the appropriate lam so that it rises or sinks, as necessary for that shed. This involves substantial tie-up but gives excellent sheds. It is ideal for weaves which are very unbalanced or where it is otherwise difficult to get a decent shed.

The closed shed on the *jack* loom has the warp threads lying at rest in what becomes the bottom layer of the open shed, well below that theoretical straight line from front to back beam. When the treadles are depressed the top layer threads move up to the top limit of the shed. The bottom shed threads remain where they are. Only the weight of the shafts is what keeps the closed shed and the bottom layer of threads of the open shed down below that imaginary straight line. When extra tension is put on the warp, as in rug weaving, the closed shed rises up somewhat in the shaft area toward the theoretical straight line. That is of no consequence when the shed is closed. When the shed opens, we find the top layer threads are deflected more from straight than are the bottom threads, hence the bottom threads are slacker and the shed is smaller in size. It becomes acutely difficult to beat the weft in properly when the top and bottom sheds are of two different tensions. The shafts can be weighted or encouraged with some spring mechanism to remain down, despite the high tension. Or a piece of wood can be fastened to the top of the back beam, with the warp passing over it. When the inserted stick is the right thickness, the top and bottom sheds will deflect equally from straight. The open shed may be somewhat smaller, but the disparate tensions should have been remedied. Jack looms present some problems for rug weaving which these modifications may help alleviate.

Beating

A good rug loom will allow you to pack in the weft efficiently and effectively. You need the high tension and a sturdy, heavy loom beater. Overhead beaters require somewhat less human energy than underslung ones to achieve the same results. Adding extra weight to the beater gives either a firmer beat to the weft or a bit less work for the weaver. This extra weight is generally in the form of a steel bar, bolted underneath the shuttle race. On an overhead beater this weight is farthest from the pivot point of the beater and consequently a bit more efficient than on an underslung beater.

Rugs require a very heavy beat. One must use the whole upper torso, not just the arms. Sitting erectly, grasp the beater in the center of the *cloth* with *both* hands, keeping the elbows straight, and move back from the hips with the whole upper body. This action is much more effective and less tiring than beating with the arms only. It resembles rowing a boat, and is most easily done with the feet extending out onto the treadles to give opposition and balance to the movement. For wider rugs, more force must be used to achieve a satisfactory beat. Weight should be added to the bottom of the beater. Multiple applications of the beater may be necessary for each pick and/or supplemental use of a rug fork every ½" or so.

Rug forks

It is not at all unusual to supplement the use of the beater with a rug fork in a weft-faced rug. The loom's beater may be light in weight or not very sturdy — or the weaver might suffer from the same limitations. The rug may have a closely sett warp or be quite wide and thus require heavier beating than seems physically possible to achieve satisfactory results. (As we increase the number of warp threads in a given rug it requires a much greater beating effort to achieve the same or even lesser results.) Because the rug fork is narrow, it concentrates the impact of the beat into just a small area of the fell instead of full width of the cloth.

The fork can beat or pack the weft into the cloth. To beat, hold the handle with the fork projecting out the heel of the hand. Smack firmly against the fell of the cloth with a quick snap of the wrist. A heavy, resonant thud resounds with each beat. To pack, hold the fork between thumb and index finger in the hand, with the fingers along the back side of the fork, gripping the handle. Put the teeth of the fork into the warp threads and *pull* it firmly against the last pick of weft. Try each method; generally one is more effective and comfortable to the weaver than the other for a given project. A rug fork is not essential to good rug weaving if the beater is adequate. Its useage can atone greatly for a poor loom. For a tapestry rug it is the only method of packing in the weft when the fell of the cloth is not straight across.

Let us look at several designs of rug forks; there are distinctly different types. Forks for vertical looms generally are very heavy. They are raised in the warp threads and almost dropped on the fell of the cloth. This weight is fine when gravity will help deliver the goods. Rug forks for horizontal looms have weight to them, but not so much as to exhaust muscles. The handle may be straight or at an angle to increase the efficiency of the beat. Some forks are sensuously shaped in the handle, lying comfortably in the hand when not in use, as the Navajo-type fork.

The teeth or tines should obviously be smooth and blunted at the ends so that they do not damage warp threads. There does not need to be a one-to-one correlation of tines to warps-per-inch. Much more critical than the spacing of the tines is their shape. They must be narrow enough to fit in the spaces between warp threads without abrading the warps. And if one is weaving where the fell of the cloth is not straight or parallel to the beater (as in wedge weave, for example) the tines must not be deep enough to distort the warps as they thwack the fell of the cloth.

Shuttles

Ski shuttles still seem to be the best designed shuttles for rug weaving. Their hooks to wrap the yarn around come slightly below the point of the ski so that they do not snag warp threads inadvertently. The hooks are 18"-21" apart and require a shed depth of only about 2". They may have a spine along the center of the ski to give a little extra weight and to keep the ski from bowing with the tension of the yarn wound on them. The hooks should be screwed or pegged to the ski. Ski shuttles move cleanly through the shed, hold large quantities of yarn, and require only a modest shed depth. The weft should be wound on them in circular fashion. There are numerous designs of ski shuttles, with subtle but distinct differences.

While most rug weavers seem to prefer a ski shuttle, I thought it might be helpful to include a list of what seems relevant criteria for selecting shuttles of other designs.

A) **Girth.** Under high tension, large sheds put much stress on the very taut warps, so a shuttle which can negotiate a smaller shed is desirable.

B) **Capacity.** A good shuttle can accommodate ½-pound of yarn without requiring a substantially larger shed.

C) **Smooth passage.** Wood, not yarns, must rest on the warps in traversing the shed. Yarn on yarn creates too much friction and slows down the shuttle. Stick shuttles are useful when they are the width of the cloth, and handed through the shed.

D) **Length.** A shuttle longer than about 26"-30" becomes impractical except on a vertical loom. It is harder to balance in the hand and requires additional space either side of the warp in order to enter and exit the sheds.

Yarns and sett

To weave durable rugs we must select durable yarns. What characteristics of fiber and spin produce a yarn to meet our needs? Whether we are spinning our own fleece, purchasing commercially prepared fibers or buying ready-made yarns, it is wise to know about the properties of a rug yarn.

The foundation of a yarn is its fiber. Regardless of the source (sheep, goat, flax, etc.), suitable fibers should be *coarse*, providing strength and resistance to felting; *straight* or *wavy*, rather than with much crimp (crimp produces loftiness which is neither as strong nor as abrasion resistant); and *long*, at least 3"-4" staple length. The more revolutions an individual fiber makes, the more securely it will remain in the yarn and resist wear. Short lengths of fiber in a yarn will cause pilling sooner or later.

There are two general ways in which fibers are prepared for spinning: carding and combing. Carding distributes the fibers evenly but orients them in all directions, higgelty-piggelty. The resultant yarn, called *woolen-spun*, has much loft and great insulating qualities. Save it for a shawl where its traits are desirable. For rugs, fibers should be combed so they lie parallel. Short lengths of fiber are also automatically removed during combing. The resultant yarn, termed *worsted-spun*, is lustrous, strong and dense, though not quite as elastic. It is desirable for both warp and weft in rugs.

Warp yarns always need to be strong. Whether on the surface in warp-faced, or hidden in a weft-faced rug, they must not break during the high tension, shed changing and heavy beating of the weaving process. They should be both well spun and plied. Linen resents too much twist but should have long fibers and be plied. Cotton, with its very short staple, should be plied and then several plied strands plied again together, as in seine twine and rope. Looser cotton plies do not wear very well. The hairs—goat, camel, and mohair—and long staple wools are excellent. Synthetics also ought to be. I can't speak from experience with them.

Weft yarns need to be abrasion resistant but not necessarily strong. Springier yarns are easier to work into the cloth. They must have plenty of spin to lock in the fibers; plying increases this locking in. If there is enough spin and long enough staple, weft yarns do not have to be plied to be durable. In weft-faced rugs warp sett must take into account the durability of the weft: a more vulnerable weft yarn should have a closer-spaced warp.

Weavers often buy commercial yarn for its texture, springiness, color. Fiber qualities are overlooked. Yet it is the fiber, its preparation and spin which distinguish a good rug yarn. Any yarn termed a rug yarn may be adequate when we start out. But as we become serious, gain skill and our rug structures becomes more durable, it is important that the structure of the yarn and its fiber suitability not be taken for granted. If you are buying commercial yarns, get 1'-2' samples of potential yarn selections, take them apart and compare them. By taking a short sample and running it back and forth between wetted fingers you can get a relative idea of how it will wear by how soon the fibers begin to work their way out of the strand. Take a sample apart to examine whether the fibers in the single ply are in parallel alignment, indicating combing. Examine the properties of the individual fibers. Coarser, straighter, longer are more durable.

Good rug weaving is not simply a matter of taking the best rug yarn and weaving it into a good rug. There is no one best rug yarn. There are only yarns more and less durable, more and less beautiful. And the ones we love best to handle, to work with, may not be as durable as some others. The real skill in rug weaving comes not from finding the best yarn, but from knowing the weaknesses and strengths of any given yarn. Matched with suitable weaves and setts, the yarn can often be adequately compensated for where it is weak; its strengths, visual and structural, can enhance the cloth.

I have worked for a number of years with a single-ply weft yarn which seems lustrous and beautiful to me. After a while I began to appreciate the vulnerability to wear of an unplied yarn. Unwilling to abandon a yarn with which I felt so much rapport, I began adding extra twist to it. This treatment has given the yarn much more of the look and durability I wanted. It articulates the visual role of the yarn in the cloth more clearly and exaggerates the spin angle well enough that one can play games with twist. This introduces a number of possibilities for experimentation with twist which produce subtle differences in yarn: single-ply yarns in both S- and Z-twist; plied yarns which are plied in the *same* direction that they are spun as opposed to the usual, opposite direction. All of these create gentle textural differences. Light will also reflect differently off opposite direction spin, much as in damask weaves.

If you are interested in exploring overtwisting or otherwise meddling with the twist of yarns the following paragraphs may be helpful. A spinning wheel seems most suited for this operation.

Overtwisting is mechanically very much like spinning, except that it is easier and quicker. One need not focus any attention on drawing out the fibers evenly; the only concern is how much twist is put in a given segment of yarn. When extra twist is added, the yarn will want to kink tenaciously.

More tension must be added to the drive belt or Scotch tensioner to prevent kinking. The amount of twist in the yarn is a factor of the size of the yarn, the size of the increment of yarn you feed in the orifice and the speed at which you are treadling. Coarser yarn simply cannot absorb as much twist as can finer.

Slowly feed increments of yarn of a comfortable length (I prefer something between 12″ and 15″). Be sure to hold the yarn firmly at the ball end of the increment or twist will rapidly gallop down the yarn toward the ball and create a mess. Feed the yarn forward toward the orifice of the flyer until your fingers, pinching the yarn, are right up at the orifice. With the other hand pinch off another increment of yarn at about the same distance from the orifice, let go of the highly-kinked yarn at the orifice with the first hand, and allow the extra twist to run down from the wheel into the new segment. Once you have established how much twist you want, continue treadling that many times per increment and the yarn will have consistent amounts of twist in each increment.

You will not know without personal experimentation how much twist you really want. And you must weave a bit of a given yarn before being able to evaluate it. You never want so much twist in the yarn that you are unable to straighten out its kinkiness despite hard tugging on opposite ends of a segment. You may enjoy its wildness in this state, but you will not enjoy trying to coax it into the cloth. Another note of caution: some plied yarns are more difficult to weave as weft when the twist of their ply is increased. Their suppleness slips away in the overtwisting; weaving them into the cloth becomes very hard work.

After finishing the twisting operation, remove the yarn from the bobbin and set the twist, discipline the yarn. It can be quickly accomplished in either of two ways, by wetting or steaming; the latter is more permanent. If you want the yarns in skeins, make a skein as even as you can. For wetting, soak the yarn in water or wash it in soap suds and rinse so that the water has been well absorbed. Hang it up to dry with enough weight attached to the bottom of the skein to straighten out the kinks. The dry skein could be first weighted and then steamed. After the yarn is dried it will be relatively straight and orderly.

A somewhat quicker procedure involves winding the yarn into balls on a ball winder, and steaming the balls for three to seven minutes. They will dry much more quickly this way, as much less water has actually been absorbed; the steam penetrates readily into the depth of the strand. Generally I overtwist a 100-gram ball at a time; that amount takes about seven minutes to steam adequately and dries overnight.

The key to this process is to have several waterproof supplementary shafts which fit snuggly on the ball winder and will come off easily. A shaft is put on the winder just before the ball is wound. The yarn is wound with enough tension to keep the kinks from appearing. When you go to remove the ball you *must* remember to remove the shaft, with ball on it. Otherwise the yarn will immediately contort and become kinky. Keeping the shaft inside the ball during the steaming and drying keeps the yarn under tension and thus it dries straight.

Shafts should have several holes in them to aid in steaming and drying. Take the permanent shaft off your ball winder or take the whole winder—kit-and-kaboodle—with you to shop for cylinders of the right size. Potential shafts include hair curlers, plastic tubes that commercial yarns come on, and small sections of PVC pipe with holes drilled into them.

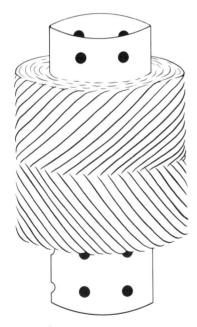

Overtwisted yarn ball on supplementary shaft.

Yarn will accept only a certain amount of twist at one time. If you desire more twist in the yarn than it seems willing to absorb you may want to discipline it and then run it through the wheel a second time. The Navajo may re-spin (as they call it) a yarn numerous times.

It is not essential to use a very expensive and beautiful yarn when first beginning to experiment with rugs, though it can help both your enthusiasm and the rug's appearance. At first it is probably good enough that the yarn be durable, suitable for the demands of rugs. Generally our skills are not so sensitively honed that we can show off its beauty to full advantage. However, as our skills improve, the cloth begins to cry out for better yarns. This may not mean more expense. It can be spoken to by giving more attention to improving the appearance of the yarn, by altering the sett of the warps, or by packing it into the cloth more evenly, to name just a few possibilities.

The notion of sett as ends per inch is easy to express and familiar to all of us. Yet it fails to take into account the size of the warp thread and hence the amount of space *between* warps. It may be easier to understand the role of sett in weft-faced rugs if we relate it to the notion of *the size of the space between warp threads with respect to the diameter of the weft.*

The more space there is between warp threads, the easier it is to weave in the weft. Less space requires more skill to work in the extra length of weft required because its course across the cloth is more circuitous.

More space between warps than the amount necessary for the weft to fit between leaves large tunnels in which the warp can move around when walked on. This can, I think, cause wear—internal wear—and should be avoided. If the warp is sett too close the weft will not properly cover the warp and the cloth may be lumpy and very stiff. Usually when the relationship between inter-warp space and weft size is about right, the individual stitch is also a very pleasing shape and the cloth, while quite firm, still has a slight suppleness to it.

Actually my own rugs have become too stiff in the past few years. But because I like the durability of the weave, the absence of extra space in the cloth, and the lozenge-shaped stitch, I am reluctant to abandon my close sett. Conversations with tapestry and other weavers suggest another alternative. I now plan to experiment with heavy steaming to see if it will make the cloth more supple without affecting durability or appearance.

Generally in weft-faced rugs we double or treble warp threads together in the final two or three heddles at each selvedge. Threads from the same heddle should be sleyed in the same reed dent also.

This bunching up of warps produces a stronger edge and a tighter interlacement at the edge. Thus the weft at the selvedge is less likely to move back and forth on the warp when walked on. The section on a cardwoven selvedge in Appendix II discusses this a little more fully.

Weaving techniques

Before looking at techniques more abstractly I'd like to make a few introductory comments about each of the paths for exploration offered in the chapters which follow for your rug weaving pleasure. While the techniques here are by no means exhaustive of the possibilities feasible for rugs, they offer a rich combination of detailed information representing several different experienced weavers' visions and approaches.

The *plain weave* rug offers the greatest potential of all weaves because of its inherent simplicity and great storehouse of variations in technique and effect. It can be the most durable of weaves for rugs when well sett and beaten. It shows off good yarns extremely well because of its simplicity.

Twill weaves offer a great range also: from lively small motifs to understated textural possibilities, all with the promise of greater thickness in the rug. Twills can also show off a beautiful yarn very well. When the weft floats on the surface are longer in these weaves, the weft yarns need to be more durable.

Rag rugs offer much promise. Patterned strips of fabric can introduce tiny bits of extraordinary color to surprise and delight the most sedate eye. When old fabric is used, they can also bring together the future and the past, recycling time and memories just as much as materials. There is an intrinsic emotional strength in both quilts and rugs made from old fabric. The unselfconsciousness and the surprise in the materials provide great honesty and visual strength. Rags also wear very well in rugs.

Warp-faced rugs have the potential for great durability because the yarns on the surface — the warps — are usually more durable than weft yarns. Because there are more warp threads these rugs may require stronger looms and much muscle to beat in the weft properly. While they do not offer as much flexibility, they can give wonderful vertical design possibilities. There is something inherently "up front" about a warp-faced rug. It is not a set of hidden elements which secretly holds the answer to what the wefts are doing and "shows its face" only in the fringes. The threads which are moved up and down by the loom or pick-up stick to form patterns are the ones you see in the cloth, proclaiming their work directly and not vicariously through the wefts.

Knotted pile techniques offer almost total freedom of design and color placement. Their luxurious thickness has kept Scandinavian households warm for centuries. Oriental pile rugs have enriched palace floors and themselves "floored" Bedouin tents.

Block weaves can produce a fairly thick rug quite quickly, since the design is essentially loom-controlled. Traditionally they have rendered most strongly those designs with heavy emphasis on horizontal and vertical color changes. They generally are reversible, with the design in the negative on the opposite side, providing the opportunity to have an "extra rug for the price of one".

After we have worked a little bit with several different techniques we begin to find much more subtle differences between them. Each technique has great and varied resources for expressing visual statements. Each technique has its own distinctive qualities. The same design may achieve greater dimension in one technique than in another. Perhaps the texture of one weave reinforces the lines of the design. In addition there are subtle nuances of some techniques which add charm. In some block weaves, for example, a peculiarity in the weft change from one block to another automatically produces a delightful transition at the border between blocks which greatly enhances the otherwise predictable design. Poorly chosen, these traits become quirks which detract from the impact of the design statement. They disturb the eye and dilute or interrupt the flow of the rug.

It seems of great import to me to try to achieve a deliberate and mutually strengthening marriage between technique and design. It results in the design becoming more than just "skin deep"; and the choice of the technique not arbitrary, not even just obvious, but intrinsic. The impact of the visual effect is much stronger when the two are closely wedded, the resulting lucidity in our thinking and approach greatly enhanced. The design shows off the cloth well; the cloth shapes the design in its boldness, and details the warmth and endearing qualities with its weaverly nuances.

This process for me seems to develop in the following way: first, to discover through experimenting a technique which my eye and hands take delight in weaving, then to evolve designs which show off that technique well. Finally, after working with it for a while, to push both design and technique into a new synthesis where each is transformed by and transforms the other. Such success does not happen often. When it does, the work preceding it becomes well worth the discovery process.

The choice of technique influences more than design. Its tempo, rhythmic progressions, tactile quality, all have subtle and very clear influence on the weaver. Let me elaborate here again from personal experience. Some techniques are much too fast for me. The cloth develops so quickly that I am unable to keep pace with the possibility for changes as they fleetingly appear. The finished rug lacks the sense of having been done by human hands because my sensitivities could not keep up with its progress. And there are techniques which are too demanding of my patience. I am unable to succumb to their natural paces. I lose attentiveness, and lust for their progress. They are painful to weave, and their results give a sense of uneasiness. This restlessness is not just a matter of speed. It is a reflection of *how* I am spending my time during the weaving and how much I like the results. I get great pleasure from the increasing flow of rhythms, as feet, shuttle, eyes, beater all become fine tuned to their interdependent roles and the cloth, the loom and I work as one. Yet this flow is still curiously unsatisfying for me if I am handling only the wood of the shuttles and beater. My hands cry for more involvement with the yarns, for more personal participation in the design. Certain pick-up weaves and wedge weave have become my dearest friends.

They weave at a speed I can keep up with. As my understanding of them grows and the cloth begins to advance more quickly I am more immersed in the process, rather than left behind. I am not a very patient person. But I have discovered which weaving techniques I work best with, which tap into that reservoir of patience which lies in me, and in each of us. Quite naturally my involvement with such weaves has become deeper and my work has improved. They have benefitted from my increasing experience; and I, I have grown from their effect on me.

Design

Rather than probe some of the mysteries of design I'd like to look at three flat weave rugs,

woven by the Baluchi, nomadic tribespeople of south central Asia. Some of the qualities of these rugs illustrate so well hunches I have about what makes a handwoven rug beautiful. Hunches are illusive, difficult to articulate and yet sometimes meaningful. I hope my descriptions of these rugs do not seem overly long. It seems important not just to look at them, but to peer at them through the eyes of the weaver, to relate the results back to the process.

Rug I

This first rug is quite deliberately arranged, with stripes and small motif bands played out in a precise relationship to each other. The weaving has been executed well, with smoothness of cloth, a pleasing shape to the individual lozenge-shaped "stitch" of weft as it appears on the surface over the warp thread; a regularity of the selvedges which is entirely compatible with the orderliness of the rug. It is 65½" long, of which all but 13½" is woven in natural dark charcoal and white wool. With such contrasting colors dominating the rug, it could easily appear quite cold to the eye. Yet there is a muted and subtle glow, too, which gives one the feeling of the warmth exuded by a dying fire's embers. This glow is achieved by introducing narrow plain stripes of two colors, a blue/purple and a red, both of which are nearly as deep in value as the charcoal and are not readily distinguished from it. They are always introduced surrounded by charcoal, insuring their subtle, rich contribution to the effect. Both the purple and red have undoubtedly been dyed over a gray yarn, so that their values are inherent, as well as intensified by the dyepot.

The bands of small motifs (dark in the light stripes, white in the dark ones) are worked in a technique termed by Collingwood (pp. 122-124) as "Skip Plain Weave". This technique is a bit slow to execute, and highly effective when arranged sensitively, as here. As you look at, admire and analyze each small motif, you realize that its shape, the articulate positioning of thread and color, is exquisite. It has movement and flow, proportions refined by much repeated experimentation with the same shape over the course of many rugs, altering its lines until the message has become clear. The dark motifs are made more interesting by fre-

Rug I. Baluchi tribal rug in natural white and charcoal, with blue/purple and red accents. Motifs are worked in skip plain weave.

quently having small centers of the two dyed colors. Here again the color does not stand out brilliantly, but rather glows, enriching the charcoal, drawing the eye closer to perceive why the drab charcoal has provided such a sense of rich warmth.

When I first looked at this rug I noticed the way it had faded at one end, the lighter gray softening somewhat the contrast of the white motifs at that end. Looking at the reverse side revealed quickly that it was not years of placement with one end exposed to more light. The gray had not faded at all; it is several shades lighter than most of the rug, a result of casual sorting of fibers prior to spinning, or running out of one gray and gradually substituting lighter shades for it—a universal predicament for weavers.

Despite the regularity of all aspects of the design motifs and their placement in the rug, the space is broken up effectively as well as sensitively. Two-thirds of the weaving is simple plain weave stripes, well proportioned to each other and to the size of the rug, with light and dark sensitively balanced. The rug never loses it sense of regularity regardless of from what distance or angle one views it. Yet it clearly retains a visual identity when seen from a distance. It does not become just an obscure shape.

Several lines of vertical soumak have been worked along both edges of the rug and set in about ¾″ from the final selvedge warps. There are two lines of purple and red alternating in checkerboard fashion with a charcoal line on either side. This soumak work functionally strengthens the edges. Visually, it also softens the horizontal emphasis given by the plain and pattern-motif stripes. And just as it introduces a sense of the vertical in the design, it also isolates the remaining ½″ of weft stripes at each selvedge into little dark and white squares. Since the motifs are never worked into the cloth out beyond the soumak lines, these little squares retain a purity of color which you do not feel in the body of the rug. Setting the soumak lines in this short distance makes the rug read much more interestingly for the way the space is broken up. The soumak stops just short of the rug at each end, ceasing with the final charcoal stripe and enhancing the lovely clasped hook motif formed by these gray stripes and the white headers at either end. These two small details of spacing the soumak contribute enormously to the visual interest of the rug, and require no extra weaving time. They do, however, require a prelim-inary plan.

There is a great sense of economy and understatement for me about this rug when I think about its conceptualization and execution. Most of it is woven in the relatively speedy plain weave stripes. The bands of the Skip Plain Weave (which is slower to execute) are carefully arranged to get maximum effect for their limited use—they occupy slightly less than one-third of the space lengthwise. Maximum effect is also achieved using a minimum amount of color. It is introduced in solid stripes for a total of just under 9″ and the tiny diamonds of color for 4½″ more. Among many of these nomadic tribespeople, dyed colors represent a much greater investment than for us. The natural white and charcoal are provided by their flocks; dyed yarns require either development of an additional skill or bartering with other people.

While I personally would prefer a rug with somewhat less regularity, with more surprise to break up the planned-ness, everything in the rug is in harmony: the regularity of the spin, of the woven surface when you run a hand over it, the sensitively spaced stripes, the quiet use of color. This whole sense of containment is broken only by a rich and unruly fringe at either end, which seems to give appropriate "zing" to it and by the tails of yarn emerging from occasional (and of course, symmetrically spaced) rows of a two-strand horizontal soumak.

Upon closer examination—and to the weaver's delight—there is something of a mystery about the use of yarn in this rug: in all the predominantly white areas there are two unplied strands of a single-ply white yarn used together as one weft. In some of the predominantly dark stripes the white motifs are worked in a yarn which has those two single-ply strands plied together. Why, we must ask, change the yarns in these areas? Even after we have closely looked at this rug to understand something of how its effect was achieved, we are confounded with new questions about what enters into producing the weaver's art.

Rug II

A potpourri of colors, designs and problems radiates from the second rug. It is effective and rich when viewed from any distance. Up close, the careful observer cannot help but wonder at how well the weaver(s) did to achieve the results. As in the first rug, there is a generally symmetrical layout of motif bands. From the bold kilim stepped diamond band the layouts of the smaller motif bands mirror each other as they fan out toward opposite ends of the rug, with the exception of one extra band just before the finish at one end. That orderly scheme has been well camouflaged, however, by color changes in motifs. We find at the beginning all of the narrowest motif bands are in natural white cotton and natural brown wool. The contrast is strong between the two colors, and the dark brown sets off the delicate white of the motifs "etched" in it. Wider bands at the same end are in blues and reds or blues and oranges, with small dots of white. The effect is mostly dark, with delicate traces of white to break up the space. For most of the second half of the rug many of the bands show a color change. The dark brown has been replaced with a light-to-medium gray cotton. The combination of gray and white cotton in these motifs stands out as a bold stripe against the background and other motifs. The effect is more fragmenting, less delicate.

The yarns contribute in subtle, pleasant, curious ways to the appearance of the rug. The wool and goat hair have become slick and shiny with wear, their hairy protrusions long worn off, to reveal the clarity of the spinning, the shape of the individual stitch. The cotton, with wear, has taken on the look of very short-napped chenille. The design becomes muted and the individual stitch difficult to recognize.

The largest motifs just to either side of the center diamonds are crisp and flowing in their statement; they follow the diagonal lines naturally suggested by advancing picks of weft (where the color moves over one warp with each additional pick). The design and color lines formed by emphasizing this diagonal line with a color juncture reflect the shape of the motif and echo the relationship of warp and weft in the cloth. Such designs present a clarity of expression and reflect the depth of the process: the making of the cloth as an intrinsic and concurrent part of the design's appearance in the cloth.

Many of the other designs in this rug, particularly the larger motifs, while bolder visually, do not exhibit this close relationship of design with threads. Through the use of stepped diagonals they develop their own shapes and present their statement. Most are more awkward than those expressing the natural diagonals of the cloth. Perhaps that is because cloth and design are not related on such

a one-to-one basis. Perhaps it is because these are new designs to the weavers or to the technique of skip plain weave, and the processes of change and refinement have not yet honed their beauty to its sharpest.

There seems to have been only poor effort to resolve the design in each motif band smoothly at the selvedges. Sometimes a motif could be said to "justify" its shape at one edge; many end awkwardly at both edges. One could almost speculate that two weavers worked on this rug side by side, beginning the pick-up work for a motif row in the center, so each could work outward toward her edge from there and have no break in the design's continuity where their efforts met. Hence neither edge really meets the selvedge gracefully.

There are also signs of the struggles during weaving to keep the fell of the cloth, the bands of pattern, horizontal. Frequent additional picks of weft have been worked into some low areas to realign the design. One sympathizes with the effort.

Two other surprises, major surprises, greet the viewer: of its 36" width of warp, 32½" are a white cotton, the remaining 3½" of warp are goat hair, and these lie at one edge! Imagine trying to weave with a warp where a broad stripe of it is of a remarkably different elasticity than the rest, and with that difference concentrated at one selvedge. It becomes easy to understand why the rug bows out at the ends the way it does.

While the rug was woven, a supplementary set of small wefts of goat hair interlaced at the selvedge along with the ground weft. We find a coarser, thicker and stronger selvedge as a result. It will withstand wear well and emphasizes a sense of unpredictability to the rug through the varied use of different colored wefts. This selvedge changes colors, changes width (it encompasses more of the rug warps at times, then fewer!). As in the first rug, it does not extend into the white header stripe at each end. The second real surprise, for me anyway, was that the left-hand selvedge was not woven with the rug! It is approximately the same length as the rug, perhaps originally an inch or two longer. It has been *cut* from another rug and sewn carefully to the edge of this one.

This is an effective rug, one with color and interesting though sometimes ungainly motifs. Though it is not well crafted and does not have the coherence of the first and third rugs, it is effective, colorful and exuberant in presentation despite the struggles.

Rug II. Another tribal rug of south central Asia. A number of anomalies in the weaving result in poor craftsmanship, though the rug is lively in design.

Rug III. The buckled surface of this Baluchi tribal rug is actually a design enhancement, bringing warmth and appeal to the serene and gently modulated design.

Rug III

The third rug presents a different kind of statement. Restrained color and vitality radiate from its entire length. One is immediately struck by its power, warmth, interesting use of space, and lumpy surface.

The space is broken up in a simple, effective and interesting manner. One can quickly relate to this rug. In looking closer at it, there is a clear sense of good planning, skillful combination of technique, shape and color. Expanse and detail reinforce each other.

The burnt orange color of large fields dominates the rug, warms the eye with its rich and subtle color variation. The plain areas are made infinitely more interesting by the serrated zigzag slit-kilim edges of charcoal brown which define and border them. These three broad fields are interrupted by bands of Skip Plain Weave motifs. Charcoal brown and white motifs enclose small diamonds of a brilliant red and blue. The sparse use of these bright colors renders them jewel-like, and softens the cold contrast of the charcoal and white motifs. The design bands are set off by single rows of two-color horizontal soumak, also in the brilliant red and blue. For the wider colored stripes demarcating motifs from broad plain areas, a more muted red and blue/ purple are used (essentially the same shades which give an ember-like glow in the first rug).

The reinforcing selvedge treatment here has some of the muted red and blue/purple in it to warm the charcoal brown zigzags as it strengthens the rug's edges. The selvedge interaction with the ends of the rug is the same here as in the other rugs: it stops in the final dark stripe, which again greets the white header with interlocking hooks.

A wasp-waisted effect appears at the selvedges where the bands occur. It is almost as if the bands collect the vast fields for a few inches of orderliness, only to have the next plain area command its full space once again.

Looking more closely we notice the lack of rigidity in the layout of the rug. The scheme is orderly, yet there are gentle variations in the scheme which prevent a sense of rigidity about the rug. The zigzag borders do not always end at the same place in their zigginess; a sensitivity to space and effect is more important to the weaver than a need to complete the repeat of the border pattern. Also one band has concentrated the stripe pattern on one side of it into a much smaller space. The order of the stripes within it has been maintained; yet fewer picks of each color were woven. The design scheme was not forgotten, clearly. Yet the change in proportions in this band and the enlarged plain field following it make the rug far more interesting.

The warp in the rug is set nearly a third again as close as in either of the other rugs, at approximately 16 ends per inch. Clearly this has been too close to allow the wefts graceful passage in the spaces between warp threads. And tension problems in the warp also have etched their way into the cloth. In a rug less well developed than this, such problems with their obviously puckery results would cauterize the design efforts. Here the uneven cloth only intensifies the rug's impact. This rug is almost geographical for me. There is much space, barren and yet warm, interspersed with intense small areas of activity and organization.

I am genuinely awed by these Baluchi rugs, particularly the first and third. It is not the beauty or the craftsmanship, the colors or the shapes. They are neither master works of art nor truly magnificent rugs. But they have presence, strength. It emanates from every part of them, holds them together. I struggle to understand this, so I can work it into my own cloth, teach it.

A really good rug reminds me of a really good actor. It is not the delivery of his lines and well executed stage movements which cause a fine performance. Rather a good actor understands the character he plays, *becomes* it.

What makes weaving convincing is not highly sophisticated design, but the weaverliness of its execution, expression. In other words it does not represent just well-formed imagery woven into cloth. That can easily be automated: stamped, molded, printed. It must also reflect the time spent doing this — the process of its creation. There is both an honesty and a consistency in the result when this happens. Look at the third rug with its lumpy expanses. They really work. Yet not because they were contrived as a "neat touch". The weaver was working the cloth — and it was a struggle because of the close sett of the warp and the nature of the weave. It arose out of immersion in the weaving process — in fact *reflects* that process — and the results are much more alive for it. Sometimes that accident, that unforeseen problem, adds vitality and freshness to the rug. Not always, by any means; but its power is great when that occurs.

There is high regard in many circles for Oriental rugs. (The Danes, in referring to Oriental rugs, simply say "genuine" rug.) There is beauty, craftsmanship and life in some of those rugs. If one looks at a lively one for any length of time, the fascination increases. For the repeated shapes are not always the same, even though they may fit in with the repetitive feeling from a distance. A color is not always constant; it may exhibit subtle variation or be replaced in the scheme by an entirely different hue. All of these charming aberrations are natural, logical weaving possibilities.

Or the lazy lines in an early Navajo rug, whose origins are in response to difficulties in the weaving process (namely the discomfort of weaving a wide span when sitting in one place). Those subtle diagonal shadowy lines in monochrome areas of the cloth enrich the results greatly, adding a reality to it.

Or, to switch media for a moment, of batik cloth, where the resist substance used in the dyeing process to prevent the dye from penetrating cloth areas continues to haunt these areas for long afterward with a slight stiffness. Sophisticated technology has produced fake batik which now even imitates the little lines where the resist would have cracked. But only the real batiked cloth hints at the richness and reality of the process with those remaining traces of stiffness.

Perhaps then we ought to spend more time enriching our process. Worrying less about how things were supposed to come out and more about what they are actually doing and how to deal with that, enhance it. Being instead of appearing as planned. To improve, one is often advised to take a drawing class. The result is more successful design but with an orientation even less weaverly. Improve design, by all means: but let us not forget the lovely nuances, subtleties of our medium. Handwoven rugs without their presence need not be handwoven.

Asymmetrical high-contrast stripes give a clean, contemporary look to this plain weave rug.
SETTING: JACK ORMAN HOME.

A Good Plain Weave Rug

Hector Jaeger and Halcyon Schomp

he plain weave rug is one of the most exciting and ultimately satisfying forms of handweaving. It is of course the most basic structure of all the handwoven rugs, and yet is by no means just a building block for other rug weave structures. Although it can be that, more importantly it is a form of handweaving which is full of opportunity for us to express ourselves and to capture two tremendously important elements of the craft. One is the technical achievement of building a piece of cloth, of constructing by hand a fabric which is both useful and strong. The other, and indeed a very different element of the plain weave rug, is creativity. The plain weave rug is a medium which allows us to express a personal vision and allows our creativity to shine through in a way which is not likely to happen in most other forms of handweaving. This opportunity for personal expression of one's own unique view of some part of the world or some feeling in one's own mind and spirit is clear and uncompromised because creative development exists separately from the technical and mechanical development of the plain weave rug. The product of the mechanical and technical achievement stands on its own with or without any other form of expression; the plain weave rug can be every bit a finished product, a complete work, even if woven in a single, solid color. Structure, strength and usefulness are all present even without the elements of color and design. Those are elements that can be literally and figuratively woven into the rug but do not in and of themselves alter it on a technical level.

In this chapter we are going to take you with us from the source of inspiration, through the development of a design and choice of materials, to the actual weaving of a finished rug. Then we will go back and dig deeper, get "a little technical", if you will, in analyzing what is actually going on in the structure of the plain weave rug, what is happening to the yarn that gives us the right finished product. Our technical analysis, however, will deal only with what we feel is important for making more intelligent, independent decisions in designing and weaving your own rugs. To proceed without this kind of information and grasp of the the principles involved would be a little like a navigator at sea knowing only one course, one destination that he had learned from another. That's a good way to get the hang of it and to build some confidence initially, but without then learning the theories and principles to apply to any situation so you can know before you start where you will end up, then it's pretty likely that either your travel will be awfully limited or you'll probably get lost!

Where we begin

To us the source of inspiration starts even before the image, the object or the feeling we want to portray. It begins with the more fundamental question of why we weave at all. Let's touch on that for just a moment.

Through weaving we constantly renew our link with the past. In the replication of the techniques and experiences of weavers throughout history, we feel our roots and our heritage, gain some understanding of what life would have been like in another time and another place and begin to appreciate technological changes through the creation of cloth. We establish a bond with people who came before us by doing with our hands what we know others did with theirs, perhaps centuries ago. To deal physically with the same mechanical considerations—problems of warp tension, of selvedges drawing in—gives us a very different quality of understanding than simply reading about and knowing that people must have done these things way back when.

In much the same way that we bridge a gap to our ancestors and to times long past through weaving, we also can at least narrow another gap, one created by technology. In a modern society where so many of the products we buy and use every day are created in a blur by machines, unseen, seldom considered, we can re-create on a loom, at our own pace and under our own control, a product of technology. The textile industry has always been at the center of technological advances, from the Industrial Revolution to the electronic age, with fabrics of all kinds being turned out at ever-greater speeds.

But we can re-establish a "relationship" with these fabrics that we wear and use every day by sitting down at our own looms. By seeing and controlling the process of making a piece of cloth, we reduce by a little bit the coldness of the mass-produced objects around us. We no longer feel quite so "cut off" from those objects.

Weaving is a personal expression of how we see things, even when it is a re-creation of a Colonial coverlet pattern, Navajo blanket or clan tartan. Our own sense of color, materials and use re-form the finished piece into something unique to us and our time. Even though we aren't expressing our own clan or familial allegiance, our personal and individual feelings of belief and identity do make their mark.

Weaving a rug by hand focuses and concentrates the values intrinsic to handweaving. A plain woven rug is the essence, the purest form of the rug because it is the most straightforward, structurally simple and sound. The tight interlacement of warp and weft forms an extremely durable structure and surface, protecting the warp from abrasion while protecting the weft from snags as well as abrasion.

For plain weave, the warping procedure is virtually identical every time, and it soon becomes a quick jump to the "fun part", bringing you as close as possible to spontaneity in weaving. Because of this simplicity of threading and treadling a plain weave, you are able to achieve the second level of purpose more easily. You are free to concentrate on color, pattern, design and self-expression since you, and not the loom-controlled pattern, are doing the designing.

The plain weave structure offers the weaver at all levels of ability a tremendous vehicle for self-expression, unhindered by the strong restraints and ability requirements imposed by more representational or technically intricate forms. The basic elements of any scene or feeling are quickly and easily accessible: the strength or gentleness of contrast, the play of light and dark, warm and cool, and most important, your personal feelings about color. These are elements which you see and use every day in your choice of clothing and furnishings, in the music you listen to and the art you like.

Although plain weave structure can have many names, may be warp- or weft-faced, may be embellished with surface design or knots, we will talk only about plain weave where the weft covers the warp and is continuous from selvedge to selvedge. We will not discuss tapestry weaves, nor will we cover surface design techniques such as soumak or rya.

Learning by doing

One of the best and most efficient ways of learning a technique and developing the confidence to strike out on your own is by working with someone else as they go through the creative and technical process of designing and executing a project. So by working through this "model", we hope you will gain an insight into how that "creative process" works and develop the hands-on technical experience to express yourself through your own handwoven rugs.

Some more technical details and descriptions will be handled more fully in the last section of this chapter. You may want to glance at them now, but the discussions of the structure of the weave are not crucial to beginning our weaving.

Planning

There are many parts to designing a rug. First is the inspiration and coloration. Size must be decided (your loom will have a lot to do with this). The determination of the specific warp/weft combination and the selection of the patterning techniques to be used to achieve your design are the final steps in planning. Some of this will take place on the loom as an idea comes out differently than planned, or changes occur to you as the design develops.

Design and sources of inspiration. We tread tentatively, timidly into the area of design and color, fearful that we will be asked for our credentials, our advanced degrees, proof of our years of apprenticeship with the great masters. We are girded in this journey, though, by the familiar assertion, that bold declaration of confidence "I don't know art, but I know what I like!"

Certainly any amount of experience and training — whether it is art school, or the insights gained with each successive piece you weave — is productive and adds to your confidence and ability to express yourself in a way that is pleasing to you. Maybe it does take just a momentary dash of disrespect to jolt us out of the feeling that to do anything more than choose a color that looks good with the drapes is somehow the bailiwick of some expert, some creative genius. *You* are that creative genius who can excite and satisfy your most demanding audience, your most discerning critic — because *you* are that audience and critic as well!

If we had a dollar for every time, in the twelve-odd years of selling handweaving yarns, that we've heard a weaver say "I just have no sense of color," well, we probably could have retired by now. We won't pretend that every weaver can be at the leading edge of the art world with their next piece, but we do believe that every weaver can bring to his or her weaving a special and unique view of some part of the world. You can look out your window at the garden and see an explosion of color that you can capture in your weaving in a different way than anyone else could. Or you can stare at a sunset and be entranced by the subtlety of color and shading, and while you may be looking at the same scene as someone else, you are seeing it in your own way. The way certain colors blend and the way you see them and how that view in turn creates a mood, a feeling in you, these are some of the unavoidable ingredients for your design. Your choice of colors and of relationships of colors will be based not on what you know but on what you see, what draws your eye and what lingers strongest in your memory.

The inspiration for many of our rugs comes from photographs, especially those of scenery: imagine vistas of sun-baked grassy plains, canyons and deserts, a tidal marsh on a crisp winter day, a springtime field in full bloom, or the burst of color in the sunrise. Use a magnifying glass to examine a piece of wood turned to polished stone. Close your eyes and remember these pictures. A treasure box of collected dried flowers, shells and stones can be a beautiful starting place for color inspiration. Let your imagination examine the endless blendings, shadows, the array of colors. Or tell the story of the change of seasons in your back yard. A very helpful aspect of photography, either your own or in a book or magazine, is that a photograph will already have imposed a square or rectangular shape and frame to the image, suggesting right then the shape that your rug might take. Similarly, to observe a scene or landscape through a window helps to outline and frame the image.

Music, too, can provide its own kind of inspiration, or be an accompaniment to visual methods. Imagine the clear darkness just before the kettledrums roll their "thunder", see the flash of lightning, the brass heralding the return of the sun and blue sky, then the flutes as the flowers unfold. Such a dramatic piece might suggest a transition of colors from strong bright tones shading into deep colors, then evolving into a series of soft, quiet hues. A simpler musical theme could be a few clear, sharp colors, random solid stripes, perhaps, which are floating on a hazy warm background color — the notes of the solo flute with a background of strings.

What we have done for our rug is to start with the recollection of sandstone formations framing a distant valley. Our image is probably a composite of many scenes, but what lingers the strongest is the impression of contrasting colors and surfaces, the strong, boldly shadowed shapes of sandstone looming in the foreground of this mental picture, juxtaposed with the soft, slightly blurry mix of colors, the pale tones of wildflowers, grasses and sun-baked brush in the distance.

To help in the often tricky process of reconstructing in a tangible form a rather vague impressionistic memory, we pored through some books of photographs of the Southwest (plus, of course, a few *National Geographics* for good measure) until we found, again in composite form, some of the elements that we were looking for. Here we carried the idea of the photograph or window as a frame for the image one step further: we used a piece of matboard (or shirt cardboard) with an approximate 3" × 5" rectangle cut out of the center to isolate smaller segments of pictures. By placing the cardboard "window" over the pictures, we could concentrate on just those parts that were especially evocative of the feeling we were trying to re-capture. The problem with looking at a whole photograph is that in seeing the actual representational image of the scene, we tend to think of the entire picture and to think very literally about everything in it. Since we are not considering representational weaving, it can be very distracting to look at the whole picture. The cardboard window helps to eliminate the distractions. It helps to take your perception of the image out of the literal and into the abstract where shadings of color, contrasts of light and dark, hazy and bright, become the only "subjects" of the picture. These are what catch the weaver's eye and lend best to the medium of the handwoven rug as a way of capturing that "essence", that mood. As handweavers, we neither can nor want to compete with the photographer's eye and lens in recording every detail in perfect clarity. But into that sturdy, useful rug we can impart the single character of a place or an image that is most exciting to us.

Depiction. Once you've narrowed down the field of ideas, bring out the colored pencils, pastels and paper to create some sketches of color blending and proportion. Outline several rectangles of the approximate proportions of the rug you plan to weave. First do bold horizontal strokes in the most prominent colors, then go back and put in blending colors, overlapping the areas to achieve a more muted effect. This will give you a general impression of coloration and proportion, as if your rug were being seen from some distance. Any method of assembling "pieces" of color can help in translating your design idea from your mental picture and any graphic source of inspiration into a form that begins to assume the look of the rug you will end up with. Paint chips, fabric swatches, paints, spools of sewing threads — anything that allows you to manipulate colors and compose different arrangements of color can be useful. We have found that pastel pencils (chalk pencils) work well because the colors can be blended easily by rubbing them on the paper so you can achieve any degree of color distinction or intermixing that you want. Keep in mind, though, that each weft shot in each color you ultimately choose will be travelling from selvedge to selvedge, so your basic method of varying colors will be weft-direction stripes, with variations in shading that we will discuss shortly.

Before choosing the specific patterning techniques to achieve the design, weft must be decided on, along with the appropriate warp material and sett (including fringe considerations).

Now is the time to pull out samples if you get your yarn by mail, or to stand in front of the bins where you buy yarn, to see which yarns offer the color range and tone that will represent your idea the best. Ideally all weavers would have suitable rug yarns available, in an infinite array of colors, and several different thicknesses so that they could achieve a rug of any chosen sett and appearance. Since this is not the case, compromises will have to be made at this point. Our feeling is that color is the most important factor; size of the warp rib (the ridge or bead in the surface of the weave which follows each warp, the width of which is a result of sett) and the surface texture appearance are secondary considerations open for adjustment if the yarns chosen for color do not necessarily conform to our initial plans for sett and surface appearance.

The weft we chose for our rug had the qualities we wanted for most of the desired effects. We used a three-ply wool with a springy twist and a particularly good color range for the soft, "grayed" shades of the valley vegetation where close blending was important. This yarn has about 265 yards per

Strong shades of sandstone formations blend into the soft hues of desert sand, sky and vegetation in this plain weave rug, which is described in detail in this chapter.

SETTING: RUSSELL KAMTZ HOME, LOVELAND, COLORADO. ERIC CALVIN, ARCHITECT.

pound. A lighter weight yarn would have allowed a more even blending of those colors in the pick-and-pick technique as you will see, but this heavier weight of yarn produced a finished piece of substantial "heft", which we wanted, and, by requiring a wider warp sett, it produced a bolder warp-direction rib or stripe in the areas where the dark "shadow" colors reach like fingers into the softer shades. That effect of shadows trickling out into the middle would have been lessened greatly by a closer warp sett and finer weft that might have given us closer shading in the soft tones. This seemed like a good trade-off, and, as you will hear much more about in our technical section, the three-ply twist produces a yarn that covers the warp relatively easily without unduly sacrificing the firm, hard surface and excellent durability which we feel is essential to the plain weave rug.

In any consideration of these compromises we always keep in mind the values which we have touched on previously. A rug, to be a "rug" rather than a wall hanging, has strength, durability, and a tightness of weave which, in the case of the weft-faced plain weave rug, we define as: the weft covering the warp completely, wefts not able to slide up and down the warps nor loose enough to be penetrated easily by a finger or pencil or to be pried open with a fingernail to expose a warp, and the weft material being sturdy enough to wear well when walked on. Those are very important attributes which will become more apparent both as we weave the rug and when we analyze in greater depth its structure and technical features at the end of the chapter. How tight is "tight" and what constitutes strength will be something we hope we'll agree on!

Later we can deal in more depth with the many possibilities for changing these elements and the overall effects that can be achieved by doing so.

Selecting a warp and sett. In selecting a warp, we looked for strength and stiffness in weights appropriate to our needs. Rug warps are available in wool, linen and cotton for the most part. Our selection of a four-ply worsted wool warp (560 yards per pound) was based on wanting a relatively heavy, full-bodied warp both to provide strength and to "fill" the weave, to produce fullness from inside the weave structure. The worsted spin is stronger than a woolen spin; to be equally strong, a woolen spin would have to be plied with a harder twist, which would very likely result in overtwists where the yarn would curl back or kink on itself. We determined that a double strand of this worsted yarn, sett at four (doubled) ends per inch would yield the best balance of tightness, fullness and strength to withstand the tension and beating required to get good warp coverage by the weft. Rather than try to develop a formula for determining the relationships of all possible warps, wefts and setts — futility probably being the hallmark of such an effort — we have found that to establish a starting point or reference point by trial-and-error (or maybe even success!), then adjusting from that according to changes in the materials you choose, is the best way of making these decisions.

Since we just happen to know already that the rug we are about to weave will come out splendidly, we can use our warp decisions here as our reference and compare some other possibilities. If we had opted for a narrower, finer warp rib in the surface of the rug over each warp, we could have achieved it, even with the same weft, by reducing the size of the warp, either by eliminating one strand or using a double strand of something finer, then shifting to a sett of five e.p.i. This would likely create the need to slacken each weft shot more to give adequate warp coverage. (More on this later, too.)

Conversely if we had wanted a wider warp rib with more pronounced bead or ridge over each warp, we could have reduced the sett to three e.p.i.; but to maintain tightness, we would have increased the weight of the warp by adding another strand, so that each warp consisted of three strands of our four-ply wool. This would have been a little more troublesome to thread in the heddles, but more importantly it would have created a slight washboard effect on the rug's surface which we weren't looking for in this case.

Linen is our "other favorite" warp for rugs. The principle difference between linen and wool is that linen is intrinsically stiffer, a characteristic derived from its longer continuous fibers that have virtually no built-in structural elasticity. This stiffness, under high tension on your loom, can mean a less resilient fell to beat against, potentially producing a tighter weave. The trade-off for that is a warp which, because of its almost brittle stiffness, is more demanding of being beamed and tied on your loom with very consistent tension. With no elasticity, the yarn itself will not "adjust" for loose threads, whereas the slight elasticity of our hard four-ply wool makes it a bit more forgiving of such slight errors. Similarly, if your selvedges should draw in slightly (yes, it can happen!) the constant wear of the reed on those threads can pull out, or effectively lengthen, the linen which has no capacity to retighten. The more brittle fibers may fray somewhat in this situation also. Here too, the wool can be a little more resilient. This quality of the wool, then, is slightly beneficial in regard to tension and wear, slightly detrimental in terms of giving under hard beating. Emphasis on the "slightly". Wool warp has a bit more natural adhesion to the wool weft than a smooth, wet-spun linen would. This can also be *slightly* helpful in holding your weft in place between shots. A rougher surfaced linen or flax, probably dry-spun, will have better adhesion, but at the same time will be more susceptible to abrasion.

Cotton does not generally have as much of the same qualities as either linen or wool in stiffness, strength, resistance to wear, or resilience. Because of its softer, shorter fiber, it begins to take on the desirable characteristics of hardness and smoothness only when it is spun into a cable cord or seine twine. At that point, it can assume the undesirable side-effects of being difficult to tie on and roll on to your loom because of the stiffness. The excessive twist, particularly in heavier weights, can actually cause a properly woven rug to curl at the corners or even buckle when it comes off the loom. Fringing or otherwise finishing your warp ends is also hampered by the twist, and while linen and wool are not without their faults (is there a perfect rug warp?), good wool and linen rug warps seem to have the best balance of qualities for the type of rug we're describing here.

Size

In determining the size of the rug, there are two major considerations. First you need to consider where you plan to put the rug and the approximate size of that space. The weaving width of your loom is the second consideration. In general you will need to figure that your finished rug will be from ½" to 1" narrower when finished than the width which you thread in the reed. For your first few rugs you should probably limit yourself to rugs which don't need to be wider than your loom, because the joining of weft-faced plain weave rugs is difficult to do well both from the standpoint of designing and weaving the sections to coordinate

well, and because the actual joining can look sloppy if not done very well.

Unless you have a specific placement in mind which determines the length needed (such as a hall runner, a long narrow piece next to a bed, or a square rug for an entryway), you must next decide on the length of the rug.

Barring some other great inspiration, we usually use the proportions of the "golden rectangle" to determine the length. To calculate this, multiply the chosen width by 1.618 to find the length to be woven. You probably don't need to include fringe in the length calculations because it doesn't add much visual body to the length of the rug.

We've chosen a 40" width because it is the width of the loom we're using and we have no specific place to put the finished piece which would dictate a smaller size. Using the "golden rectangle", we have decided on a woven length of about 65" using the following formula:

width of approximately	40"
	×1.618
finished woven length should be	65"

Specific patterning

Before choosing specific patterns for a rug, we need to review the ways of presenting or changing color in a weft-faced plain weave rug woven selvedge to selvedge.

Solid color. The strongest and most basic effect is simply a single mass of one color. The first variation on the solid color is to use multiple weft strands together (either close shades, or for a tweedy effect, light and dark values together) to create a color from the combination. Although this may be a good way to use up scraps and mill ends, we do not like the "thready" and rougher surface texture it creates. Selvedges are also harder to control because of differing elasticities and tensions winding on to the shuttles. Our personal feeling is that multiple weft is best used in a wall hanging or in cut pile techniques (such as double corduroy or rya) where the inconsistencies may actually be desirable. For the remainder of this discussion we'll assume that each weft shot consists of a single color strand, though any technique could be done using blended weft strands of an appropriate thickness.

Stripes. Another variation is stripes: big or small, two colors or a rainbow. Stripes are easy to do,

solid color

two-thread stripe on
solid ground

two-thread stripes of
alternating colors

spots

pick-and-pick
alternating blocks

long warp stripes with one
color constant, the other
color gradually changing

alternating wefts
in one shed

alternating, decreasing
blocks

chain link

carrying only one shuttle at a time, and starting and ending each weft color before proceeding to the next color. These offer bold, geometric planes to show off color blocks.

Alternating weft techniques. For the blended color changing so useful in depicting natural color effects, wefts must alternate quite closely. The minimum solid stripe in a plain weave is produced from two consecutive weft shots of the same color (sheds A and B). This may be in the form of a single pinstripe introduced in a larger field of color, or such stripes could be moved successively closer until they alternate equally with the background. The selvedge remains quite neat in this technique, especially if the stripe color is started on the opposite selvedge from where the background weft is. If these pinstripes are to be widely spaced it will be easier to begin and end that weft color with each stripe by bringing the end back into the weave. If there is less than ¾" between pinstripes, it may be easier to carry the stripe weft inside the weave at the selvedge. Where pinstripes are alternating equally (2/2 alternating), a neat selvedge will form very naturally.

Spots. For just a suggestion or sprinkling of a color we use "spots". The spot weft is just a single weft shot, woven in one shed. If spot weft shots are in opposite sheds, several shots apart, their appearance will be more spontaneous and random.

Pick-and-pick. Our favorite technique is "pick-and-pick". Other names may be applied, but a rose is a rose. Here the warp direction stripes and color changes within them blend color from a distance while providing subtle and interesting detail up close. The pick-and-pick effect is achieved by using two colors, weaving one in shed A and the other in shed B.

Harness: 1 & 3 (or 1)	2 & 4 (or 2)
Shed A	**Shed B**
lt.	
	drk.
lt.	
	drk.

Countless variations for intricate color change are possible in this technique. An interesting source of ideas is inkle woven bands turned sideways (look at the warp as if it were your weft). Some larger scale designs are shown here.

Alternating blocks.

Harness: 1 & 3 (or 1)	2 & 4 (or 2)	
Shed A	**Shed B**	
lt.		
	drk.	as desired up to about ¾".
lt.		
	drk.	
drk.		
	lt.	as desired from 2 shots per color up to 1" or more.
drk.		
	lt.	

These can appear in a constantly changing checkerboard, or with the addition of one or two extra shots between the blocks (in the example above, the dark weft), can create a "pole and ladder" effect. The addition of a single shot between the blocks will cause the blocks to be in the same warp stripe (same shed) for a strong, slightly formal look. The addition of two shots between the blocks will cause the blocks to be in opposite sheds making alternating rungs on the ladder. Although this is not shown in the woven sample, it can be drawn as follows:

Long warp stripes. The technique we use most often is the long warp stripe, changing colors in one of the stripes.

Harness: 1 & 3 (or 1)	2 & 4 (or 2)	
Shed A	**Shed B**	
lt.		
	drk.	[as desired.
lt.		
	drk.	
med.		
	drk.	[as desired.
med.		
	drk.	
pale		
	drk.	[as desired.
pale		
	drk.	

A spot in one shed. "Spots" of an accent color can be introduced in one shed by introducing only one weft pick of the accent color, turning the ends back in to the weaving; or if several spot rows of the same color will be used only a few shots apart, the weft may be carried inside the selvedge.

Harness:

1 & 3 (or 1) Shed A	2 & 4 (or 2) Shed B	
lt.		
	drk.	[as desired.
lt.		
	drk.	
med.		
	drk.	[as desired.
spots		
	drk.	
pale		
	drk.	[as desired.
pale		
	drk.	

Alternating, decreasing blocks. An interesting diagonal illusion is created when blocks of decreasing size are alternated.

Harness:

1 & 3 (or 1) Shed A	2 & 4 (or 2) Shed B	
lt.		
	drk.	[as desired.
drk.		
	lt.	
drk.		
	lt.	
drk.		
	lt.	
drk.		
	drk.	
lt.		
	drk.	
lt.		
	drk.	
drk.		
	lt.	
drk.		
	drk.	
drk.		[as desired.

Alternating wefts in one shed. It is also possible to alternate colors in one shed, but since it is difficult to get a satisfactory selvedge with this technique we use it sparingly.

Harness:

1 & 3 (or 1) Shed A	2 & 4 (or 2) Shed B
lt.	
	drk.
med.	
	drk.
lt.	
	drk.
	drk.
pale	
	drk.
pale	
	drk.

Chain link. The last example shown on the sample is the "chain link or ladder" which creates a fairly strong image.

Harness:

1 & 3 (or 1) Shed A	2 & 4 (or 2) Shed B	
drk.		
	drk.	[as desired.
lt.		
	lt.	
drk.		
	lt.	
drk.		
	lt.	
drk.		
	lt.	
lt.		
	drk.	
drk.		[as desired.

If the last light colored weft had been left out, the effect of spires on a horizon or blocks on a base would have occurred.

An interesting thing to note on our sample is the effect of doubling the warp size. When we stitched the cut warp ends back into the weave next to the warp, effectively doubling warp size, an interesting thing happens — the weaving draws in quite dramatically. (Honest, it did come off the loom exactly the same width as the rest of the sample.) There are two lessons to be relearned from this: 1) given a particular sett and weft size, it will take more weft length (slack) to accommodate the thicker warp, and if you don't give it the rug will take it, in the form of drawn-in; and 2) if you want to use a stitched-in warp for your end finish rather than a fringe, you'll need to put in extra weft slack for 1" to 1½" of weaving at each end of the rug. Plan ahead for this type of finish.

We will discuss weft placement at the selvedge when we get to the actual weaving.

Finalizing the design. Now that we have decided on size and looked at some methods of introducing color into the plain weave design, we can finalize the design for our rug. A small dilemma arises here, because it is easiest to do this with your yarns in hand, to lay out whole skeins and see the different relationships of colors. Yet until you have done this, it can be difficult to determine how much yarn in each color you will need. We start with the total amount needed for the whole rug, regardless of color distribution; and again, we have a "first rug" as a reference point. In this case, we happen to know that this particular combination of materials and structure calls for about ⅓ of a pound (or around 5½ ounces) of yarn per square foot of area. The rug will be 40"×65" or just about 18 square feet; 5½ ounces×18 square feet=99 ounces, or about 6 pounds, 3 ounces of weft. Now we can start dividing this total figure up among the colors we have chosen and according to the apparent, approximate proportions of color that our sketches indicate.

Dark brown and a deep brownish red will be the main colors representing shadowed sandstone formations in the foreground at the end of the rug where we'll start weaving. To suggest their looming presence in the foreground, we'll devote about 2' of the length to them using solid color and continuous pick-and-pick *warp stripes* in those two shades. The deep red will predominate here.

Approaching the colors of the valley beyond the rock formations, the dark shades will be broken by small amounts of a lighter sandy brown and a subdued salmon pink. These will be brought in in the pick-and-pick with short *warp stripes* or *blocks* to suggest highlights on the rocks created by rays of light among the shadows.

Next the colors will shift to the desert valley of sun-parched sand and stone in beiges and pale sandstone tones of orange. These will be pierced first by continuous, then intermittent, fingers of the deep red as the shadows of the rocks dissipate across the distant rolling valley floor. This will bring us a little past the middle of the rug and to very sparing bits of the colors of tough, low desert vegetation. The suggestion of sagebrush and blooming cacti, in soft pink, yellow and green tones is made for about 8" with the spotting technique against a background of soft orange and gold tones.

This transient-seeming, distant life will rather quickly fade as our gaze continues — and our colors progress — into a hazy, far distance. Here the horizon is lost in pale blue and gray-purple shades done in the decreasing blocks technique that might seem like the wavy lines of heat rising from the earth's surface or of a mirage.

At a point about 48" or 50" through the rug's length, this haze then dissolves into the vague silhouette of a mountain range at some indeterminate distance, seemingly floating across the horizon with only the slightest variation in their purple tone indicating more than a two-dimensional form. Most of this last section will be pick-and-pick warp stripes, to maximize the color blending, to appear almost as a wash of color.

On the next page is a color guide that we planned, and the actual order that we ended up with. Remember that such a guide is not meant to lock you in to each shot of color, but simply to help you execute your whole idea within the size rug you have chosen. Deviation from specific measurements of color or from color blendings may well be dictated by your eye as you weave any given design of this type. But be sure to keep your overall dimensions and your original "vision" in mind as you go. The changes we made were not substantial, but seemed to be called for as the weaving developed. You'll notice, for example, that the sage green was eliminated entirely, as too bright.

From this kind of guide, you could calculate every last square inch of each color and determine

PLANNED COLORS			ACTUAL COLORS		
	Shed A (1-3)	Shed B (2-4)		Shed A	Shed B
4"	deep red	deep red (solid)	4"	deep red	deep red
6"	deep red	dark brown (pick-and-pick)	5¾"	deep red	dark brown
2"	deep red	deep red (solid)	2"	deep red	deep red
5"	deep red	sandy brown (alternating blocks)	1"	deep red	sandy brown
1"	deep red	deep red (solid)	⅛"	deep red	deep red
4"	deep red	salmon	2"	deep red	sandy brown
3"	deep red	pale sand	¼"	deep red	deep red
3"	deep red	gray sand	2¼"	deep red	sandy brown
2"	pale sand	gray sand	1"	deep red	deep red
3"	deep red	terra cotta (grayed)	1"	deep red	salmon
4"	pale orange	terra cotta	⅛"	deep red	deep red
(with spots and short blocks of yellow and pale green)			1¼"	deep red	salmon
			¼"	deep red	deep red
3"	gray sand	terra cotta	1½"	deep red	salmon
(with spots and short blocks of coral and sage green)			3"	deep red	pale sand
			2¾"	deep red	gray sand
2"	gray sand	sage green	2"	pale sand	gray sand
2"	gray sand	gold sand	3"	deep red	terra cotta
4"	gray sand	gray purple	4"	pale orange	terra cotta
5"	pale blue	gray purple	3"	gray sand	terra cotta
3"	gray purple	blue purple (in decreasing blocks	*(with spots of pale green and pink)*		
½"	plum	plum ending the section)	2"	gray sand	pale green
2½"	plum	blue purple	*(with spots of yellow and pink)*		
3"	plum	dark purple	2"	gray sand	gold sand
3"	eggplant	dark purple	4"	gray sand	gray purple
			5½"	pale blue	gray purple (plain pick-and-pick;
			3"	blue purple	gray purple no decreasing blocks)
			3"	blue purple	plum
			2½"	dark purple	plum
			3¼"	dark purple	eggplant
			65½"		

exact quantities. But don't! You'll throw your fun/ drudgery index all out of whack. Besides, most yarns are available in a unit measure that will make such precision pointless, and it would inhibit your freedom to change as you go.

The yarn we used comes in about a four-ounce skein, so with 16 shades plus a few for spots, you already have four pounds of yarn if you just bought one skein of each! The deep red is clearly the "biggest" color, being about one-quarter to one-third of the entire area, so we'll use about 1½ pounds of that color. Next are the gray sand and gray purple—12 ounces each. Then terra cotta— eight ounces, and a skein (four ounces) each of the other 12 colors and the smallest possible amount of yellow, pale green and pink for spots (a full skein may be the minimum). This will total close to seven pounds, which leaves a minimal amount of leftover yarn considering the number of colors. Cutting it close will probably work out, though, if you remain somewhat adaptable as you weave.

The loom

Before we put any yarn on the loom, we'll take time out here to discuss equipment.

One general area of concern when approaching rug weaving is what kind of loom is suitable, or more specifically "Can I weave a rug on my loom?". First of all, keep plenty of grains of salt handy to take when hearing almost any response to that question. There are no hard and fast rules as to what is or isn't an adequate loom and there probably should not be because each weaver will get different results from any piece of equipment. In architecture, by contrast, there are endless standards for what materials and engineering methods are required for a building according to its proposed use. Everything from public safety to politics enters into those standards, as for automobiles, as for so many products. Mercifully, not so for looms. We are fortunate to have little more than common sense, trust, trial-and-error, and practicality to guide us in evaluating our looms—another of the distinct pleasures of handweaving. And we have each other to compare notes with and seek advice from. Suffice it to say that practically any reasonably well-constructed floor loom with two or more harnesses and of 30″ weaving width or greater will *probably* work. The types of looms where there is some question are folding looms and "portable" floor looms. These will mostly be of a size that would not suggest rug weaving anyway, such as 25″ weaving width or less, but some folding looms in the 36″ range can serve quite adequately, if not ideally, to weave a rug. And some cannot! If the warp and cloth beams look suspiciously like closet poles, and the best feature of the loom is that you can fold it up and toss it in the closet or your car trunk single-handed, then be a little wary of weaving a rug on it. The demands that the necessary tight tension and hard beating will put on your loom may be too great for some of the lighter weight and portable models. To be able to fold and carry a loom conveniently is a great asset in many cases, but we can't recommend possibly damaging that loom trying (probably without success) to do something for which it is not really designed. Similarly, of course, table looms will be best applied to rug weaving only as sample looms to test possible patterns and color ideas. To permit the weft to cover the warp, however, you'll probably need a wider warp sett than you would use for the actual rug, so your sample will not be structurally the same as your finished piece.

Softer pieces that may be woven in rug techniques or apparent rug weave structures, such as finer weft-faced material for pillow covers and purses or looser pieces that are often used as wall hangings, can work well on lighter and smaller looms. The critical distinction that makes a rug a rug is the tightness and firmness that will require a more substantial loom to execute. With some of the portable floor looms, there may be a rug or two available to the ambitious and energetic weaver who might compensate for the equipment by bracing the loom with hand and feet with each beat, but at some point you'll just be trying to squeeze water from a stone.

Since the principle function of any loom is to hold the warp square and taut, and not let that tension vary during weaving except when desired, a simple test of how well a given loom might perform that task in weaving a rug is to stand at the front, brace your foot against the middle of the front foot rail or treadle rail at the bottom, grip the breast beam at the center and pull toward yourself.

(Depending on your own construction you may want to have someone heftier than you do this.) If the frame of the loom feels as if it is "giving", flexing, or almost wanting to fold slightly, or if one side does so without the other, then it may not be stiff or square enough for a very tight warp. Some side-to-side or diagonal "looseness" is not very important, since the warp stresses are only front-to-back. Many floor looms will actually lift off the floor at the back when subjected to this test and tilt forward. This is not a problem, and indicates that the loom is rigid. Stability and stiffness should derive more from structure and design than from sheer dead weight.

Most floor looms, of course, are built for the full spectrum of weaving from feather light scarves to rugs, so most of the adjustments you make from one kind of fabric to another will be in technique rather than alterations to your equipment. However, as a practical matter, most looms are designed to be easy to move as opposed to being "built in", and so immobilizing your loom will provide a fixed structure for beating against a tight warp. While you do not need a ponderous beast of a loom to weave rugs, we have found some relatively simple ways of enhancing your "full spectrum" loom for the more specialized purpose of rug weaving.

1. General condition and maintenance: A loose or sloppy feel in your loom can often be cured by simply checking all the screws, nuts and bolts for tightness. All the shaking and pounding of normal weaving will naturally loosen up almost any loom. Pay particular attention to warp beam brackets or bearings, and just routinely tighten everything. Don't force or overtighten, especially wood screws which might strip out the wood threads or even break the screw. Just get them firmly snug.

2. Blocking, bracing or weighting your loom: Any tendency for your loom to move when beating will decrease the effectiveness of the hard beating necessary to a successful rug. Such movement has the effect of a shock absorber and should be minimized so that all of the force available is concentrated on the fell of the rug. The harder beating of rugs can cause your loom to shift or slide on the floor, or even to rock slightly. If your loom is on a smooth floor, consider foot blocks to prevent creeping (see boxed material). This will help save your floor, too, if it's wood. Some looms come with a rubber pad under the feet, but if yours does not, some form of thin pad (such as two thicknesses of a bicycle inner-tube, cut to fit and glued on) will reduce sliding and scratching, and lessen the noise. Keep it thin, though; remember, you do not want a shock absorber!

**Installing floor stops for the
front legs of the loom (on a wood floor)**

MATERIALS: Two pieces of ¾" plywood, 3" × (the width of your loom's leg + 4¼"). Six 1½" #14 panhead sheet metal screws.
TOOLS: Jigsaw with plywood blade, ¹¹/₆₄" drill bit, ¼" drill bit, screwdriver to match the screws.
PROCEDURE: Mark the plywood pieces as diagrammed. Using the jigsaw, make the cutout in the plywood as follows:

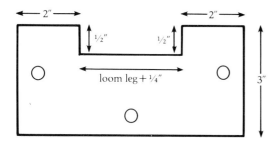

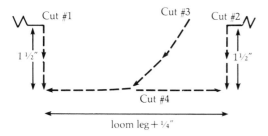

Using the ¼" drill bit, drill holes through the plywood in the approximate positions shown. Do this on both pieces of plywood.

Position your loom *exactly* where you want it for weaving. Change to the ¹¹/₆₄" drill bit. Place one of the blocks in position (the front of the loom leg should be in the cutout). Hold block in place while you drill through it into the floor about ¾".

Screw in the first screw. Check the position of the block, adjusting if necessary, and drill the second hole in the floor. Put in the screw. Then do the third hole and screw. Repeat the procedure for the other leg.

If your loom is on a heavy rug or carpeting, it will embed itself somewhat and thereby anchor itself much better than on a bare floor. Some movement may still occur though, and since installing floor blocks is not practical here, consider bracing your loom. Turn the loom so that the front is 3' or so from and parallel to a wall. Cut two 2 × 4's to the 3' length, and place each on the floor squarely between the front leg of the loom and the base of the wall, pulling the loom tightly up to the end of each brace.

If your loom is stiff but not heavy or has a high castle and a tendency for the back legs to lift from the floor when beating hard, a simple ballast of sand bags or bags of shot which can be placed on the cross piece of wood at the base of the castle (place one on each side) or below the warp beam if there is another cross piece there, can help anchor and stabilize the loom. These should be approximately two to three pounds. Placement will vary with different looms, but obviously must not interfere with your treadles.

And, finally, another method of immobilizing your loom that we have used successfully on a solid hardwood floor is to use L-brackets or hinges to attach the back legs of your loom to the floor. (On many looms, this would mean attachment at the base of the castle.) Using L-brackets with each arm 6" to 8" long, simply screw the brackets into the floor in such a position as the upright leg is pressed against the side or back of the leg or castle. Rather than screwing or bolting into the loom, simply drill a hole, in alignment with the uppermost hole of the bracket, through the leg of the loom and use a snugly-fitting steel pin (¼" in diameter or so) to secure loom to bracket. This will be easier to remove when you want to move your loom.

This method is the most extreme as far as altering your house and your loom is concerned, but it also is the most effective in eliminating shock absorption in your beating.

These are merely suggestions, not requirements, to make your loom better suited for more easily weaving a rug.

3. Beater weights, added to your beater to increase its mass and momentum for rug weaving, are probably the most common additions made to floor looms. The range of attitudes about them is the widest possible: from "You *must* have them on any loom or you can't weave a rug", to "If you think you need them, then your loom just isn't suit-

Adding removeable beater weights to a 36" to 45" loom

MATERIALS: These should be readily available at a good hardware store. Two 2" 10/24 hanger bolts, two 10/24 wing nuts, one 1½" × ¼" × 36" steel bar, one 1½" × ⅛ × 36" steel bar.

TOOLS: Electric drill with ¼" bit for drilling steel bar, ⁹⁄₆₄" bit for wood, screwdriver for removing shuttle race, two pairs of pliers.
PROCEDURE: Drilling bar: Mark spots on the ⅛" bar *accurately* as in the diagram below.

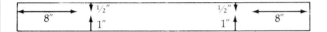

Mark the top of the bar with a piece of tape. Use the ¼" drill bit to drill the two holes. To keep the bit shart and drilling better, drip oil in the hole frequently. Use the ¼" drilled bar to mark the hole positions on the ⅛" bar, Use the same drill bit to drill this bar.

Preparing the shuttle race: Mark the back side (nearest heddles) of the shuttle race with a piece of tape; also indicate which direction is up with an arrow. (Note: the shuttle race is the part of the beater holding the bottom of the reed.)

Take out the reed, but leave the top of the beater on. Carefully unscrew the shuttle race screws. Do this by unscrewing each screw about halfway, then while someone else holds the shuttle race for you, finish unscrewing it. Take it to a work bench to drill it.

Position the shuttle race with the tape mark up and the arrow facing away from you. Use the ⅛" bar as a marking guide. Center it *very* accurately left to right (mark center of bar, mark center of race, the align the two marks). Make sure the top of the bar is toward the top of the shuttle race.

Maintaining the right-left position, lower the top edge of the bar about ⅛" below the top edge of the shuttle race (Figure 1). Lowering the top edge of the bar slightly will keep metal from rubbing on warp threads.) Now mark the hole positions, through the holes in the bar, into the wood. Remove the bar.

Drilling the shuttle race: Before drilling the holes in the shuttle race, mark the ⁹⁄₆₄" drill bit by wrapping a strip of tape around it ⅞" from the tip.

Keep the drill *very straight* while you drill each hole. Drill a ⅞" deep hole (just to the tape mark on the bit). If your hole isn't straight, your hanger bolt will be crooked.

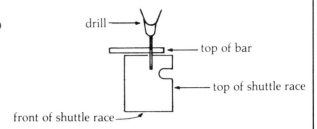

Installing the hanger bolts: Lock the wing nuts together on one of the hanger bolts. Put one wing nut on upside down (Figure 2) winding it down just enough to get the second wing nut on top, right side up (Figure 3). Tighten the second nut down on the first by holding the bottom wing nut securely with one pair of pliers and using the second pair of pliers to tighten the top wing nut down very firmly.

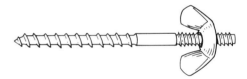

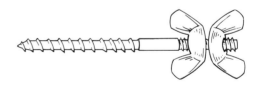

Now you can screw the hanger bolt into the shuttle race. Rub the wood thread of the bolt with soft soap or Vaseline before starting it in the hole by hand. When it is screwed in as far as it can be by hand, use a pair of pliers to finish turning the bolt until the smooth part of the bolt is just out of the wood. Remove the top wing nut and then the bottom one. Repeat this process for the second bolt.
Replacing the shuttle race in the loom: Hold the shuttle race in position while someone else starts the screws back in very carefully. Screw each one in about half way, then go back and finish screwing them in tightly.

Put the bars on the hanger bolts, making sure you have the top on top, with the edge just below the shuttle race surface.

Screw on the wing nuts.

able for rug weaving." Well, we all tend to be a little dogmatic now and then, but after eliminating the extreme points of view, we've settled for the belief that some looms, and some weavers, of course, will benefit more than others from beater weights; but the addition of them to most contemporary floor looms will reduce the physical effort required of the weaver and will improve the quality of the finished product. You can probably live without them, but do better with them. The preceding boxed material is a method of installation that is well-suited for most looms.

4. Aprons, apron cords, apron rods or sticks: The increased tension on rug warps requires good condition of cloth aprons and of apron cords or straps. In the case of apron cords that are laced through your warp and cloth beams, check for stretch in the cord and for alignment of the apron rod or stick parallel to the beam. The rod should be parallel when each section of cord is equally taut. If the cord seems to stretch, you might replace it with a heavier, stiffer cord; usually a core-braided or solid-braided nylon or a hard-braided cotton is used.

The size of apron rods supplied with your loom often needs to be "beefed up" for rug weaving. Heavier rods can be cumbersome with light, delicate warps, so the loom makers are not just economizing with lighter rods. But for rugs, a ⅜" thick steel rod is good. The greatest tendency to bend occurs when a narrow warp is put on a wider loom; full width warps distribute the loads more evenly. In either case, the stiffer the rod that the warps are attached to, the less the chance of uneven warp tension arising from the rod bowing. In our own method of warping, we attach the loop end of the warp over the rod, then strap the rod to the flat wood apron stick of the loom with ½" or ¾" fiberglass reinforced "strapping tape". As you'll see, this is quite sufficient.

5. Harness "float": This is the term for the tendency of harnesses, in a jack-type loom only, to rise from their intended lowest position at rest because of the warp tension. The geometry and design of some jack loom sheds is such that the warps are pulled down in the harnesses to an at-rest position that is below the plane of or straight line between the back beam and breast beam (see illustration). When the warp tension on a relatively inelastic rug warp becomes great enough, it overcomes the weight of the harnesses and begins to rise, trying to stretch straight from front to back. The pur-

pose of this designed "low point" is to equalize as much as possible the stresses on the warp threads, when harnesses are raised, between the yarns being pulled up by the rising harnesses and the yarns being held down by the weight only of the harnesses still at rest. (Countermarch and counterbalance looms achieve even better equalization by separating warps up and down, equal distances, from an at-rest position which *is* the plane of breast and back beams.)

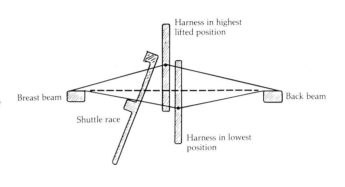

Harness in highest lifted position

Breast beam

Back beam

Shuttle race

Harness in lowest position

Small amounts of harness float are almost inevitable in rug weaving on jack looms, and, to the extent of ⅛" to ¼" or so, are nothing to be concerned about. Greater amounts than that, though, can begin to cause some problems if the warps on the bottom of your shed are lifting off the shuttle race of your beater and possibly causing you to snag or pick up bottom threads as you throw your shuttle. Also, excessive harness float can cause a smaller shed and even restrict free movement of your shuttle. If this is the case, you can check the following:

a) Be sure that your treadle tie-ups are adjusted, if possible, to give maximum lift. This will ensure all available shed above the floating selvedge line. Note: if you increase this too much you may find that the heddle bars of the rising harnesses will start to lift the threads which are "at rest". You do not have to worry too much about tension and stress equalization with a rug warp because it will be a tough, sturdy yarn anyway. (Shed equalization as it pertains to warps is designed to reduce potentially damaging stresses on more delicate yarns.)

b) If your loom has any back beam adjustment, set it in the lowest possible position to minimize the amount of shed that the loom will be trying to create below the floating selvedge line anyway. Not many looms allow this by design, and while those that do not can usually be altered, we do not recommend "customizing" your loom without being very sure you understand what you're trying to accomplish. On most looms, such an alteration would probably consist of replacing the side-bars that hold the back beam/warp beam assembly at a fixed distance from the back of the castle, provided that assembly pivots or folds out from the base of the castle, with longer bars or braces. This would permit the back beam to be positioned, rigidly, at a point farther from and therefore lower than the original position. The two sets of side bars would, of course, be interchangeable.

c) Another fairly common method of reducing harness float is by using harness weights to increase the effect of the harness pulling the warps down to the at-rest position. Some looms are actually supplied with such weights, and indeed power looms use what are called "lingoes" in the industry which are suspended weights used similarly to bring the harnesses down properly, although the requirements on such machines are based on speed and other factors slightly outside the realm of the hand-weaving loom. On our looms, the weights can be simple iron bars, square sections of ¼" or ⅜" stock, 24" to 48" long, depending on the size of the loom and the amount of weight desired. Such weights can be taped securely on the tops of the harnesses for easy installation and removal.

Every jack loom will have a slightly different amount of "down shed" designed into it, so the need for compensation or adjustment for harness float will vary accordingly.

Remember that anything you do to reduce harness float by either minimizing the amount of "down shed" below the floating selvedge line or increasing the dead weight of the harnesses will increase the amount of physical effort required to raise the harnesses. Everything is a trade-off, particularly when you're dealing with such immutable forces as gravity!

The risk of discussing harness float at such length is that you'll infer some great importance from it. Don't! It is simply another consideration that is a little different in weaving rugs than in your other weaving. Our main purpose in analyzing it this way is so that you will: 1) be aware of it and 2) un-

derstand what's happening. It is far more important and useful to know *ahead of time* what can happen and to not worry about it than to be surprised and confused later on!

Warping

Since we can't dodge this little chore any longer, we'll try to lend a few hints for making it go more smoothly. You may have your own procedure but we'll share some ideas, keeping in mind that the relative ease of the set-up for a rug should help make it an almost negligible task.

When we wind the warp onto the warping board, we guide it through a hard cardboard or plastic tube (6" to 8" long, ½" to ¾" diameter) such as you will find inside some yarns. For this particular warp, in which two strands work as one, we: threaded both ends, each from a separate cone, through the tube; attached them to the starting peg on the warp board; then guided them around the pegs with the tube in one hand, loosely guiding them from the floor with the other. The tube does two things: it guides the yarn between pegs accurately without your having to stick your whole hand between them, reducing knuckle wear and allowing greater speed; and it prevents you from squeezing the warp in your fingers, which causes uneven and usually too much tension on the yarn, causing uneven length and at least several documented broken warp boards! Also, with multiple warp strands in each working warp (and here doubled), it prevents dropping one of them. The tube can be used for any type of warp.

For our rug, 40" wide by four warps per inch (unless otherwise noted, a warp or end will mean the doubled strand) means 160 warps; but to give balanced color effect in pick-and-pick, i.e., the same weft color at each selvedge, we would have 159 working warp ends. Since the first and last warps are double for selvedge strength and body, 161 actually were wound. The length of the warp on the warp board was about three yards (almost two yards for the rug plus one for the loom).

We wound two separate warp chains and recombined them on the lease sticks later to prevent overloading the warp board. With each chain, be sure to attach tight chokes, or ties, around the warp at least every yard before taking it off the board (don't forget to tie the cross, too). The choke ties will minimize the natural tendency of almost any hard-twisted rug warp to twist as a bundle. Because of this same characteristic of rug warps, we do not recommend the "non-cross" methods of warping.

We beam the warp before threading so that the warp is not dragging through reed and heddles while we tension it and roll it onto the warp beam. This is by no means mandatory, but we find it more convenient to see the entire warp stretched from back to front, unencumbered by heddles, as we beam. If your harnesses lift out of the loom easily, that helps, too; likewise the reed. Lease sticks should ideally be positioned as firmly as possible between the castle and back beam, spaced at least 1½" apart. If your loom has a horizontal surface here, the sticks can be securely taped or even clamped down. Most looms, however, have a gap that requires suspending the lease sticks by cords or improvising front-to-back slats that the sticks can rest on and be affixed to. In any case, the sticks should be held tightly at about the plane of the breast and back beams.

Without threading first, a raddle is needed to spread the warp out. We recommend a raddle with 1" spaces, especially for rug warps; any finer spacing just means more work dividing threads. Run a steel apron rod through the loop end of the warp and strap it to the rod or stick in the warp beam apron (at the ends only for now) with ½" or ¾" strapping tape (fiberglass re-inforced). The tape should encircle the two rods three or four times, and the rods should be spaced about ½" apart and be *parallel*. Spread out the warp in the raddle, arrange it similarly on the apron rod, tension the warp slightly from the front of the loom, then strap the two rods together at about 8" to 10" intervals across the warp.

Probably the most important area for emphasis and extra effort in beaming a rug warp, as opposed to a softer warp, is rolling it onto the warp beam. If each thread is sufficiently and equally tensioned onto the beam, then your weaving will not be "haunted" part of the way through your rug by slack threads or sections of threads. To ensure this tightness, it is critical to pull any slack off the beam before consecutive turns of warp have rolled over it. The circumference of the warp beam, therefore, will determine how often you should stop rolling and tighten. Most plain warp beams are solid wood with a circumference of 9" to 15", compared to open "reel" type beams of 24" to 36". With either, you should stop and retighten warps every 1 to 1½ turns of the beam. On the smaller beams, three or

four wooden warp sticks should be inserted on every other turn or so. On the larger beams, no sticks or paper are needed on warps under three yards; sticks may be used beyond that and placed over the solid cross-rails of the beam only. Warp sticks can be additional lease sticks, or may be made from smooth softwood such as flat molding stock or narrow lattice. Softwood should be ⅜" thick or more, and at least ¾" wide. Paper or corrugated cardboard, as you may use on softer warps, can compress inconsistently with a rug warp and may actually do more harm than good.

The best method of tensioning to prevent slack from rolling onto the warp beam is to stand sideways to the breast beam at the front of the loom, take 3" to 4" worth of warp at a time and rather than just pulling—and possibly towing your loom around the room—hold the bundle firmly in one hand about 15" from the breast beam and *push down* evenly on the bundle mid-way between the breast beam and your hand with your other hand, or even with your knee. This downward force allows no limit to the force you may apply without sliding or tipping your loom. This should be done all the way across your warp each time, eliminating any need to have tension on the warp when you are rotating the warp beam. You can do this alone every bit as efficiently as with a helper (with whom you would only end up having a tug-of-war to be half as effective).

If you need a tighter grip to hold the bundle, wrap the warps evenly around that hand, but be sure not to twist them when you do so. Now don't laugh, but gloves can be very helpful (especially with linen warps) both for this and for tying the warp onto the cloth beam apron. Golf or sailing gloves, which protect the palms and sides of your hands, but have no fingertips so you can still feel and tie, work well. You look like either Arnold Palmer or Ted Turner, but they work!

Naturally, you should smooth back the threads in each bundle before tightening. If your warp is wound evenly, very little smoothing is needed; usually just snapping and tugging the warp chain will reveal any individually loose warps. If you are smoothing individual warps by pinching (never combing) and sliding the pinch back toward yourself, do so carefully and gently; remember that each warp is continuous with an adjacent warp, being looped over the apron bar, and near the head of the warp, you may actually pull the other end back.

If you do thread the loom before beaming, the rest of this procedure will work better if you lift your harnesses to a position where the heddle eyes are in line with the breast beam and back beam so that the weight of the harnesses will not interfere with the tensioning. Put blocks or books under the harnesses to keep them in this position. This will apply only to jack-type looms with the "down shed" position.

If you want to give our method of warping a try, but haven't because you felt that the reach to the harnesses from the front of the loom was too long, a good way to make threading from the front easier is to raise your harnesses, using blocks under the harnesses, so the heddle eyes are about 4" to 6" above the line from breast beam to back beam.

This allows you to sit straighter and reach more comfortably to the harnesses for threading rather than having to look and reach down into the harnesses while wishing your eyes were on your collarbones. On most contemporary looms this generally means, too, that rather than wishing the breast beam were out of your way, you will have a convenient brace to lean into with your hips.

When you elevate your harnesses for threading, bring your cross in the lease sticks forward also, and try to position it as close to the center of the back harness as you can. This will probably mean suspending the lease sticks at the back of the castle.

Threading

We used a straight threading starting on harness one and ending on harness three. Because of the bulk of the two double warps that form the selvedge we threaded them in two heddles. This will also make the "split selvedge" which we will use easier. So the threading is:

For our sett of four ends per inch, we used a four-dent reed. Clever, eh? Every other dent in an eight-dent work as well, but in that case the "doubled" double selvedges (four strands of yarn) should be split into two dents to avoid squeezing them in the reed. In the four-dent reed the double selvedges occupy one dent.

Tying on the warp to the cloth beam apron is done largely as you would do it for any warp. Because of the extra tension, however, it is very important to avoid slanting or bowing the apron rod or stick. Keep your bundles down to 1¼" to 1½" worth of warp (five or six threads) except for the selvedges, which we usually attach as a smaller bundle so that the point of attachment on the rod will be directly aligned with the selvedge threads' position in the reed rather than flaring out from a knot. This will help prevent any tendency to draw in the selvedge at the outset. A diagram of the tie-on sequence is shown below.

3rd	5th	1st	4th	2nd
others	others	others	others	

Heading

After tying on and checking tension we're ready to begin the heading to spread out the warp. We use strips of toilet paper for a cheap and easy-to-find-and-measure heading weft; others use old nylons or multi-stranded scraps.

In *Shed A* put one strip across about halfway between the apron rod and the beater. Change to *Shed B* to put in another strip next to the first. Close the shed and beat both strips into place. Change back to Shed A, and proceed as before putting in one strip, changing to shed B for the next strip, then beating. You'll need five or six heading strips to spread the warp. Now is a great time to check for threading errors. Look carefully at the heading weaving because after this point it is very hard to correct a mistake.

To create a very neat base for the fringe, we're going to twine the edge before beginning weaving. For an especially closely twined edge we used a single strand of the four-ply warp twined around *individual* warp threads rather than around the doubled warp threads (eight twists per inch). It would work almost as well to have used a doubled strand of warp to twine around the doubled warps —four twists per inch.

Cut a piece of warp four yards long and fold it in half. Bring one end of the strand up between the left hand doubled selvedge threads. Twine around them double. Then begin twining around the individual strands. Be careful not to miss any warps. Every 1" or so stop to beat the twining in against the heading and at the same time check to see that you haven't missed any. At the right hand selvedge, again twine around the double warps as illustrated and bring the ends back around the last pair back through the loop and tighten gently.

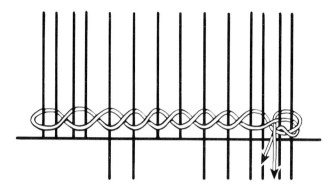

Beginning weaving

All through the weaving, as new wefts begin and inactive wefts end, we *taper and fluff* them to reduce bulk so that they can be woven in, virtually eliminating the need for working them back into the warp direction with a needle or hook. To taper the end, cut one ply about 3" from the end and strip it off the end. Cut one of the two remaining plies about 1"-1½" from the end and strip it, too. Untwist each ply slightly and pick at it to taper and fray out the end of each ply. This could be done with any plied yarn.

A note about shuttles: We recommend medium length ski-type shuttles (18"-21" long) because they hold at least four ounces of yarn easily while leaving you a smooth sliding surface to go through the shed, and a turned up tip to avoid warp snags. You should have a least two, and three or four would be real handy for all of the color changes.

Wind two shuttles full of deep red yarn. (Yes, even when weaving a solid color area in a rug which is mainly pick-and-pick we use two shuttles because the appearance of the selvedges will be more consistent.) Taper and fluff the end of each weft.

Begin the first weft in *Shed A* (1+3) by leaving the last 2" of weft hanging outside the selvedge. This will be two-ply only, as the third ply ended about 1" before the selvedge. To bring the tapered end back into the weaving in the same shed without creating a two-thread skip-over at the selvedge, bring that end back in by splitting the double selvedge and bringing the weft around and back in between the two warps. This same technique will be used throughout. (Since only two of the plies

are making the trip around the selvedge the extra bulk which normally occurs is reduced.) Leaving some slack in the weft, beat it in place — more about leaving slack in a minute. Put the shuttle down on the weaving.

Begin the second weft in *Shed B* (2+4) in the same way starting from the opposite side. It will be quite helpful to tape a label to each shuttle designating the shed for which the shuttle is used. Leave slack, and beat the weft in place. Put the shuttle down on the bench beside you.

Now that the weaving has begun the next consideration is how to achieve consistent, non-wavy selvedges that don't pull in. The secrets to this are: 1) how the weft is placed and beaten, and 2) how the wefts intertwine at the selvedges. Weave another shot in *Shed A* and as this active weft comes out of the shed (it will pass out under the doubled selvedge) use your thumb and index finger to hold the opposite selvedge edge at the fell while the active weft is pulled snug in against that selvedge. Then allow the weft to go slack, *put the shuttle down on the weaving* and arrange the weft as follows: Release the edge of the weaving and use that hand to create a small bubble near the selvedge edge by pinching the weft (index finger below and thumb above the warp) 1½" to 2" from the edge and slide the weft toward the fell. Do not pull the weft tight against the fell, just to about ¼" from the fell. Now use the same hand to pinch the weft about 13" to 15" from the selvedge and begin to push the weft toward the reed. Simultaneously use the other hand to nudge the weft down at a point about 13" to 15" from the opposite side. The weft should take about the path shown.

Grip the beater with both hands and start to pull it toward you. As the beater moves toward you, begin to close the shed. As the weft arcs are flattening, the shed should be completely closed. Lean back and pull hard with your whole body, not just your arms.

As you begin to develop a "feel" for the springy character of the weft, the way that it constricts in thickness when stretched then recovers to its full thickness when slackened, you can start to see how different wefts might behave and how you would need to handle them differently. Where the three-ply pulls itself back into the shed somewhat, giving itself slack to curve over and under the warps and "fill in" the weave (a stiffer, less elastic yarn, one lacking the "coil spring" nature of the three-ply) would need to be given more of the necessary slack

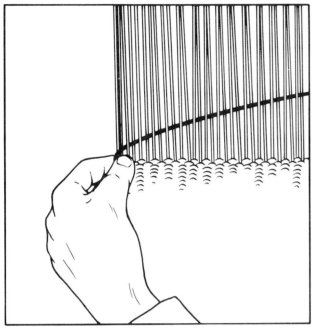

Use your thumb and index finger to hold the selvedge edge at the fell while the weft is pulled snug against it.

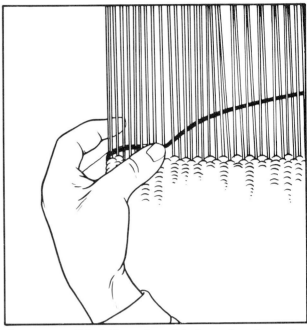

Create a small bubble 1½" to 2" in from the edge and slide the weft toward the fell.

With your left hand, pinch the weft about 13" to 15" from the selvedge and begin to push the weft toward the reed.

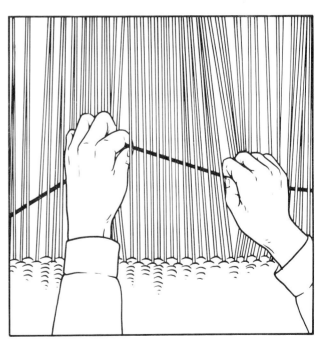

At the same time, use the other hand to nudge the weft down at a point 13" to 15" from the opposite side.

manually by increased waving or bubbling before beating. Our technical section will analyze the differences in yarns further, but for now, as you weave, try to visualize what is happening to the yarn.

Weave a few shots with too little slack, then with too much, and see what happens (then take them out, of course!). With the wefts stretched through the shed before beating, you'll see that no matter how hard you beat, they do not cover the warp because they have insufficient length to travel over and under the warps and fill out over the surface, but have been constricted by trying to stretch to reach from selvedge to selvedge. As you can imagine, in addition to not covering the warp, that poor weft will be desperately trying to pull back some slack from the ends, the effect of which is to pull the selvedges back in toward the middle.

Now you should be ready to continue with the actual rug in *Shed B*. The second important action to get consistent selvedges is just that — be consistent in how the wefts intertwine at the selvedge. We suggest you tape two labels to the front of the first harness or the breast beam. These should say:

out under —
  put it down at the fell

out over —
  put it down on the bench

This will serve as a constant reminder to do just that. When the shuttle comes out of the shed under the selvedge, put it down on the weaving at the fell. When the shuttle comes out over the selvedge, put it down on the bench next to you!

Pick the shuttle up from the bench and enter the shuttle in the shed. As you take the shuttle out of the shed but before you pull it taut, use the opposite hand to hold the nonactive weft at the selvedge. Use your middle, ring and index fingers to hold the loose weft gently. Use your thumb and index finger of the same hand to grasp the weft right outside the selvedge at the fell (index finger under the rug, thumb on top). While holding the nonactive weft slightly taut, use the shuttle-holding hand to pull the active weft up tight against the selvedge and the non-active weft. Leave plenty of slack, put the shuttle down on the bench. (This latter technique will be used whenever both shuttles are on the same side.) Bubble and beat as before. Continue alternating these two shuttles in their designated sheds. (Here we think you'll find the labelled shuttles very helpful, especially with just one color.)

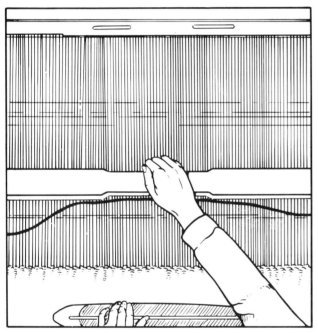

As the beater moves toward you, begin to close the shed. As the weft arcs are flattening, the shed should be completely closed.

We're going to continue these two shuttles for 5" so you'll have plenty of practice before we get to two colors. It is a good idea to measure your weaving every couple of inches to assure yourself that you're keeping the right width (about 39¼") and that the distance from beater to fell is the same in at least three places. If it is narrowing more than ½" you'll want to take out some of the weaving and add a little more height and depth in your waves. If the distance from the fell is not the same or if there is a hump toward the reed, your tension is uneven and you should re-tie at the apron stick.

After 5" of red we're going to end one red weft and begin a dark brown. In a pick-and-pick rug, when one color stops and another starts, the most convenient way to do this is to overlap the tapered and fluffed ends a couple of inches in from the selvedge. If you don't like the looks of this transition, end the tapered red weft at one selvedge in the same way it was begun (only two of the three plies go around and back in to the shed to reduce bulk — split the double selvedge). Begin the brown weft on the opposite side (this is to reduce any bulk build-up caused by the turned back ends).

Alternate the red and brown for 6". End the brown and begin again with another shuttle of red. Then continue following the overall guide using your own judgement for placement of spots.

When a spot is introduced you will need to use the split selvedge technique to avoid the two-thread skip-over at the selvedge. The next shot (of background) will probably need to have the selvedge split also, or possibly just circle the selvedge creating an extra loop around the selvedge before re-entering the shed. After weaving the spot weft check your shuttles to make sure you've got the right one for the shed you're weaving.

When the rug is finished duplicate the twining at the end. Weave an "ending" of three or four picks of your heading material and cut the rug off the loom, leaving about 8" of warp to be worked into fringe. Remove the rug from the cloth apron bar by untying. You should have about 8" of warp to use for fringe.

Finishing

When a rug comes off the loom, it is almost inevitable that there will be bumps and bulges in places they shouldn't be. We usually devote an hour or more to working them out. Do not take out any

headings or endings yet. Just tie groups of warps loosely in overhand knots to hold them in place.

Spread the rug out on a large, hard, flat surface that can take moist heat. We have a big countertop, but a clean floor or a sheet of exterior plywood would work, too. Begin by smoothing and pulling at the rug to achieve the best shape you can at this point. If your surface is plywood you could tack corners in place and even out small variations in selvedge width.

First, we attack bulges and bumps with steam, and then give the whole rug a thorough general steaming. You'll need a steam iron and a spray bottle filled with water (distilled, if your water has any particularly troublesome residues such as iron), and a washcloth or similar sized piece of terry cloth fabric. If your hands are sensitive to heat a pair of good fitting gloves will probably save some wear and tear on your skin. Be prepared to donate them to rug finishing though, because the heat and moisture will probably ruin them for anything else.

Wet the washcloth thoroughly with the sprayer. You want it quite moist but not soaking wet. Lay the cloth over a bulge and "iron" the washcloth very gently with a resting and lifting motion. Do not put the full weight of the iron on the rug, just enough to get the iron to steam the water in the cloth. Once the area is quite hot and steamy remove the cloth and use your hands to push, pound, pull and smooth the bump. You may want to go over one area several times in a row, or come back to the area after working on others. With two people working together some variations in selvedge width can be stretched out after steaming the 8"-10" in from the edge.

Since we work with wool wefts, this process is relatively easy and effective. Synthetics will not respond to this treatment by easing, stretching and shrinking to smooth out imperfections.

Gently pull (unweave) about six warps out of the heading (three of your doubled warps which are now individually separated by the twining) and divide them into three groups of two. Braid these in a standard three-strand braid. Finish the end of the braid with an overhand knot or wrap the ends for a smoother finish. Continue across in this way.

Analyzing what we have just finished

Now that we have completed our rug and can look at the process as a whole, it's a good time to go back and analyze what the plain weave rug structure is all about in more detail. What have we made the yarns do to come up with the desired result, and how can we apply what has happened here to other possible materials and warp setts we might use in other rugs?

To organize the sequence of thinking here, we offer the following:

1. desired result: the tightest, firmest rug possible.
2. this result will derive from the closest possible warp sett which allows proper warp coverage by the weft.
3. this, in turn, requires the proper balance or relationship of the variable elements, namely, the warp size and sett and the weft size and characteristics.

Point 3, then, is what we need to learn how to do in order to get the desired result from whatever choice and combination of appropriate materials we might be working with. The central fact of life of the weft-faced plain weave rug structure (which affects how we achieve the proper balance and arrangement of materials) is what we call the "dilemma"! It is simply that each weft can cover only one side of a segment of warp at a time as it intersects with that warp. The segment that it covers will be equal to the maximum expanded diameter of that weft, of course. Therefore, the opposite side or exposure of the same segment of that warp must be covered by the next weft. The fact of one weft passing over a particular warp and the next passing under it is a function of the two sheds of plain weave. The dilemma, however, arises when those consecutive wefts must then be pressed together *between* warps, one passing from above one warp to below the next, the other passing from below the one warp to above the next. At that point between warps where the tooth of the reed beats each weft against the previous one, sufficient compression is necessary to ensure proper coverage on the rug's surfaces. Those two wefts, which together are covering the front and back surfaces of the same segment of warp, must compress to occupy effectively the space of a single weft.

Three terms that we will use in discussing how to deal with this dilemma are:

- *compression point:* the point where consecutive wefts meet between warps and are compressed by beating.
- *expansion point:* the point on the surface of the weave where a weft crosses (intersects) a warp and expands to its maximum diameter to cover the warp.

- *axis* of the yarn: the imaginary center line of a yarn, like a core thread inside the yarn.

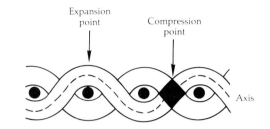

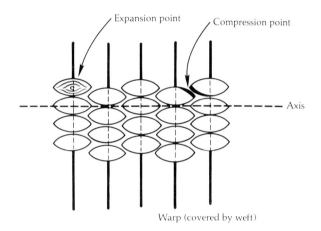

To begin to develop an eye for this, let's take a look first at what the yarns are doing in some other familiar weaves.

In a balanced plain weave, or tabby, warp and weft do the same thing as each other (assuming they are the same yarn); all they do is bend slightly over and under each other as they intersect. All that changes is the axis of the yarn as it curves up and down, allowing warp and weft to conform equally to each other. Depending on the characteristics of the yarn, it may flatten out somewhat where it intersects (soft yarn) or it may retain its natural roundness (harder yarn).

In a classic overshot, we have the same tabby fabric forming a ground weave plus a pattern weft of a heavier yarn which embellishes the ground weave almost as stitchery would. The pattern weft must pass through the ground fabric, then float over it for varying distances according to the pattern. As you can see, or may have experienced, a puffy yarn will compress to squeeze through the tabby (here the tabby yarn may compress somewhat as well) and then will expand in the overshot floats to cover the tabby and create the solid surface of the pattern block. Conversely, a hard or stiff pattern yarn, while apparently the correct thickness, will distort the tabby where it passes through by merely forcing the tabby open rather than compressing, and then create a stringy, sparse pattern block by not expanding the floats.

What we are seeing is the importance of changes not only in the axis of the yarn, but in the *shape* of the yarn as well, in producing the desired result. Compression and expansion are the ways in which a yarn can change shape that are most critical.

The biggest problem with *seeing* what the yarn does in our plain weave rug is that by the time one weft has been forced or molded into its final configuration in the weaving process, it is obscured by a succeeding weft. If you unweave the last shot to see what happened to the one before it, what happened to it isn't happening any more, because it was only being made to happen by the subsequent shot being beaten against it! (Sound like Catch-22?)

So, unlike in balanced weaves where everything is fairly visible, our rug weave forces us to rely more on deduction and logical speculation to determine what is happening. At least we know that the only yarn that changes at all in either its axis or its shape is the weft. The warp remains straight, neither compressing nor expanding, and remains in a single plane.

Think of a single weft shot somewhere in the middle of our rug. Imagine it as a nice round piece of yarn travelling in a straight line from selvedge to selvedge. Obviously, that's not what it looks like in the rug! Its axis is bending constantly as it passes over and under the "non-conforming" warps. Since the plain weave structure demands more bending over and under warps for a given sett than any other structure of weave, then it is clear to see that the weft will need more length (slack) to accomplish this without causing draw-in.

Basically, every weft shot must change shape regularly (alter its natural roundness) as it crosses the warp. In the tabby each thread merely interlaced warp with weft evenly, by bending. In our rug, the weft has had to change direction or bend to pass over and under each warp in turn, plus it compressed weft against weft between the warps (i.e., at the compression point) then expanded as it passed over the warp. It is this compression of consecutive wefts together and expansion over warps that, given proper warp sett, sufficient warp tension and strong enough beating, produced the weft-faced effect. Conversely, if the weft did not compress or expand, it would only bend, and the result

would be that each warp would show wherever a weft passed under it.

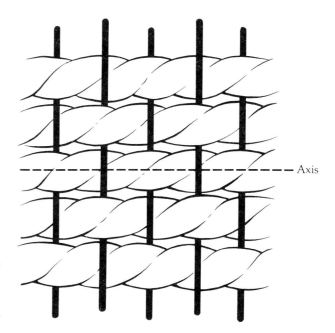

Axis

This is a fairly obvious concept, but it is central to selecting appropriate yarns and matching them to a warp sett that will result in a well-crafted rug. Because the plain weave structure is the tightest, resulting from the maximum number of yarn interlacements, it places the most stringent requirements on the weft to "perform". A looser weave structure such as twill is less demanding of both yarn and weaver because the structure itself allows easier coverage of the warp. But if you can master this concept for the plain weave rug, it will apply in varying degrees to all rug structures.

The firmest, most solid and therefore (as we have said right along) the most desirable plain weave rug, will derive from the closest warp sett which still allows warp coverage. If there is room for the compression point to move side to side, then the compression points of consecutive wefts can also shift around between warps (see next page). This quite simply means that the structure of the rug is insufficient to prevent shifting of its materials within the weave, and, in practical use of the rug, it means that under the wear of footsteps the materials can wear internally, that is, grind against themselves within the weave. It also means that the surface of the weft yarn is exposed for a greater distance at a time than necessary, exposing longer lengths of individual fibers to snags and greater wear from abrasion against foot and floor.

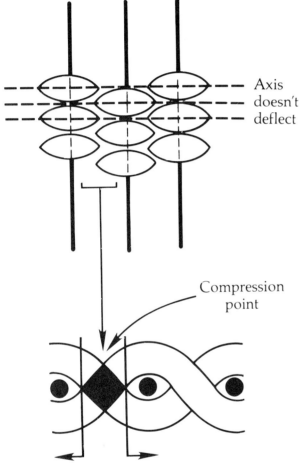

Axis
doesn't
deflect

Compression
point

Compression column is
wider so compression
points can shift from
side to side between
warps (wider sett in relation to diameter of
weft).

Therefore, it is most desirable that the warp sett *confine* the compression point where consecutive wefts cross to a straight line or column, mid-way between warps, and not allow room for that point to shift side to side.

The weft must reduce its natural diameter (in the warp direction) so that when it passes over the adjacent warps, the axis or selvedge-to-selvedge center line of that weft has been pushed (beaten) down far enough toward the fell of the rug that its natural expansion from the axis can then cover the exposed segment of the warps. In a plain weave rug weft, just as in most wefts, the axis will change direction only in a two-dimensional plane which is perpendicular to the warp as it goes over and under the warp. The axis *does not* curve or turn in the warp direction into the spaces over warps that must be covered. Those spaces are filled by weft expansion only, the puffing out from the compressed dimension. If you were to sight across the fell of your rug from selvedge to selvedge and imagine the axis of each weft, it would be going straight away from or toward your eye—up and down, over and under warps, but *not* bending side to side as you view it.

From these requirements of the yarn, we see that the characteristics of weft, and the size and sett of the warp, must be carefully coordinated to produce a successful result. To illustrate, let's look at some different wefts and apply these principles and requirements to them, starting with the yarn we just used in our rug.

We have already seen the benefit of the natural *spring*iness of the three-ply twist in producing the right amount of slack in each weft shot as you weave. The three-ply twist also makes the yarn compress and expand more easily because it makes a bulkier or loftier yarn than if the same number of wool fibers found in a cross section of the yarn were spun into a suitable single, heavier ply. The three plies create air space between themselves in much the same way round logs, stacked parallel, do, compared to taking the same wood, sawing it into flat boards and stacking it that way.

The effects of this increased ability to expand and compress are obvious in relation to the need for it to do so in the weave structure. Furthermore, because they are separate, unlike the single spun mass of fibers of a one-ply, the three separate plies tend to realign themselves at these two critical points, and additionally can actually mesh with the plies of next weft rather than meeting surface to surface. At the compression point, the plies can align themselves side by side to become flatter in relation to the warp direction. Then as they rise over the warp, they can similarly realign themselves to flatten out over the warp and cover it. The natural crimp of wool fiber does some of the expansion and compression, and the plied structure does the rest.

It is clear that a single ply offers the most contrast with our three-ply weft. A single ply with yardage equal to this three-ply (265 yards per pound) and spun of the same fiber blend, would be a smaller diameter yarn it if had sufficiently hard twist in it to be as durable. Durability derives from both twist and fiber quality; of course, the number of twists per inch in a ply determines how much of the surface of individual fibers is exposed to abrasion on the surface of the yarn. The three-ply can have a fairly hard spin in each ply to protect the fibers, but maintain its loft and spring through its plying as we have discussed. The single ply yarn, therefore, to be equally durable as each such smaller ply, must have proportional twist and so will be stiffer over its length and less compressible and expandable in the weave. To get proper warp coverage then, adjustments must be made in both weft slackening as you weave and possibly in beating and warp tension. Since a stiffer yarn will not slacken itself to the extent of a springy one, you may have to manually arrange slack in the weft shot by creating waves that approach the technique of bubbling, as in tapestry weaving, depending on how stiff the yarn is. This is to provide enough length of yarn for the weft to go over and under all the warps without causing draw-in. A less compressible yarn will actually require slightly more length for this because the yarn is not flattening out as much on top of warps as it passes over, and therefore the axis is travelling a bit longer, "curvier" path.

A "Pin Warp" for Yarn Analysis

Because the warp in a weft-faced rug does not change shape or alignment, you can make a "pin warp" device like the one below to analyze what goes on in rug weave structures. We developed this simple device to magnify and "freeze" what happens to various weft yarns as they conform to the warp. Just weave the weft through the "warp" pins to duplicate any weave structure you like, and see where and how the weft must expand or compress to beat down and cover the warp.

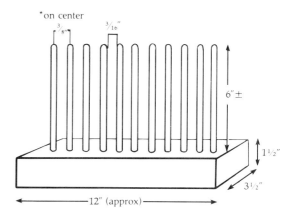

*Spacing of pins can vary according to different weft yarns to be used.

Materials: A 1' piece of 2×4; 6' of ³⁄₁₆" steel rod, cut to approximately 6½" lengths, rounded smooth cone end. Note: drill pilot holes for pins as straight as possible so "warps" will be parallel.)

Axis—must follow "curvier" path in harder yarn because yarn is not flattening against the warps on surfaces of the rug.

Axis—follows straighter path in more compressible weft.

You might imagine using a closer warp sett when using a hard twist one-ply, because its smaller diameter leaves some empty space between warps. But a closer sett would narrow the space for the weft compression to occur, and if the compression point for a yarn with very little compression/expansion capacity is limited in side-to-side movement to a column, the axis of the yarn may not be beaten close enough to the fell for the yarn's limited expansion to cover the warp. So we are finding that as a trade-off for the harder weft yarn, (which may have the colors we need or whose more pebbly surface texture and pronounced warp ridges may be desirable in the finished rug), we may need to allow some shifting or movement of the compression point if we are to get proper warp coverage. Despite the slightly increased wear and structural looseness compared to our sample rug, this shifting lets one compression point beat in *next to* as well as *on top of* the previous one, thereby letting the axis of the yarn beat down closer to the fell. Remember that even if you are comfortable with this kind of trade-off, you will be working a little harder to achieve the best possible results because of the extra manual arrangement of each weft shot.

Another change that makes warp coverage a little easier is to reduce the size of the warp from two strands to one or to a finer warp yarn. This will reduce the radius of the warp itself which the weft will have to curve over and under, as well as increase the space between warps for compression /intersection to occur. These benefits will be only very slight, however, and will obviously decrease warp strength; so again, you must weigh the pros and cons.

Increasing warp tension will generally help warp coverage; additional beater weights and just plain beating harder will help to force a little more compression (but not expansion) into a hard weft; but at some point any given yarn just won't compress any more.

Many weavers might feel that all else being equal, a *softer* spun single ply, again with the same yardage and fiber blends as we've looked at so far, would be a way of getting a one-ply to beat in properly on the same warp and sett. If the yarn were spun softly enough to have similar loft and compression as the three-ply, it would indeed beat in much the same (although the coil spring effect of the three-ply still makes weft slackening, etc., easier). But to induce that much loft a generally un-

acceptable trade-off would be made: the soft twist would leave too much of the length of the wool fibers exposed on the yarn's surface and therefore on the rug's surface, and more rapid deterioration from abrasion would be inevitable in practical use.

With the rug we have woven as a reference point, and now with the other comparisons of weft we have made, we should have the basic tools for determining appropriate warp setts for other wefts. A three-ply with similar characteristics of fiber and spring, but with twice the yardage and so half as much fiber in the cross section, should work well on a sett of eight ends per inch and with a warp of effectively twice the yardage of that we used.

We actually tried what we believed at first to be just such a "half-scale" yarn, however, and found that it worked better with the warp sett at six. We realized that the yarn was spun and twisted to yield twice the yardage, but it was spun from the *same* fiber blend as its big brother three-ply. So to truly create a half-scale yarn, it would have required using a wool fiber of half the count or coarseness, i.e., a very fine wool. This would not be suitable for a rug yarn, but would have produced closer equivalent characteristics of compression and expansion to the heavier yarn. Without such adjustment of the fiber, however, we had a yarn which was proportionally harder or denser, requiring the slightly wider sett.

If, then, a more pronounced warp ridge or beaded surface were sought with this smaller three-ply, increasing the warp size would be called for. And that, in turn, might require a wider sett still, though not necessarily. Slightly more work to produce the additional weft slack needed to follow the curvier path over and under a heavier warp would be our preference to ensure greater overall tightness.

Another application of this concept is to again take a springy three-ply, but with just slightly more yardage, i.e., slightly lighter weight, of 300 yards per pound (about 10% to 15% lighter). If our most critical consideration is to retain the solid structure, and warp size and sett are the elements we can adjust, what do we do? A 10%-15% increase in the warp sett, using the same thickness, is impractical because 10%-15% of four is .4 to .6. A warp sett of 4.4 to 4.6 ends per inch? Every other dent in a nine-dent reed would be close, but nine-dent reeds are uncommon. So we can either go to five ends per inch and reduce the size of the warp slightly or stay at four ends per inch and increase the effective

A plain weave rug with strong, crisp, asymmetrical design lines is as appropriate on the wall as on the floor.
All three rugs in this chapter could have been woven on the same warp—evidence of the versatility of plain weave.
SETTING AND ACCESSORIES: GALLERY EAST, LOVELAND, COLORADO

warp size by perhaps adding another strand to have a tripled warp.

A four-ply rug yarn with 300 yards per pound is not significantly different from the three-ply. From what we said about the characteristics of the three-ply, you can imagine that the four-ply will also be fairly springy, although with four smaller plies there will be a bit less air between the plies, so slightly less expansion and compression. Probably the only adjustment needed for such a yarn is a somewhat harder, repeated beat compared to the equivalent three-ply, and possibly a bit more work in arranging weft slack.

Another fairly common rug yarn is the two-ply "rya" type yarn with a sharp twist of the plies around each other. The traditional twist is designed into the yarn so that it will remain firmly plied in cut-pile techniques, but as a flat, plain weave weft the distinct separation of the plies tends to produce little shadows on the surface of the rug which, at least to the very particular eye, can detract from the visual firmness of that surface, although no appreciable loss of durability results. The somewhat irregular surface texture and shadowing of the two-ply derives from its less round cross-section than either a one-ply or three-ply. This type of yarn's ability to compress and expand is similar to the three-ply's, and it will require only slightly more manual weft slackening to produce satisfactory warp coverage and tightness.

We have spoken so often of trade-offs and compromises that another general style of rug yarn which illustrates compromise is good to mention here. The Swedish-style one-plies that usually yield around 500 to 600 yards per pound offer some interesting variations. The coarser, harder twisted yarn, traditionally with up to 25% goat or cow hair blended with wool, will need a wider warp sett of five or six ends per inch due to less compression capacity and depending on how much manual arrangement of slack you are game to do. There are also versions of the same style of yarn which are more loosely twisted and spun from all wool fiber of a noticeably softer grade. Here a tighter warp sett is possible and therefore necessary to achieve a

firm-bodied rug and to protect the more delicate fibers from abrasion. The construction of the yarn makes for less work, but also for commensurately less durability.

Finally, using multiple strands of yarn in a single shed as weft can, as we've mentioned, be an effective method of color blending for a tweed or "ragg" effect, but the possibility of each of several strands lying in the weft equally smoothly is practically nil. The result is usually an uneven, thready surface texture that, in terms of the smooth, solid, regular surface we want for a plain weave rug, is visually less pleasing to us. Any such unevenness indicates certain strands of weft being less tightly integrated into the rug's surface and therefore, technically, more susceptible to wear than others.

Depending on the character of the individual yarns in a multi-strand weft, the compression/expansion characteristics will be roughly similar to those of a three-ply or four-ply, probably not quite as good, but your fundamental considerations of warp and sett will about the same.

Yarn is such an imprecise thing, imperfect, perhaps, in the sense that it is never an *exact* size, or *exact* weight or count. Yet that very aspect of yarn and the resulting imprecision of weaving itself accounts in large part for the joy of it. If we were seeking precision and scientific perfection, we might be better off as machinists or engineers. We have not constructed charts and graphs with every warp/weft/sett combination for plain weave rugs carved in stone. Instead, we have given you a better way, a clearer way, we hope, of looking at the plain weave rug, both to understand what it should be as well as how to make it that way. Probably everyone would agree that if a house were constructed using only half as many floor timbers or wall studs as usual, it might, at a glance, look the same, but it would be "shoddy". So too would a rug woven just to *look* like a rug, but with only half the warps, be less than a true rug; it would, in fact, be "sleazy". Without imposing standards that can be strictly measured, we hope the standard of craftsmanship reflected in a properly woven plain weave rug can be embraced by anyone.

The Weft Face Twill Rug

Marilyn Dillard

ne of the basic weaves, the ever popular twill with its many threading and treadling possibilities, is durable as well as interesting and versatile in weft-face rug weaving. The natural characteristic of the twill threadings allow the weft yarn to float over more than one warp end. When these weft floats are beaten into a warp set at 4-6 e.p.i., the result is a smooth, thick weave structure suitable for rugs. Because the weft floats pack in on top of each other, a twill rug is thicker than a plain weave rug.

The minimum number of harnesses for a twill is three. Four harnesses offer more possibilities, and with more than four harnesses the threadings can be even more complex. Twill weave threadings can be straight, pointed, double or triple pointed, skipped, undulating and maybe more! The treadlings can be straight, broken, reversed, extended and treadled on opposites. Considering the many twills found in any weaving book, or the ones you can dream up, along with all the treadling variations, the possibilities in patterning seem endless—narrow verticals, wide verticals, short diagonals, long diagonals, sometimes squares, and even triangles.

A well crafted handwoven rug should be durable, have strong edges and lie flat on the floor. A weft face twill rug can easily meet these requirements by the nature of the threading. Equally as important as the weave structure for a well crafted rug are the equipment and materials. A good portion of this chapter discusses looms and other miscellaneous equipment, warps and wefts, and how to use each of them in rug weaving.

Next is some basic information on design. Good design can make a well-made rug even better. I'll get back to some twill possibilities—threadings, treadling, sampling.

The equipment

Let's consider some of the usual weaving equipment owned by the typical handweaver. The floor loom—counterbalance, countermarch or jack—is suggested equipment for rug weaving. A table loom is sufficient for samples or weaving a small mat, but beyond those small items, you'll need a floor loom to weave a durable rug (unless, of course, you're weaving Navajo-style). Whatever kind of floor loom is available to you, it can probably weave a rug.

It's often suggested that you attach an iron bar to the beater. This is done by many rug weavers, but if you have any reservations about doing that, don't worry. Using your own body strength to beat can add a good deal of weight to that loom beater. But weighted or not, the heavy beat necessary for a well crafted rug will usually cause the loom to jump or move across the floor.

One way to deal with that problem is this: Tie the loom down so that it is stationary and cannot move even an inch across the floor. You will need two heavy duty screw eyes or hooks and several yards of good quality heavy rope, such as clothesline. Nylon ropes will usually stretch, so cotton is preferred. First place the loom so that the back beam is parallel to a wall. The distance from the wall should provide enough space for the weaver to comfortably work at the back of the loom threading or tying the warp ends.

Second, find a good place along the baseboard of the wall where a heavy duty screw eye or hook can be screwed into the wall. It is best to locate a stud. If the floor area where the loom is placed is concrete, a special heavy duty screw eye made expressly for concrete can be drilled into the concrete floor where the wall and floor meet. Check with a hardware store about how to do this properly. Screw the eyes or hooks into the baseboard or floor.

Third, determine which part of the loom is a major support structure. It might be the legs in front that hold the breast beam, or it could be a wide middle leg that holds the harnesses. Tie the cotton rope to that support and then extend the rope through the inside of the loom to the hook or screw eye at the floor or wall, and tie securely. Repeat on the other side of the loom. A word of caution: keep the rope as close to the floor as possible in order to avoid tripping over it later. With the loom now rigid, a great deal of force is possible with each beat.

Good ski shuttles are a sound investment for rug weaving. They hold a good deal of weft and they are designed to slide through the shed easily. However, some ski shuttles seem to be better than others. Ski shuttles have a hook at each end to hold the weft as it is wound, and the shape of that hook is important. A well designed ski shuttle should have a hook that is gently curved down so that it will not catch on the warp ends while it is traveling through the shed. Some ski shuttles just do not have enough hook, and some do not have any.

The height of the ski shuttle is also important. It should be minimal in order to slide through the shed easily.

Rug temples are more widely used by weavers today than ten years ago. I was introduced to a rug temple, or stretcher, through Peter Collingwood's *The Techniques of Rug Weaving*. Without reservations, I purchased one immediately and have used one for every rug since. Each weaver approaches a project differently and I have always given careful consideration to the selvedge draw-in. If the draw-in is more than ½", it is too much. One way to eliminate that draw-in and have nice even edges throughout the woven project, is to use a temple. A temple can alleviate special problems caused by a close sett or a good deal of interlacement.

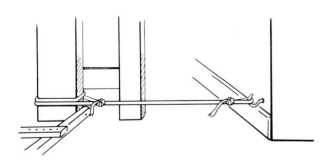

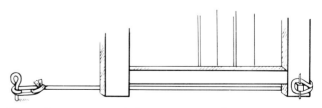

Heavy-duty screw eye drilled into concrete floor.

A large-eyed tapestry needle is handy for darning in the weft ends. There are many satisfactory kinds on the market; my favorite is a straight one, 5" long.

The materials

Proper materials in rug weaving result in a well crafted, handsome and durable rug that will wear for many years. The warp ends are under a great deal of tension throughout the entire weaving process and, therefore, the warp yarns must be very strong.

There are several kinds of warp yarns to consider for rug weaving. The three most commonly used are cotton, wool or linen. Horsehair, cowhair and some synthetics are sometimes used. The strength of the yarn is significant. The warp yarns will affect the overall feel, or handle, of the rug. Generally speaking, a cotton or wool warp will produce a softer, more limp rug, while linen produces a firmer rug.

The warp is completely covered by the weft in weft-face weaving, and is visible only at each end. Some thought should be given to the color. Cottons and wools are available in many colors, while linen warp is usually white or natural.

The common sizes of cotton carpet warp are 8/4 and 8/6. Cotton twine, such as seine twine, is available in many sizes. Common wool warp is two-ply or three-ply, tightly spun, and the Navajo wool warp. Linen rug warp is available in dry spun (rough) or wet spun (smooth). Common sizes are 6/3, 8/2, 8/3, 10/5, 10/6, 20/11 and 30/12.

Realizing there are so many weights, it is difficult to give an exact formula that will always work when choosing a warp. My own simple rule is: the warp and weft must be compatible. The heavier the warp, the wider the sett, the heavier the weft. The finer the warp, the closer the sett, the finer the weft. In order for the warp and weft to be compatible, one may need to be doubled or tripled to be a companion to the other. A warp may be used single, doubled or tripled; a weft can also be used single or grouped. The amount of warp yarn to be used for a rug project should be figured by the yard. Remember there is no warp take-up in weft-face weaving.

The weft yarns must also be durable, and I suggest they be wool. "Rug wool" is a common term used by yarn suppliers. It is available in weights of two-ply (to be doubled or tripled), three-ply, four-ply, and even six-ply. Single wool yarn with a firm twist in medium or heavy weight is also good. Rug wool should be firm and tightly spun. Twist is important, as it affects the durability of a rug, especially if it is to withstand the wear and tear of being walked on. At the same time, the weft yarn should be pliable enough to beat well and pack nicely in order to cover the warp.

It is a good idea to wash all the weft yarns before weaving them, especially if the yarns have been wound on a cone. Washing opens the yarn; it will weave better and beat in better after washing.

Skein the weft yarns before washing. Use warm water and a mild soap for washing. In order to wash several pounds at a time, use a large utility sink or bathtub. After rinsing, squeeze out as much excess water as possible or, use the spin cycle of a washing machine. Air dry the skeins of yarn. A washing machine can be used for washing the yarn if you are careful to never let the machine agitate; work the machine manually.

The amount of weft yarn to be used for a rug project is figured by the pound. A weft-face twill rug usually requires ⅓ to ½ pound of weft per square foot, though a sample will give you more precise information for figuring quantities.

A warp separating material, such as 1" strips of rags, is needed at the beginning and ending of the rug. It holds the extra inches of warp ends necessary to do the finishing techniques after the rug is removed from the loom. A minimum of 5" in warp separating material should be woven, and 6" or 7" is even better. The finishing techniques are easier to do with longer warp ends. Sew or glue several 1" strips of rags together in order to have a continuous weft. Other heavy, firm fibers can be substituted, but I personally prefer the rag strips.

The weft base, or temporary weft protector, should be a rug wool, though it is not part of the actual rug. It plays an important role at the beginning and ending of the rug. I think of it as a weft *base* because it provides a firm, straight fell line to beat the first picks of the rug against. (The fell line is the last beaten pick.) The warp separating material does not provide the kind of firm, solid interlacement necessary for beating in the first picks of the rug, nor is it solid enough to hold the rug wefts in place when the rug is removed from the loom. One inch of weft base should be adequate. You won't remove the weft base until you're ready to do the finishing techniques; it is keeping the first and last picks of rug weft yarns from working loose.

Warping

Any usual method of warping a loom — front to back, back to front — is satisfactory for weft face rug weaving as well. Typical setts are four, five, six or eight ends per inch, depending on the size of the warp and weft yarns to be used. Double floating selvedges are important when weaving a twill weft face rug because they provide durable outside warps on every pick. In general, if you are sleying an end in every dent, sley your floating selvedges in the *same* dent as the edge warps. If you're sleying every other dent, or some other more open sequence, sley your floating selvedges in the dent *next to* your edge warps. The floating selvedges are not threaded through the heddles. They must be allowed to "float" in a neutral position.

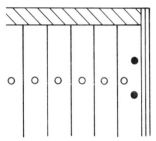 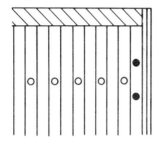

5 e.p.i., 5-dent reed   5 e.p.i., 10-dent reed

The floating selvedges can be tied and beamed along with the other warp ends. Some weavers prefer to add the floating selvedges after the other warp ends have been beamed by tying them to the front apron rod, then threading them through the reed in the proper position, then weighting them at the back of the loom. Warping from the front, I always beam the floating selvedges with the other warp ends because the very heavy beat in rug weaving causes the weights to dangle in the back.

If you're warping from the front, tie the warp ends to the back tie-on rod or stick in even knots, not too large. The outside warp ends, including the floating selvedges, should travel in a straight line from the reed to the back or front apron rod or tie-on sticks. The knots at the front will be small, only eight to ten ends each.

Before winding on the warp, make several sheds with wooden dowels or molding strips. They should be longer than the warp is wide. This adds extra tension to the warp ends as they are being wound over the beams. For warping front to back, make the sheds in front of the reed. For warping back to front, make the sheds in back of the harnesses, so that spreading the warp evenly doesn't cause too much deflection.

Wind the warp on slowly and evenly. Pull the warp ends firmly and often in order to have even tension. It is very important to have even tension on all the warp ends; this comes with experience. After the warp has been beamed, tie the knots firmly and evenly at the front. Then tie them again and again and again, each time pulling out any ease that might be in the warp. If the warp yarn is linen, expect to have blisters on your fingers!

The weaving procedure

The loom is properly warped; it is time to start weaving. Begin weaving with the warp separating material. The warp tension should be very tight. Use a tabby treadling if possible; otherwise a straight twill, twill on opposites or any two sheds that will give a good interlacement are suitable.

On most twill rug threadings, you will enter each pick by placing the shuttle over the floating selvedge, and exit each pick with the shuttle going under the floating selvedge. Some twill threading variations have floats along the selvedges and the floating selvedges may be handled differently. Sometimes it may be necessary to enter the shuttle over the floating selvedge and exit over the floating selvedge. Here are some other variations: Enter over the floating selvedge and exit over the floating selvedge on a certain pick. Or, enter over the floating selvedge and exit between the two floating selvedges. Occasionally, the floating selvedges can be wrapped around once.

It is important to pre-plan exactly how the floating selvedges will be woven, and then be consistent with that method throughout the entire project.

As soon as there is 1½"-2" of warp separating material woven, begin using the rug temple. Set the temple width the same as the warp width in the reed. The temple is placed just below the fell line, the teeth penetrating the web between the outside warps and the floating selvedges. Weave ½"-1", then lift up the temple and insert it again just below the fell line. Continue to move the temple every ½"-1", throughout the weaving procedure. Bubble, or wave, excess weft into each pick, *even the warp separating material!* Even though the actual rug web is not being woven yet, it is still important at this point to not have the selvedges drawing in.

Once again, in order to have straight selvedges and an evenly woven rug, be consistent throughout the entire weaving procedure.

The weaving sequence should be:

1. Open the shed, throw the shuttle from left to right, weaving the floating selvedges as preplanned, then put the shuttle down (on the loom bench or on a small table next to the loom bench).

2. Close the shed slightly. Smooth the weft over the left floating selvedge with the left thumb and forefinger, then push it firmly against the fell, making a neat edge.

3. Bubble the weft left to right, placing it against the fell at the right selvedge.

4. Change to the next shed.

5. Place both hands on the beater, grasping it firmly, and beat, leaning back to use your body as well as your arms.

6. Throw the shuttle right to left, then put the shuttle down.

7. Close the shed slightly. Smooth the weft over the right floating selvedge with the right thumb and forefinger, then push it firmly against the fell.

8. Bubble the weft right to left, change the shed, and beat as before.

Changing the shed before beating helps the pick of weft to beat down firmly. The amount of excess weft bubbled in should be the same on every pick. The weave structure affects the amount of excess weft needed—more interlacement requires more weft; minimum interlacement requires less weft.

After weaving 5″-7″ of warp separating material, begin weaving the weft base, or temporary weft protector. Choose any compatible rug wool for the weft base. The weft base is not part of the rug; it will be removed later. Weave 1″ of weft base, using the temple and the same weaving sequence as outlined before.

After the 1″ of weft base is woven, the actual rug begins. The weft base now provides a straight, firm fell line.

Throw the first pick of rug weft, leaving an end about 3″ long. The weft end in the first pick can be left to hang freely most anywhere along the fell line—it will be darned up after weaving 2″-3″. It should not be wrapped around the selvedges.

A heading may be woven in the background weft. It is usually in a tabby, if a tabby is possible. A straight twill, or twill on opposites, is satisfactory for a heading, too. The heading, usually 1″-2″, is optional, but it is a good idea to at least weave the first and second pick of the rug in tabby or other tight weave before beginning any pattern.

A note on adding additional weft yarns: Generally a weft can be started anywhere across the web.

Because of the color in a pattern, and in order to have a color all the way across the width, it may be necessary to start and end a weft at the selvedges by wrapping around the floating selvedges and inserting the weft end into the same shed for 1½″-2″, then leaving an end to darn in later. But be cautious about creating any buildup of weft along the edges when doing this.

Join wefts of the same color by overlapping them approximately 1″-1½″, then leaving an end to darn in. If the weft yarns are doubled or tripled, separate them and leave ends along different warp ends so that the weft ends can be darned into the web individually.

The weft ends are best taken care of as the weaving progresses. The beginning weft end(s) and any other ends within the first 2″ of weaving will be darned "up" into the web along an adjacent warp. All other weft ends will be darned "down" into the web along an adjacent warp. Darn the ends in about 1″-2″ with a tapestry needle. However, there are some alternatives to consider when handling weft ends:

If the weave structure is very tight, and a plied weft is being used, or a doubled or tripled weft, unply the weft and darn the ends in individually along different warp ends.

Handspun wool or wool singles yarn should not be cut with scissors. It is better to untwist it slightly and pull apart gently, leaving a soft, irregular end. These ends can be overlapped and beaten in, omitting any darning.

If the rug has a right and wrong side, the ends can be pushed to the back, or wrong side, and darned in after the rug is removed from the loom.

The last pick at the end of the rug can be ended anywhere across the web, leaving an end to darn down.

Before the rug can be considered completed, another 1″ of weft base, or temporary weft protector, must be woven. Last, weave 5″-7″ of warp separating material. Continue to bubble these wefts and reset the temple every ½″-1″—even though this material will be removed later. It will help prevent draw-in and curling at the corners. Now the rug can be cut from the loom.

The finishing technique

The warp separating material can be removed, if desired, as soon as the rug is cut from the loom. Do not, however, remove the weft base, or temporary weft protector until there is sufficient time to do the rug finishing. That weft base is holding those tightly beaten picks of rug weft.

The decision on how a rug is to be finished should actually be made before the rug is woven. The warp ends, finished, are a part of the total design. The finishing techniques involve the warp ends, and usually require two steps:

1. A weft protector does just that, protects the initial and final weft picks from working loose.

2. A warp protector is done to prevent the warp ends from fraying.

The length of excess warp you allow is determined by what kind of weft protector and warp protector will be used. You can find a number of different rug finishes in Appendix I; more are shown in detail in Peter Collingwood's *The Techniques of Rug Weaving*. These weft protectors are all ones I have used successfully for the weft face twill rug:

- Overhand knot
- Philippine edge
- Damascus edge, and variations of the Damascus
- Double knot
- Indian edge
- Maori edge
- Chained edge
- Four strand sennit edge

Once the weft protectors are completed, the loose warp ends must be finished or they will unply and eventually wear away.

Suggested warp protectors:
- Overhand knots on the ends of small warp end bunches
- Plying ends together and knotting at the end
- Any one of the numerous methods of braiding
- Darning the ends back
- Swedish fringe

Instructions for some of these warp protector techniques are found in Appendix I.

A word of caution about darning the ends back into the web. This should only be done on a loosely woven rug, and careful preplanning is necessary in order to do this successfully. When the initial warp separating material and weft base are being woven, the temple should be set at least ½" wider on each side, and kept that size until the first 2" of the rug are woven. Reset the temple to the width of the warp in the reed and weave until the

last 2" of the rug. Reset the temple again, ½" wider on each side, and weave the last 2" of the rug, the weft base, and the warp separating material. The web will look distorted on the loom, but this excess width is necessary for the take-up that occurs when you darn the ends back.

The completed rug can be steam pressed or dry cleaned.

Trouble shooting or solving weaving technique problems

The first few rugs you weave may reveal some problems, the most common of which is the weft not covering the warp. The usual solution is to bubble more excess weft into the web. Or, the warp sett could be too close for the weft.

If the rug ends pull in after the rug is removed from the loom, it may be because you used a rug temple for the body of the rug, but not for weaving the warp separating material and the weft base.

Should one side of the rug be a little longer than the other after the rug is removed from the loom, it is probably because more weft was bubbled into that longer side.

Sometimes a finished rug will appear to have "bowed" ends after it is finished. It may be because too much weft was bubbled into the edges. More weft is needed in the center of the rug than the edges. Bowed ends may also occur if the tie-on sticks, or apron rods, need to be replaced. Because of the very tight tension on the warp in this kind of weaving, the sticks begin to bow, especially if they are not very thick. It is good to replace these sticks periodically.

If the warp ends are darned in without preplanning, the rug ends will be distorted. The method of finishing the rug should be determined before the rug is woven, so that this kind of problem will not occur.

Designing the weft face rug

A weaver learns to use many tools in order to produce an end product. Design should be thought of as another tool. Anyone can learn to use it. As the weaver continually explores weaving techniques, he should, at the same time, explore basic design techniques. Design fills practical needs; it is problem solving, and there are design problems unique to weft face rug weaving. The first design problem is the fact of being limited to a two-dimensional plane, usually a rectangle. The second design

Symmetrical arrangement of design elements provides balance for the intricate twill patterning in this rug.
Note how the varying rib sizes add textural interest.   SETTING: RUSSELL KAMTZ HOME. ERIC CALVIN, ARCHITECT.

problem is to consider the weft face weave structure itself—all the weaving techniques are loom-controlled and the shuttle is usually thrown selvedge to selvedge. The third design problem is of equal importance—the rug is functional, and must therefore meet certain requirements such as being durable, lying flat on the floor and having strong edges.

The basic style of the rug to be woven is of prime importance. A good design is a plan for execution and among the first decisions is to determine the basic style of the rug to be woven. The style will dictate the material, weave structure, and general design concept.

A border design rug has a design around the edge and the center is treated as a separate but related design unit. Striped rugs can have horizontal bands of color or pattern. Plain weave, twills and block weaves are all good weave structures for creating horizontal bands. Vertical bands of color are created by certain treadlings of twill and block weaves. The all over patterned rug is very suitable for twills and twill derivatives. Numerous patterns can be created by repeated treadlings. The center plan rug emphasizes a design area in the center against a neutral background. The design can be horizontal or vertical.

Design, definitions of design and methods of designing are discussed thoroughly in numerous textbooks. The guidelines presented here are to help the weaver be more aware of self-expression along with weaving techniques.

The visual elements of design are evident to weavers. They are color, size, shape and texture. Color can vary endlessly—personal preference or the colors being used in the interior for which you are weaving usually guide choices in rug design. Size, in rug weaving, is determined by the overall dimensions of the rug. That measurable size affects the scale of the pattern motifs and the arrangement of stripes or blocks. Shape in two-dimensional design is a flat form having only length and width. Texture, specifically visual texture, is an innate quality in weaving.

Fundamental design principles—proportion, balance, rhythm, emphasis—offer guides for organizing these elements.

Proportion in design is based on quantitative comparisons of elements. The amounts of each color used, the background area versus patterned areas, stripe widths and the intervals between the stripes, small to large areas, or smooth to rough

texture should be given careful consideration in the earliest planning stages.

There are several basic principles that have guided designers again and again over the years:
• Uneven numbers are more interesting than even.
• A rectangle contains more differences and is therefore more interesting than a square.
• Diversity is selected over uniform regularity.
• Variations in the intervals of stripes on fabrics are more interesting than equal spacing.
• Subtle variations and relationships among the design elements create added interest.

A ratio known as the "golden section" or "golden mean" was formulated by the Roman architect, Vitruvius, and was much used by the Greeks and artists of the Renaissance and became an established canon of proportion. A simplified ratio based on the golden section is 2:1.618. You can use this ratio to determine a pleasing rectangle for your rug. The width in inches, multiplied by 1.618, gives the length in inches.

For example:
A 25" wide rug could be about 40½" long. (25 × 1.618 = 40.45).
A 30" wide rug could be about 48½" long. (30 × 1.618 = 48.54).
A 32" wide rug could be about 51¾", or 52" long. (32 × 1.618 = 51.78).

A related system of expanding relationships was formulated by Leonardo Fibonacci, medieval Europe's greatest mathematician. This number system is known as the "Fibonacci series". This is a series of numbers that has been found to reveal the secret of much of nature's structural design. Each number is the sum of the two preceding numbers: 1,1,2,3,5,8,13,21,34, etc. The numbers from the Fibonacci series can be used to determine area within a total rectangle, or quantitative areas of color, pattern, stripes, or texture.

Example 1:
13" of background
21" of pattern
13" of background
Total rug length is 47".

Example 2:
5" of background, 8" of pattern, 3" of background, 13" pattern variations, 3" of background, 8" of pattern, 5" of background. Total rug length is 45".

Example 3 (an asymmetrical design):
13" background, 3" pattern, 21" background, 13" pattern variations, 5" background, 1" stripe, 2" pattern or background, 1" stripe, 5" background. Total rug length is 64".

The second design principle, balance, is the quality that gives visual security or stability. Balance exists when all forces present are in a state of equilibrium. The handwoven rug can be symmetrical, or formally balanced, or it can be asymmetrical, or informally balanced. A symmetrical rug has the same design on each side from the center in the exact reverse of the other. An asymmetrical rug uses the design elements in an irregular, though balanced, way. Formal or informal balance is another personal preference choice. It is best to not combine the two in one design. A symmetrical design could be described as having dignity, order, restraint, uniformity, and static balance. An asymmetrical design could be described as having charm, intrigue, characteristics of nature, and kinetic balance. The numbers from the Fibonacci series can be used to give balance the

same way they are used to give proportion.

Rhythm is regularity and recurrance which lead to expectancy. The rhythm in the handwoven rug can be established by repeated lines, textures, colors, light and dark patterns, and the intervals of the background weft. Rhythm facilitates the movement of the eye from one part of the design to others; it provides progression or movement.

The numbers from the Fibonacci series can be used to establish rhythm by applying them to the actual number of repeats of a color or picks in a pattern motif.

Example 1:
AAAB, repeat 3 times; AABB, repeat 5 times; AAAB, repeat 3 times.

Example 2:
AABAABBB, repeat 8 times; 13 picks of background; AABAABBB, repeat 8 times. This could become a pattern motif that is done for a total of 13".

Example 3:
Color A, 5 picks; color B, 2 picks; color A, 5 picks; color C, 13 picks; repeat.

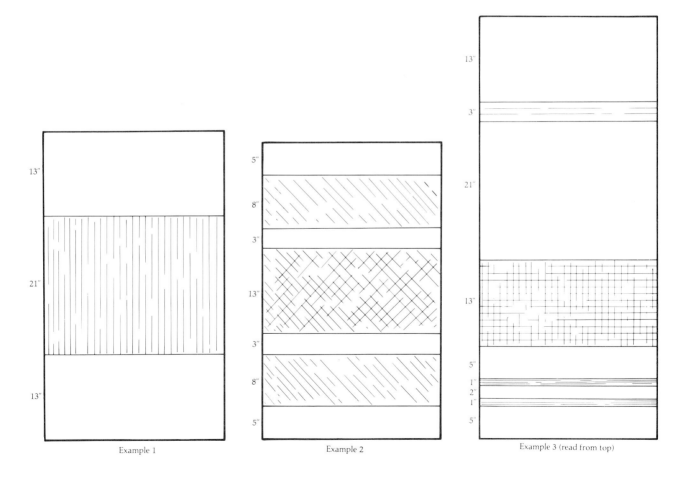

Example 1   Example 2   Example 3 (read from top)

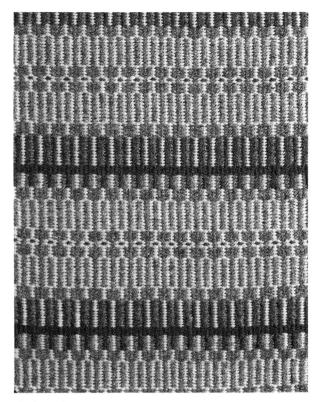

A three-harness point twill (Krokbragd) sampler.

A sampling of two-color pattern possibilities on a four-harness straight twill threading.

Four-harness point twill sampler.

Four-harness point twill sampler.

Emphasis is the repetition of a design element, or the contrast of a design element in order to catch the viewer's eye. A color can be emphasized by using it again and again and again. A patterned area can be emphasized by repetition. On the other hand, emphasis can occur through the preplanned creation of a conspicuous difference — a change in color, an exaggeration of the pattern, or perhaps a minimizing in one area of color or pattern. A bright, intense color can be used in a small amount to create a surprise, or emphasis.

Unity is the result of all the design elements and principles working together. They are compatible for the needed function; there is an ordered arrangement to the whole.

The best way to begin designing your hand-woven rug project is by making many preliminary sketches on graph paper. (Cutting and pasting with colored paper is a good exercise in determining proportions.) Begin to notice the basic layout, or graphics, in magazine advertisements, calendars and brochures. Contemporary paintings also are a good source. Any printed material showing lines or blocks dividing spaces can be an inspiration in designing a special rug. Utilize the guidelines that have been given, and you'll be amazed at the ideas that will emerge.

A sampler of twill weaves

The last section of this chapter is full of suggested twill threading and treadling graphs intended to be exercises for exploring some of the weft face twill patterns. The drafts have been limited to four harnesses, but there is no limit to what you can do on your own if you have more harnesses.

Set up a sample warp, 10"-12" wide. Refer to the kinds of warps and wefts discussed earlier in the chapter. A minimum length for each sample is about 12", but you'll probably get excited about all those pattern possibilities and want to weave at least 18"-20". Add the loom waste necessary for your loom plus the length for weaving warp separating material and a weft base.

As you weave a sample, be aware of what each weft is doing. The twill threadings allow the weft yarn to float over or under two or three warp ends, and sometimes the floats may even extend over or under four, five or even six ends. When planning your own rug threadings, it is best to not have floats traversing more than six ends, or about 1" long. The best way to learn about color and weave

effects in weft face weaving is by experimenting on the loom. Fortunately, this kind of sampling is fun — full of surprises. You will discover that some color and weave effects in the suggested sequences are more interesting than others, but they all have possibilities. The treadlings and threadings given are suggestions for a starting point. Feel comfortable about trying other treadlings, or working out various threading alternatives. Record every treadling sequence you do, as well as each color sequence, on note paper. When the sample is removed from the loom, it should be labeled accordingly. Each sampler will become a source of reference for future rug designs and the labels will be very helpful.

The capital letters in the weaving instructions represent different colors. It is helpful to label your shuttles accordingly, especially when three or more colors are being used in a sequence.

In order to have nice edges, you will need to rotate the shuttles in a consistent manner. For example, in a three color sequence:

> Throw color A, and place that shuttle next to you on the bench or table.
> If color B is next, throw that shuttle and place it next to A.
> If color C is next, throw that shuttle and place it next to B.
> If color A is next, it is at your side, and colors B and C are in proper order to be used. Color A should enter the shed *over* colors B and C.

If the shuttles are always handled in such a methodical way, no matter what the color sequence is, the selvedges will look good. Also note that patterned areas have quite a bit of weft bulk at the selvedge edge because of using two or more shuttles. When weaving areas of solid color background, in conjunction with patterned areas, it is good to use two shuttles for weaving the solid color in order to have more bulk at the selvedge edge. Remember, your rug will look like it is handwoven. Do not expect the selvedges to look like those on a commercially woven carpet!

Three harness point twill, the Norwegian Krokbragd weave

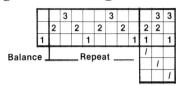

Note the weave structure as you are weaving: a tabby pick and two picks with floats under three warps.

Following are some suggested color sequences; experiment on your own as you see other possibilities. Do these three pick sequences several times in order to see the pattern develop.

1. ABA
2. ABB
3. ACB
4. BCB
5. BCC
6. AAB, AAB, BAA, BAA, ABA, ABA, repeat
7. ABC 5 times, CBA 5 times, repeat
8. AAB, ABB, AAB
9. AAB, AAB, ABC, ABC, AAB, AAB, BAA, BAA, CBA, CBA, BAA, BAA
10. ABB 5 times, CCA 5 times, ADD 5 times
11. AAA, AAB, AAB, AAB, ABC, ABC, ABC, BCA, BCA, BCA, BCA, ABC, ABC, ABC, AAB, AAB, AAB, AAA
12. AAA, AAB, AAB, AAB, ABA, ABA, ABA, BAA, BAA, BAA, ABA
13. AAB 8 times, ABB 5 times, AAB 8 times, ABB 5 times
14. AAA 3 times, ABA 4 times, ABB 4 times, BBB 3 times, CBB 4 times, CBC 4 times
15. AAB 8 times, ABB 8 times, ABC 8 times, BBC 8 times, BCC 8 times, BCD 8 times, CCD 8 times, CDD 8 times, CDA 8 times, DDA 8 times, DAA 8 times, DAB 8 times, AAB 8 times, ABB 8 times, ABC 8 times, BBE 8 times, BEE 8 times, BEF 8 times, EEF 8 times, EFG 8 times; reverse from this sequence.

Here are some additional three-harness threading and treadlings; they only suggest the many possibilities. Try the color sequences given above, or develop your own.

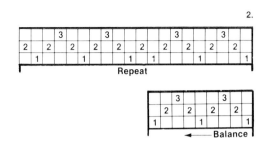

2.

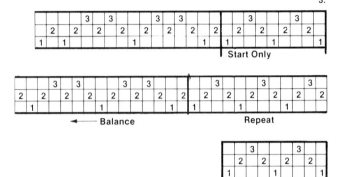

3.

Other treadling possibilities:

A)	12	23	13	
B)	13	23	12	(reversed)
C)	1	2	3	
D)	12	1	23 2 13 3	

Four harness straight twill

I—Three pick repeats

1. When doing a three pick repeat, the treadling should be:

(AAB, reading across)

Treadle—	12	23	34	14
	A	A	B	A
	A	B	A	A
	B	A	A	B

Repeat as desired

(ABB, reading across)
```
Treadle  —  12   23   34   14
                A    B    B    A
                B    B    A    B
                B    A    B    B
```
Repeat as desired

Other three pick repeats could be: ABC, ABA, BAB.

2. The treadling can be reversed:
```
                14   34   23   12
```

3. The treadling can be a broken twill:
```
                12   23   14   34
```

4. Omit any lift using a three pick repeat:

(AAB, reading across)
```
Treadle  —  12   23   34 (omit 14)
                A    A    B
                A    A    B
                A    A    B
```
Repeat as desired

(ABB, reading across)
```
Treadle  —  12   34   14 (omit 23)
                A    B    B
                A    B    B
                A    B    B
```
Repeat as desired

II — Four pick repeats; these repeats can be treadled straight twill, reversed twill, or broken twill.

AABA AAAB AABB ABBB ABAA ABBC
ABBA ABCC

Repeat any sequence enough times to have a stripe

III — Complex repeats; treadle straight twill.

1. Five pick repeats:
   ABABA ABBBA ABCBA AABCC ABBCA
   ABACA ABCCA
   Repeat any of these four times for a full sequence.
   Put any three together as a fifteen pick repeat, for example: AAAAA BAABB BBAAB, or
   AAAAA BAACC CCAAB
2. Six pick repeats:
   Combine any two of the three pick repeats.
3. Seven pick repeats:
   AABBAAB AABAAB or combine any three and four pick repeats
4. Eight pick repeats:
   AAABABBB or combine any two of the four pick repeats

5. Nine pick repeats:
   AABAABBBB or combine any four and five pick repeats
6. Ten pick repeats:
   ABBABABBAA or combine any two of the five pick repeats
7. Twelve pick repeats:
   ABBAABAAABBB or combine any of the given repeats to make a total of twelve picks
8. Treadle any of the given complex repeats in a broken twill (12 23 14 34)
9. Combine any straight twill sequence with a broken twill sequence.
10. Reverse a treadling at any lift.
11. Reverse the color order at any lift.

IV — Treadling on opposites.

Treadling "on opposites" means to treadle a given lift, then treadle the opposite lift next. For example:

    Treadle 12, then treadle the opposite lift, 34
    Treadle 23, then treadle the opposite lift, 14
    Treadle 34, then treadle the opposite lift, 12
    Treadle 14, then treadle the opposite lift, 23

A second color is usually woven on the opposite lift.

To treadle the sequence AABA, on opposites, reading across:

```
Treadle    12    34
            A     B
Treadle    23    14
            A     B
Treadle    34    12
            B     A
Treadle    14    23
            A     B
```

A different color and weave effect can be woven by treadling AABA, on opposites, this way:
```
Treadle  —  12  (34)  23  (14)  34  (12)  14  (23)
             A    A    B    A    A    A    B    A
```
Another interesting way to weave a solid color area is to weave the same color weft on all the lifts, treadling on opposites.

Treadle any of the given repeats, on opposites.

V — Extending the twill lifts

Extending the twill lifts means to first treadle a given lift, then treadle the opposite lift, and next treadle the first lift again. For example, reading across:

Treadle — 12 34 12
         A B A
Treadle — 23 14 23
         A B A
Treadle — 34 12 34
         A B A
Treadle — 14 23 14
         A B A

1. Treadle any of the three pick repeats, extending the twill lift.

2. Treadle any of the four pick repeats, extending the twill lift.

3. Reverse the treadling, extending the twill lift.

Treadle — 41 23 41
         34 12 34
         23 14 23
         12 34 12

VI — Think about combinations in treadling, in color effects, and in reversing. For example:

12	A		23	A
34	B		14	A
12	A		12	B
34	B		34	A
23	A		14	B
14	B		23	A
34	A		34	B
12	B		12	A
14	A		34	B
23	A		12	A
14	A		34	B

Skip twill, or broken twill

The original draft:

Any twill threading can be converted to a skip twill (or broken twill) by excluding certain ends in some regular order. On the above draft, every fifth end was excluded. The original draft is rewritten for the Skip Twill:

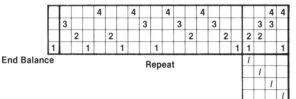

End Balance   Repeat

Following are some suggested sequences; experiment on your own as you see other possibilities.

1. Treadle straight twill: AAB AAB AAB AAB repeat, or ABB ABB ABB ABB repeat.

2. Treadle straight twill: ABBAABAAABBB repeat, or ABBBAABBABAB repeat.

3. Treadle broken twill: AABBABABABBB repeat.

4. Treadle straight twill: AABAABB.

5. Treadle straight twill: AABB 5 times
                              ABBB 5 times
                              ABBA 5 times
                              BBBA 5 times
                              BBAA 5 times
                              BBAB 5 times
                              BAAB 5 times
                              BABB 5 times.

6. Try any of the suggested treadling sequences given on the straight twill threading.

7. Remember to try treadling on opposites and the extended twill lifts.

Skip twills offer many opportunities for experimenting with your own threadings. Here are two more drafts, converted to skip twills, to get you started.

The original draft:

By omitting every second and seventh end, the resulting twill repeats on 20 ends:

The original draft:

By omitting every sixth end, the resulting twill repeats on 20 ends:

Point twills and point twill variations

All the pattern repeats and treadling sequences suggested for the straight twill and skip twills can be used for the point twills. Two special color and weave effects on point twill are saddleblanket designs and flamepoint designs. These are especially interesting when treadled on point twill threadings. A few suggested threadings follow:

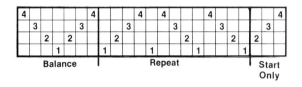

Balance   Repeat   Start Only

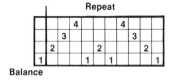

Repeat

Balance

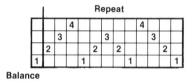

Repeat

Balance

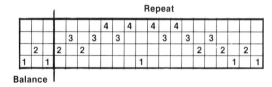

Repeat

Balance

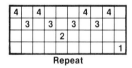

Repeat

I – Saddleblanket designs

The Navajo twill weaves, commonly called saddleblanket designs, were originally woven by the Navajos for their own use, or for sale. The blankets were woven on the Navajo tapestry looms in a single size or a double size. The contemporary weaver, using a floor loom, can duplicate those early twill weaves, or develop unique designs by using weft color rotations. Saddleblanket designs are done on a straight twill treadling, using only three colors. The colors are always used in a regular rotation. Be sure to label your shuttles and keep them in proper order!

1. Four repeats of ABC, reading across:

Treadle –	12	23	34	14
	A	B	C	A
	B	C	A	B
	C	A	B	C

2. The characteristic diamond shapes found in saddleblanket designs are done by reversing the treadling and color order.

Treadle –	14	34	23	12
		B	A	C
	B	A	C	B
	A	C	B	A

The color order can be changed at any time: ACB, BAC, BCA.

3. Vertical stripes can be woven by using the same color rotations, but eliminate one lift.

Treadle –	12	23	34	(omit 14)
	A	B	C	
	A	B	C	
	A	B	C	
Treadle –	23	34	14	(omit 12)
Treadle –	12	34	14	(omit 23)
Treadle –	12	23	14	(omit 34)

II – Flamepoint designs

Flamepoint designs are woven by using the straight twill treadling and four colors. In traditional flamepoint, the colors are four shades of one hue. The colors are shifted to create pattern.

ABCD, reading across:

Treadle –	12	23	34	41
	A	B	C	D, repeat 4 times
	B	C	D	A, repeat 4 times
	C	D	A	B, repeat 4 times
	D	A	B	C, repeat 4 times

III – Other design possibilities

Many other designs can be created by changing color rotations while keeping a constant treadling sequence. Each four-pick sequence, when repeated, creates a series of color blocks that can be used to build design motifs. The wefts will have floats and usually one weft will not appear on the surface as part of the design, but is used to bind the web. For a rug, I usually change threadings so that the floats are not more than 1" long. Think of the floats as little blocks in planning a design. After experimenting at the loom with these suggested sequences you'll begin to understand how a series of color blocks can be developed. Then you'll be able to design your own motifs on paper and come up with the threading and treadling necessary to weave your own design.

Reading across:

Treadle —	23	12	14	34
	A	A	A	A, repeat 2 times
	B	B	B	A, repeat 2 times
	C	C	B	A, repeat 2 times
Treadle —	12	14	34	23
	C	C	B	A, repeat 2 times
	B	B	B	A, repeat 2 times
Treadle —	14	34	23	12
	C	C	B	A, repeat 2 times
	B	B	B	A, repeat 2 times
Treadle —	34	23	12	14
	C	C	B	A, repeat 2 times
	B	B	B	A, repeat 2 times

Repeat from this point, backwards

2. Reading across:

Treadle —	12	23	34	41
	A	A	A	A, repeat 3 times
	B	B	B	A, repeat 4 times
	B	A	A	A, repeat 10 times
	B	B	B	A, repeat 10 times
	B	A	A	A, repeat 4 times

3. Reading across:

Treadle —	34	14	12	23
	A	A	A	A, repeat 3 times
	A	B	B	B, repeat 3 times
	A	B	C	C, repeat 9 times
	A	B	B	B, repeat 3 times
	A	A	A	A, repeat 3 times

4. Reading across:

Treadle —	12	14	34	23
	A	A	B	B, repeat 6 times
	B	A	B	A, repeat 8 times
	B	A	B	B, one time
	A	A	B	B, repeat 6 times

5. Treadle any of the boundweave sequences given "on opposites."

12	A	34	B
23	A	14	B
34	A	12	B
14	A	23	B

6. Try any color and weave effects given on the four harness straight twill.

Putting theory to use

To illustrate some of the principles presented in this chapter, I designed a rug that is somewhat of a sampler. The threading is the pointed skip twill given in the section on skip twills.

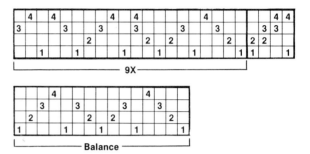

The sett is 6 e.p.i. using an 8/3 linen warp. The colored pattern wefts are wool singles: three shades of red, rust, tan, gray and dark brown. Three background wefts are used. Background A is one strand of two-ply camel berber wool and one strand of two-ply dark natural. Background B is one strand of the same camel berber wool and one strand of two-ply medium natural wool. Background C is one strand of the same camel berber wool and one strand of two-ply light natural wool. Using the slightly different naturals along with the camel berber gives the background of the rug more visual interest.

The treadling is straight twill throughout, unless noted otherwise. I decided this rug would be finished with a four-sennit braid, so the temple is set according to the width of the warp in the reed.

The general weaving procedure for this particular rug follows:

1. 6" of warp separating material. At 2", the temple is set.

2. 1" of rug wool for the weft base, or temporary weft protector.

3. Using background A, weave the first pick of the rug, leaving the loose ends near the center. Because a doubled weft is being used, the two are separated in order to be darned "up" different warps. Weave 4" of background A, using two shuttles to give more weft bulk at the selvedges. . Two shuttles are used for all the single color areas.

4. Fine lines of gray are made by treadling 12 background, 23 gray and the opposite treadle 14 gray, then 34, 14, 12, 23, 34, 14, 12 all in back-

This rug samples many different twill effects, but maintains design coherence through careful attention to balance.
SETTING: RUSSELL KAMTZ HOME. ERIC CALVIN, ARCHITECT

ground. Next 23 gray and the opposite treadle 14 gray. By repeating this treadling any number of lines can be woven. This is a good time to use the numbers in the Fibonacci series to determine the number of stripes.

5. Background A is continued, treadling straight twill until the total rug length is 8".

6. Six picks of dark brown are woven, treadling 12, 23, 34, 14, 12 and 23.

7. A twelve pick sequence, ABBAABAAABBB, woven on opposites, provides the small pattern using two colors. Color A is gray and color B is tan. It is best to write out a sequence like this on paper before weaving it. Read across:

12	A	34	B
23	B	14	A
34	B	12	A
14	A	23	B
12	A	34	B
23	B	14	A
34	A	12	B
14	A	23	B
12	A	34	B
23	B	14	A
34	B	12	A
14	B	23	A

This sequence is repeated three times, then followed by another six picks of dark brown.

8. 3" more of background A.

9. The saddleblanket design on this threading is quite different from those described in the sampler section. Three colors are used, and the treadling is straight twill. The shuttles are labeled according to color in order to avoid getting them mixed up. Color A is gray, color B is tan, and color C is rust. Working left to right, the shuttles are rotated:

Treadle 12, throw shuttle with color A, then place that shuttle right next to you on the right.
Treadle 23, throw shuttle with color B, then place that B shuttle to the right of shuttle A. Treadle 34, throw shuttle with color C, then place that C shuttle to the right of shuttle B. Treadle 14, throw shuttle A, picking it up from your immediate right. Place shuttle A right next to you on the left.

Continue to rotate the shuttles in this manner. The saddleblanket design is repeated for 5".

10. The background weft now is B, the camel berber wool with medium natural. Using two shuttles, 1¼" of background is woven. The colored bands in this portion are intended to give some accent color. Even though each band is a single color, two shuttles are used. The sequence is ⅝" dark brown; ⅝" background B; ⅝" gray; 1" background B; ⅝" red; 1½" background B; ¾" tan.

11. Background B is now woven until the entire rug measure 42".

12. A 1" band of gray.

13. 3" of background B.

14. Three shades of red have been chosen to do another wide band in the saddleblanket design. 4" are woven in straight twill, then the treadling is reversed for 1".

15. A 1" band of the medium shade of red.

16. The background is now C, camel berber with light natural. 3" of background C are woven, then the fine red lines are done by treadling the same way the gray lines were woven at the beginning of the rug. There are 5" of red lines.

17. 2" more of background C complete the rug.

18. 1" of rug wool for the weft base, or temporary weft protector.

19. 6" of warp separating material, and the rug can be cut from the loom.

20. A Damascus edge variation, steps 1 and 2, is done from the wrong side of the rug. The warp ends are then plaited in a four strand sennit. (See Appendix I.)

Weaving a Rag Rug

Inga Krook

Picture yourself in your home in a small village off the beaten track. You are a weaver, you have a loom, you have some warp yarn but no weft yarn whatsoever. You are aching to weave. There is no store in your village that sells yarn, there is no mail-order business to order from. You have no sheep, you have no patch of flax growing and the climate is not suitable for cultivating cotton. Your neighbors are not into spinning or weaving at all. It will be weeks before you get to the faraway town and the market next.

What do you do? Yes, you invent your own weft material. You suddenly think of those old worn-beyond-further-repair clothes that you laid aside long ago and did not have the heart to throw away. Could they be used? "Why not. I can cut them up in narrow strips and use the cloth strips as weft. I can have use for a coarse weave like that." Thought, said and done. The rag weave is a fact.

In my imagination this is the way the first rag weave came about some hundreds of years ago. I would like to know exactly when and where on earth it occured. I would also like to know if the same thought came to several people at about the same time in different parts of the world, or if it was one person's invention which was then spread to other people and places from that one weaver.

What I do know, however, is that in Sweden, my home country, pieces of rag weaves dating back to the 1700's have been recorded in a not disdainful number. Those rag weaves were used as covers over the hay or straw, which was the common mattress material in the beds of that time. The covers were woven with rag strips of natural linen cloth on a linen warp in plain tabby. Some of them also have a stripe or two in colors.

Later on the women—I am sure it was women, knowing the Swedes— wove rag coverlets, with which they adorned the beds. These coverlets were also woven in plain tabby as a background weave with colored rag strips woven in on top in different patterns; either in small pieces, in rya knots, or in continuous strips, making an overall surface design. The back of the weave was thus plain. These weaves, so called tatter coverlets or tatter weaves, were inspired in their designs by other ornamental weaves of different techniques.

A great number of the tatter coverlets are mentioned in inventories of estates, so it is easy to track them down to the exact times and places where they were made. The earliest dated, preserved tatter coverlet is from 1834. Many are saved in museums and they make an interesting study in the variation of patterns and colors from different parts of Sweden. Besides, they are very stimulating and inspiring for a modern weaver to explore.

It is not known if the idea of weaving with rags is a Swedish invention, or if it originated in some other country, but surely it suited the Swedes very well. People were poor, most of them self-providing farmers who were forced to take good care of their possessions as well as save everything that could possibly be used over again in some new form or shape.

One would think that the rag rug is an old, yes, ancient product, but the fact is that it did not appear in my country until the 19th century. Before that time it was common among the majority of the people to strew the floors with juniper needles or sand, and at big celebrations, with straw. In the homes of the nobility and the gentry, rugs had been in use for some time — probably imported embroidered or Oriental rugs or what was obtainable at the time.

The forerunner to the rag rug was a rug woven with straw or rush for weft and sometimes in a combination with rags. Eventually the rugs woven only in rags took over and became common.

The rag rugs from that time preserved in museums and old homes in the country are not colorful. They were made from rags of clothing, which in those days generally consisted of white linen garments for every day use and black wool for Sunday. The colorful folk costumes we have seen pictures of, and which are fairly common even today — they have experienced a renaissance — were hardly ever cut up and used in rag weaves, mainly because the clothes were seldom worn out. They were used so sparingly, only at great celebrations like weddings, at Christmas, Midsummer and other big yearly events; and in addition, they were inherited.

The rugs are thus striped in black and white and are often exquisite in the designs and proportions of the stripes. Some rugs are patterned with black stripes on a natural white warp, or vice versa, and with the stripes in the weft make a plaid effect, which many times adds considerably to their interest. There is a lot we can learn from their beautiful simplicity.

It was not until the latter part of 1800, with the coming of the industrial age and machine-made cotton fabrics, that colors started to appear more and more in the rugs. By and by people in general experienced a somewhat better economy, they could afford to buy the machine-made fabrics, and there was a greater variety to choose from. Thus the women could have the heart to discard clothes and other textiles more often and use them in their rug weaves. The standard of living had also risen in the respect that larger houses with more than one room were built, so there was more space, which created a new need for rag rugs.

At this time, and on into the present, the rag rugs became very popular both to weave and to use. The common kind was the plain weave runner with stripes or borders in colors. Sometimes a geometric pattern in an inlay technique, the Swedish *rölakan*, was added in a border or spread over the whole rug. Now and then the rölakan was more elaborately done, showing flowers or leaves, and the weaving was more tapestry than rölakan.

Another technique that became very popular, especially in this century, was rosepath. The rugs were woven in tabby with more or less intricate borders in rosepath, sometimes narrow, bright colored stripes in rosepath and sometimes wide fields of shaded colors spaced out over the whole rug.

All this decoration of the simple striped rag rug added a further interest to their final beauty. It is amazing to realize how much time and effort these ancestors of ours spent on their rug weaves, and we have to admire their skill and artistry.

The runners of those days were always between 24" and 28" wide, probably depending on the widths of the looms available. This size was also practical, as narrow rugs were easier to handle in cleaning, both the regular house cleaning and the washing. These narrow runners were usually placed side by side covering the entire floor, which generally consisted of wooden boards.

The cheerful informality of rag hall runners just asks for exuberant use of color, as in this pink, purple, red and cream one by the author. SETTING: RUSSELL KAMTZ HOME. ERIC CALVIN, ARCHITECT.

At one time in the "good old days" it became fashionable to place the newest invention, linoleum, in a square under the dining table and place the rag runners around it. Later again, when the linoleum had conquered the people and the floors completely, the runners appeared more sparingly on top of the linoleum. It also became a practice to place rag runners as protection over more valuable rugs, like large store bought or maybe even Oriental rugs, where the traffic in the room was intense.

Another type of runner, which likewise served as a protection rug, was the *ripsmatta* (rep rug). The technique dates back to the latter part of the 1800's and was, as well as is, fairly common. The ripsmatta is a warp-faced rep — the warp preferably cotton — which makes the pattern in blocks, and with a rag or heavy cotton yarn alternating with a thin cotton thread for weft. These rep rugs were often called "summer rugs" because of their protective use as covers over the more distinguished rugs during the summer time, when people were outdoors more and often came in with dirty shoes.

The materials used in the old rag rugs were of course of natural fibers. At first linen yarn was used for warps; later on, when cotton had arrived in Sweden, that material became the most common. Since there were no man-made fibers as yet, the weft strips were cut from rags of natural fibers, sometimes used in a mix but more often with the same fiber through and through. The all-cotton rugs seem to have been the most popular kind, probably because they were the easiest ones to take care of.

Some years ago, in my time, rag rugs were the most popular item to weave in Sweden. I think there was hardly a Swede who had not at one time or another tried a weft or two in a rag rug weave. It has been considered the simplest and easiest kind of weaving there is. Consequently there was no end to all the types that were made. There were also all kinds of designs and color combinations created. Some of them were absolute museum pieces, but some of them were really bad, even in looks, and wore out pretty quickly. The great majority were ordinary, pleasing pieces of weaving that were used and used and served their purpose very well.

Rag weaving today

In the United States as well as Canada, rag weaving was practiced in Colonial times, and also came with later waves of immigrants and has re-mained rather persistently in some areas. For example, in the Scandinavian settlements and bordering areas people have woven rag rugs for their homes since the time they arrived. Beautiful proofs of the craft still exist.

Rag weaving has been "discovered" recently in other areas, especially in the eastern states and on the west coast, where it has become very popular and very "in". There the rag rugs have been revived, more fashionable than ever.

Today's rag weaving is quite different from what it was, both in the United States and in Scandinavia. First of all it is not a necessity to recycle old material anymore and, second, we have invented new uses for rag weaves more in line with originality and attraction than need. Now rag weaves are designed for practically every purpose and use, for the homes as well as for garments. All kinds of techniques, qualities and designs are used and weavers make curtains, bedspreads, table mats and runners, cushions, rugs, coverlets, rocking chair mats, hammocks and wall hangings as well as material for clothes. The list could go on and on. The imagination is endless and it is wonderful to see all the attractive and fanciful items that can be produced from rags.

Even contemporary rag rugs have a new look, although they are mostly made in the traditional way regarding technique, quality and material. Most rugs are still woven in tabby; but twill is also used often as well as rosepath. Monk's belt, overshot and other techniques that create floats are not traditionally used in rugs, but occur fairly often nowadays and make interesting overall patterned designs.

An ancient technique which was used in the traditional rag rugs, as I have mentioned earlier, and which is woven today as well, is rölakan. The technique is more common in rugs woven in wool yarn than in rags though.

The double binding technique, which is a contemporary invention as far as I know, is not widespread as yet — I am working on it — but a most fascinating technique, which, like rölakan creates geometric designs.

Regarding the material, we still use the natural fibers in warp and weft in our rugs, but added are the many new fibers that have appeared in fabrics in our time. The man-made fibers might be very different to handle and to weave with, but the finished rugs do not necessarily look different from the conventional ones because of the fiber content.

The new look of contemporary rag rugs is more a result of design and color combinations. A number of rugs are still striped, but in a modern way and often shaded from one color to another or from light to dark. Sometimes bold color combinations are woven in wide bands or abstract figures on the rug and sometimes the entire rug is a single but unusual color.

Now we have more colors to choose from or we make a color we need by dyeing the rags and we have less respect for how things are "supposed" to look or always have looked. We want to try any wild idea we can think of, and it has given us many effective results for modern interior decoration.

The sizes of the rugs have also changed from the traditional runners. Large rugs covering a good part of the floor have become popular. They are easier to handle and maintain today with all our mechanical aids. Many weavers have acquired wider and bigger looms, so large rag rugs are easy to accomplish. The earlier way of sewing several narrow runners together to get a large rug is still a good solution for weavers with narrow looms and demands for big rugs.

So with an option of sizes as well as designs, the use of the rugs has also altered from the old days. Now we have more homes with carpeted floors and the rag runners have in many cases been dismissed to the kitchen, the bathroom or the basement. Here and there large rag rugs are used as throw rugs on top of the carpeting, more for the looks of them than for protection of the carpet underneath.

In the many homes with wooden boards or parquet floors, there is still a market for rag rugs, runners or large ones. Many, many are still taking the Carl Larsson look to their hearts.

Preferable equipment

I do not quite agree with the old concept that weaving rag rugs is the simplest and easiest thing that can be done on a loom. Rag rug weaving takes just as much planning, consideration and thorough work as any other weave.

Initially the equipment should be well considered.

When weaving a rag rug, or any kind of rug, the tension of the warp should always be taut and the rug should be beaten hard and tight. The result has to be a firm weave. Therefore it is important to choose a loom with a heavy construction that can take the continuous hard beating without being

ruined and without moving or bouncing for every beat. The beater in itself should be heavy and help the weaver to pack together the wefts tightly.

Another vital concern is, the ability to tighten the warp as much as necessary. I have found that counterbalance looms are more sufficient in that respect than jack type looms.

In jack loom construction the warp is meant to sit at an angle, seen from the side, and that angle prevents the warp from being tightened enough. Or rather, if the warp is tightened sufficiently, the harness frames are pushed up and distort the shed; in other words, the shed gets narrow, the treadle is pressed harder to get a better shed, and the threads lifted will make a larger angle than the threads that remain down. The upper threads are thus tauter than the lower ones, the shed has become uneven in tension and the beat will not be adequate.

In a counterbalance loom the warp can be tightened as much as desired, because the warp goes straight from the breast beam through the heddles on the harnesses to the back beam. Because of its counterbalance action the two layers of warp threads pull apart evenly when the shed is opened. It is said that this kind of loom has a sinking shed, and so it has as far as the tie-up on the draft is concerned; but the fact is that when a treadle is pressed to open the shed, one set of threads goes down, sinks, and the other set goes up, rises, just as much. The threads counter balance. Therefore all the threads have the same tension and the shed and the beat will be proper.

By this I do not mean that a rug cannot be woven on a jack type loom. It can very well be done. The main concern is, as always, if the loom is sturdy and heavy enough. The matter of the relationship between a taut warp and an adequate shed can be worked out. See page 10 for illustrations of these shedding mechanisms.

Another important tool is the shuttle for rug weaving. The regular boat shuttle is not large enough for this use. Big shuttles are needed and there are various kinds in the market, such as stick shuttles, ski shuttles and combinations and variations of the two. Both stick shuttles and ski shuttles come in different lengths.

The stick shuttle is very simple and easy to make if necessary. It can take a good amount of rags, but the more rags that are wound on, the more difficult it is to slide through the shed, because the rags cause friction against the warp threads. To help out, very long stick shuttles, corresponding with the width of the weave, could be used; but then they are often too long to be comfortable to work with.

I prefer the ski shuttle, which also takes a large amount of rags wound sidewise on the shuttle, leaving the wooden ski part to slide through the shed with ease. There, too, a moderate length of shuttle is the handiest one to weave with.

Another tool which is very useful when weaving rugs is the stretcher bar, or temple. Stretcher bars are obtainable in different lengths each length adjustable, and are made of wood or metal. I prefer the wooden kind, which is merely a matter of habit. The metal temple serves its purpose just as well and both kinds are easy to manage and to attach to the weave.

General viewpoints on rag rug weaving

Other matters to consider when making rag rugs are the material, the execution and the final look of the project.

The warp has to be of a strong material, the thread fairly heavy and smoothly spun.

The rags to be used for weft should be of a suitable quality, so the cut strips do not fall apart or ravel when handled. The strips have to be well cut and equal in thickness (note: not necessarily in width) so there will be no bumps or uneven parts in the rug. Thin strips mixed with heavier ones make the result bulging and wavy and the selvedges crooked. The selvedges should be straight with smooth, neat turns for each weft.

The rugs ought to be firmly beaten. There should be no possibilities to poke fingers through the weave. The rugs should lie flat and evenly on the floor and not slip or wrinkle when stepped on. They should also look square with right angles showing an equal width, as well as length, all over the rug.

The edges at the beginning and the end of the rug, if woven with a different material (such as yarn), must not be drawn in, which makes the corners curl and easy to stumble on. Besides, it looks awful.

All hanging threads and "mouse ears" sticking out should be trimmed off, if there is no danger of cutting off a weft strip in doing so.

The finish, such as fringes, hems or whatever, should be neatly done and appropriate to the quality and look of the rug as well as suitable for its purpose.

Material for warp: yarn

As just mentioned, the warp used for rag rugs—as well as for any kind of rugs—should be a multi-ply yarn of strong and good quality.

Cotton carpet warp is specially made for rug or carpet weaving, as the name implies, and is strong, durable and easy to work with. Some makes of carpet warp come in different sizes and are double twisted.

Double twist means, for example in 12/6, that two and two threads are twisted together first, then three sets of these 2-ply twisted to make the 6-ply. As a result there is a large amount of twist in the thread, which is needed to give the extra strength and insure that it will be long lasting.

For comparison, look at an end of 8/4 carpet warp that is not double twisted. There all the four threads are twisted together in one group and the thread has not nearly as much twist as the 12/6. It is softer, yet it is the same weight as 12/6. Both these types of carpet warp are excellent in thinner and medium qualities of rag rugs.

A highly twisted, several ply wool yarn as well as a heavy linen warp, for instance 8/4 or 8/5, both kinds very strong, will help in making thicker rugs. The wool warp will create a pliable and soft rug, while the linen warp makes the rug stiff, a stiffness that diminishes with wear and washing. When a rug with a linen fringe is placed on the floor, care should be taken to always keep the fringes flat and in order. If tangled and bent and constantly stepped on, the fringes will eventually break and fall off. This is due to the character of the linen fiber, which in addition to its strength, stiffness and rigidity also is very brittle. A linen warp in a rug is nevertheless considered more elegant and of a higher class than a simple cotton warp.

Many synthetic yarns, if heavy enough—the strength is usually there whether it is thick or thin—also work well as warp yarn for rag rugs.

Material for weft: rags

We still use the word rags, indicating old, worn clothes or other textiles, but so often today new fabrics are used. We go to the fabric store and buy a new piece of cloth that is attractive and cut it up for use in our projects. Sometimes it is necessary, and I have done it myself a couple of times when I absolutely had to have a certain shade—and found it!—but I am not very fond of that solution. The

This rug is reminiscent of early Swedish ones woven of old clothing—black wool, white linen. Judicious use of printed fabric adds a special "sparkle" of tiny red and yellow random spots.
SETTING: STUDIO OF JACK ORMAN, LOVELAND, COLORADO.

tradition to produce a new thing out of old material, the recycling process, appeals very much to me.

Naturally it is a question of supply. So many people do not save old garments and other fabrics, but throw them away when they are worn out or have become tiresome to look at.

If I had not been a rag weaver from the very beginning of my weaving career, maybe I would not have been such a pack rat. But I am. I have boxes and boxes full of old worn out, washed out, faded, disregarded, thrown away, torn and tired garments and other textiles. I have probably announced my love for rags and what I use them for, in a loud voice, so kind people come to me with bags full of their throw-aways. The rags accumulate . . . it makes me so happy.

If you are not a pack rat and have not saved old rags at all and want to weave a rag weave, there are places to obtain old garments. You can find a lot at garage sales, at the local thrift shops, or in good-will stores. Also ask your relatives, friends and neighbors if they have anything of old textiles that they want to get rid of.

There are different companies that sell remnants from their mills, or stores that sell distressed goods or left-overs inexpensively. Fabric stores sometimes have sales. Fabrics from these stores are of course new and unused material, but they are surplus and rejects, so they are in line with the tradition. A thing to remember is that new material has to be washed to shrink and prove colorfast before it can be mixed with old rags in the same weave; otherwise the rug might show up very uneven and bubbling after washing and maybe with colors that have run. Needless to say, the old garments and textiles, the rags, should also be washed and be clean before they are cut up and used in a weave.

My preference in rags is cotton rags, and nowadays cotton/polyester, since pure cotton textiles are less easy to find. Cotton rags are soft and feel good to handle, they are easy to cut, and they pack together well in the weave.

Wool rags are also soft and beat together nicely, but are mostly more difficult and tiresome to cut, especially if the material is thick and heavy. Linen is easy to cut, but because of the stiff and non-elastic character of the fiber, it can be difficult to pack into the web well. Only when the linen fabric has been washed a number of times does it become soft and "packable".

Man-made fibers, like polyester, acrylic, nylon and similar, are mostly both painstaking to cut and

difficult to beat, especially the knit fabrics, which are very springy. They are not my favorites. Rayon is easy to handle and can be very appealing, but I am a little hesitant about its wear in a rag rug.

It is a good rule to use rags of the same fiber through the entire rug. Different fibers have different take-ups and shrinkage, and if they are mixed can cause the rug to bubble and draw in here and there and destroy the intended good look. After washing it can even be worse.

On the other hand, there is nothing that says that, for example, a cotton warp cannot be woven with linen or wool strips in the weft, or vice versa. A mix with a wool warp and cotton weft might not give the most desirable quality, but can very well be done. Often a linen warp is used either with wool or cotton rags, and the combinations make very appropriate and long lasting rugs as long as only one fiber is used throughout — either in the warp or in the weft — it does not make the rug uneven, either in the weaving or in the laundry. Naturally a wool warp might shrink more than cotton or linen in the washing, but it will shrink evenly.

Cutting the rags

There are many ways to cut rag strips for weft. The old fashioned way, of course, is to cut with a pair of scissors.

One procedure is to cut around and around on the piece of fabric, thus getting one continuous strip. The disadvantage is that the strip will contain all the different directions of the material; some parts are straight, some on the bias and the rest in between, and this can cause problems in the weave. It will stretch unevenly and make the finished rug wavy.

Another way is to cut strips straight with the warp or weft direction of the rag piece, almost to the end of the fabric. There another strip is started in the opposite direction, leaving the strips hanging together in about ½". Continue cutting and again stop ½" before the edge, start a new strip beside the second one and so on. Thus you will get one long continuous strip again, this time in the straight direction but with "turns" every so often. These "turns" should be trimmed by cutting off the sharp corners. When weaving, the "turns" have to be folded and manipulated so they do not stick out of the weave. It is almost impossible to do this neatly

— it also slows down the weaving considerably — and the weave will show little "mouse ears" forever.

The best way to cut strips with a pair of scissors is to cut straight — again with the warp or weft direction — all the way through the material and end up with a bunch of individual strips. Strips can also be cut on the bias, but they should not be mixed with straight cut strips in the weave. Unless, of course, the wavy effect is planned for and part of the design.

Whichever way you choose to cut the strips with a pair of scissors, it will take time. In the beginning of my rag weaving I used the second way described, but soon changed to the third. It seems to me I sat there for weeks and weeks, cutting and cutting, getting more and bigger blisters on my fingers, before I had enough rag strips for a rug.

Then, just a few years ago, I learned the absolute best and quickest way to cut rags. The knowledge was given to me in a somewhat roundabout way from another Swedish weaver. A friend of mine — a Frenchman and a non-weaver — showed me how his landlady, the Swedish weaver mentioned, used to cut her rags. I have been grateful to both of them ever since.

The trick is to lay aside the pair of scissors entirely. Take a flat piece of fabric, roll it straight to a tight and hard roll, take the very best and sharpest kitchen knife available and the cutting board, and then cut slices from the roll like cutting a loaf of bread. The "slices" unroll to nicely cut strips. This is quick!

What still takes some time is the trimming of the garments before the rolls can be made. All seams, collars, cuffs, pockets, buttons, buttonholes, zippers, etc., have to be cut away so the pieces will be flat before they can be rolled properly. Save small pieces like collars, cuffs and pockets, if you do not cut them at once. They might come in very handy and give you that extra strip you absolutely need to finish your weaving.

Sheets, curtains, yardage and other large pieces of fabric first have to be cut in narrower sections to be comfortable enough to roll. The most convenient way to get these big pieces in narrow parts — and straight — is to tear them. That is the only time I tear fabrics for my rag weaving. Tearing is otherwise another way of getting strips. I do not particularly care for the frayed look in the finished rugs that results from torn strips, but in certain cases it can look great and add to the design.

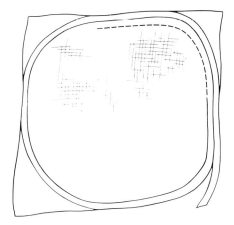

To cut around.

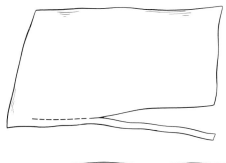

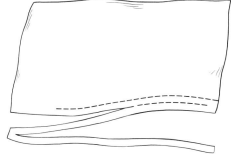

To cut straight with "turns".

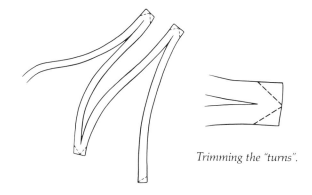

Trimming the "turns".

The harder the roll of fabric is, the easier it is to cut. Naturally it helps keeping the knife really sharp. Serrated knifes do not work, only the straight ones. Some material will not roll tight at all; then you just have to do the best you can. Most fabrics give a tighter and harder roll if you continue to roll it long after the material is ended. Wide ribbed corduroy rolls better one way than the other. If the right side is up, roll it against the nap; if the wrong side is up, with the nap. On narrow ribbed corduroy it is sometimes difficult to tell which way the nap goes and it has to be rolled the way that seems best.

Blended fabrics are more difficult to roll and to cut straight than an all-natural fabric. It happens, if a roll is not tight enough, or the knife is dull, that the cut strips look like rickrack. And the joke goes: 'It takes skill to cut rickrack.' However, it does not work well in the weave, so strive for tight rolls.

The width of the slices you cut will be the width of the strips, which is rather needless to say. It is a good help to mark the cutting board with the desired width in order to keep an even measurement. The width is naturally dependent on the quality of the rag material. Thin and soft fabrics have to be cut wider than heavy and stiff fabrics. In other words, the width has to be adjusted to the character of the rag, but also to the quality and the appearance of your weave.

Before cutting anything at all, you have to decide whether you are going to weave with single or double strips. As a rule a strip used singly should be cut a little wider than it would be when used double. A single strip in the weft gives a thinner result and is faster to weave. The colors will be solid and emphasized because of the one material. When weaving with double strips, you will get a heavier product, which is good when making rugs. The weaving will be slower because the two strips have to be adjusted in the shed to give the best result in shading the colors.

The main reason why I use double strips in my rag rugs is that I like to play with the colors and vary the shades in different areas of my design. For instance, a print can make a subtle blend with a one-colored fabric, a dark shade can enhance a rather dull color and a mix of two "impossible" colors can turn out amazingly beautiful.

Another reason is that two narrow strips pack together better than one wide strip when beating.

A question that often comes up is: "How much rag do I need for my project?" In a medium quality

rug, woven with double strips, I count on three to four pounds of cut rags per square yard. Naturally the amount can vary depending on the quality of the rug that is being made—what is medium?—but also on how well beaten the rug will be, on the weight of the rag fabric and on how thrifty the weaver is with the strips.

When it comes to the individual colors of the design and how much rag is needed of each, I usually measure them instead of weighing. By test weaving I know how many wefts there are per inch, and from my design I know how many inches I need of each color, so I multiply the figures and get the total number of wefts. That figure I multiply by the width of my weave to get the yardage I need.

Joining the rag strips

When the individual strips are cut, the ends have to be trimmed off at about a 45° angle and joined. They can be sewn together, either on the sewing machine or by hand, or they can be glued together with textile glue. Place one strip with another one overlapping about ¼" or ⅜" along the slant and sew. Or put glue on the first strip along the slant and press the joining strip on top, slants—and

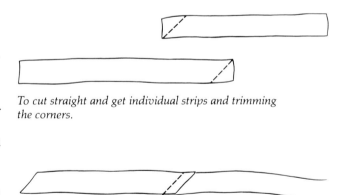

To cut straight and get individual strips and trimming the corners.

Joining the rag strips.

strips—in the same direction. When there is a printed material or other fabric with a definite wrong side, you can choose to glue all strips with the right side up, or glue them alternately with the right and the wrong side up. I do the latter many times, when I want a varied effect in an otherwise too solid color.

Use the glue sparingly. It stains white fabric with yellow spots after a length of time and on solid

Short strips of rags can be joined in a planned sequence for tapestry effects, or they can be simply laid into the shed with an overlap. SETTING: HOME OF JACK ORMAN

colored fabrics it can leave dark, sticky spots if you are too generous with the glue. If dropped on a hard, smooth surface or on your fingers, the glue can be rubbed off, but be careful not to get it on your clothes. Then you will have more rags for your rag pile.

The glue comes in handy tubes obtainable in fabric stores. I have tried a couple different makes and prefer one over the other. Both of them work well, however, especially on natural fibers; on polyester or acrylic blends the glue does not stick so easily and quickly. The glue is said to remain through laundry. I am a little doubtful about that, but in our case it does not matter much. The gluing is mainly done to keep the strips together during their handling in the weaving. When the strips are beaten in, they will remain in the weave whether there is glue or not, on account on the slanting joins which are secured between several warp threads.

This also indicates that the strips do not have to be glued or sewn together at all, but can be laid in by hand, overlapping to join. To glue is merely a practical matter when there are many short strips that would take a lot of time to place in the shed piece by piece. What you lose in time gluing, you gain in weaving in that case.

There are other ways to join strips: for example, loop the strips together in cut "buttonholes" at the ends, or sew them together with a seam straight across the width. In both cases pronounced bumps will show up in the weave. It can be added for effect sometimes, but for ordinary rugs for everyday use I prefer the smooth slanted joins.

Planning for a rag rug weave

To plan a rag rug and prepare for the weaving is a time-consuming but very pleasant task. A good way to get started is to consider the location and the purpose of the intended rug.

For instance, if the rug is going to be placed in the kitchen in front of the stove or the sink, we know that it will be subject to stains and a lot of wear. The rug should therefore be light and easily manageable, but tight and firm, so that it can take frequent laundering in addition to the heavy traffic.

A rug for the living room can perhaps be a large one in a soft but thick quality with color and design to match certain furniture or objects in the room.

For the dining area, where chairs constantly have to be moved and where crumbs are spilled, a flat and firm rug without bulky borders or design elements is the most wearable and practical kind.

A stairway rug has to be bent and shaped over each step, maybe even curved, so there a thin, smooth quality with a less close sett might be the best solution.

Direct questions can also be asked, like: What kind of floor will the rug be placed on? Will it be exposed to heavy and frequent wear from dirty shoes? Is the space for the rug limited? Is there a demand for an extra thick or soft rug? Can the design be bold and conspicuous? Are there certain colors in the surroundings that have to be matched?

When all these and other pertinent questions have been answered, already a vast number of possibilities have been diminished to a manageable few. It is now rather painless to decide upon quality, size, technique and design.

I have already mentioned that 8/4 or 12/6 cotton carpet warp are good choices of warp for making thinner rugs. Of course the weaving technique, the sett and the rag weft also have something to do with the quality. To get a smooth and lightweight rag rug that at the same time is firm and dense, I would use either of the mentioned warp materials, thread the weave to a tabby, set it 8 or even 10 e.p.i., and weave with a single rag strip. And beat hard, of course. The result will be a very thin rug, and if placed on a slick surface it might even need to have a pad underneath to prevent it from slipping when walked on.

If a little heavier rug is desired, I would set the warp 6 or 8 e.p.i. and weave with double strips. A linen warp can also be used in this sett to make a thicker, and at the same time stiffer, rug. Since tabby is the densest weaving technique we have, a tabby rug will always be firm and strong, provided it is beaten hard and tight. Apart from that, it is enjoyable to play with colors and designs in a tabby when there is nothing in the technique that competes or interferes.

A twill rug will be less dense than a tabby, but thicker and more pliable because of the weave structure. If set in a fairly coarse reed, say 5 or 6 dents per inch, and woven with double strips, twill will create a very thick rag rug. The warp can be linen or cotton, but with cotton I would choose a heavier carpet warp than 12/6. The rule that twill should be set closer than tabby does not apply to rag weaves where the structure is weft-faced. It is important only when the same yarn is used in both warp and weft to make a fifty-fifty quality.

The twill I have been talking about here is naturally the reversible kind, looking the same on both sides. This four-harness twill, also called batavia, is (next to tabby) our most common weaving structure, and is used very often in rag rugs.

Rosepath is another technique that is frequently used in rag rugs. Rosepath can be woven two ways: either with a tabby weft between each pattern weft, which is the most common, or with the rosepath woven "on opposites" all the way. "On opposites" means that if the pattern weft is woven with harnesses 1 and 2 raised, the background weft weaves with 3 and 4 raised; if the pattern is woven with 2 and 3 raised, the background weaves with 4 and 1 raised; and so on.

This latter way of weaving rosepath makes the rug very thick and pliable and is most suitable for an overall design. When making a rug with only narrow borders of rosepath, the combination with tabby is the best way.

I chose this way to weave a dining room rug with narrow borders of rosepath to give to my sister many years ago. At that time I did not care for rosepath in general and particularly not in rugs. I had the most uninspiring and drab rags and probably thought that borders in rosepath would pep up the rug a little. I wove unwillingly. The result was one of the most elegant rugs I have ever woven. The colors had become subtle and soft and blended well with the rosepath borders, which did pep up, but just enough to add elegance, and the rug fit perfectly with the colors and the furniture in my sister's dining room. Once in while a luck like that can be bestowed upon us!

Double binding is a technique that makes thick rugs with geometric designs, which are loom-controlled, as opposed to the designs in rölakan, which are laid in by hand. The double binding technique is a two-block weave and can be woven in tabby on four harnesses or twill on eight harnesses. It can easily be mistaken for a double weave, but does not have two layers of web. The blocks are of course decided by the threading, but in the treadling you are free to combine and alter colors infinitely and that is what makes the technique so intriguing and fascinating.

My love for the double binding technique goes back about ten years, when I first saw a rag rug in the tabby version of the weave. I was invited to the summer home of a friend of mine, and there, in her outhouse, I saw this beautiful rag rug woven in equal squares in soft shades of light turquoise, blue, aqua and white. It was a large rug and a large room and the most pleasant outhouse I have ever been to. I spent a lot of time there down on my knees on the rug to find out how it was made. Later I discovered that we had briefly passed the technique in my weaving school, when we were taught weft-faced structures. At that time we were required to weave samples and were asked to make a rug in the eight-harness twill version with wool yarn for weft. I happened to choose the ugliest color combination and hated the rug and the technique deeply for years. Until I was introduced to this beauty in the outhouse! I have made many, many rag weaves and rag rugs in double binding since then and yet the technique seems completely unexplored, barely touched.

Often it is difficult to decide on the most suitable size for the intended rug. It is tricky to visualize the best proportions of a rug for a certain area. Some practical guides can help; for example a rug under a dining room set should be large enough so the chairs have room to be moved on the rug and not get stuck on the edge now and again, or that a rug does not necessarily have to be placed under heavy furniture like couches or cupboards, where it would not show anyway.

An aid to that visualization of size is to outline the anticipated size with cords — or rag strips! — or to place newspapers in the full size of the planned measurements. It is amazing how much it helps to get a good view of the proportions of a rug in the room.

Planning the rug for this book

My aim in designing a rug for this book was to create a modern-looking rug based on the traditional way of making it regarding quality, technique and material, and at the same time inform step by step how to do it.

I chose a tight but fairly thick quality; a tabby set 6 e.p.i. with a 12/6 cotton carpet warp and with cotton (and cotton/polyester) rags for the weft. The design is in a way traditional with its stripes, but in the proportions and in the color combinations, the rug looks contemporary. The size is not too large. The rug is easy to manage and maintain and intended to be placed in a hallway or as a throw rug in a living room.

Using double strips of rags allows for gradual color blending between stripes — a subtle and contemporary effect.

Rag rug

Size: 90″ × 35″.
Technique: Tabby.
Warp: Cotton carpet warp 12/6, black.
Weft: Cotton and cotton/polyester rags, double strips, three main colors.
Sett: 6 e.p.i.
Reed: 6 dent, one thread per dent, double threads twice in each selvedge.
Width in Reed: 38″.
Number of Threads: 6 × 38 = 228 + 4 selvedge threads = 232.
Length of Warp:

length of rug	90″
take-up 10%	9″
shrinkage 6%	5″
fringes, 6″ per side = 12″, (included in the loom waste), loom waste	36″
	140″

(approximately 4 yards)

Making the warp

When making the warp I chose to wind it with two threads. It cuts the warping time in half and is just as easy as winding with one thread. I hold the two threads separated with my little finger so they do not twist around each other in the winding. They have to be held firmly and with the same tension all along. I never let go of the tension. If I have to leave the warping for some reason, I secure the threads around one peg on the warping board, or lock the two warping threads under the made warp on the warping reel in order to keep the tension. When returning to the warping, I make sure I do not slack the preserved tension when I start again. I make the warp with only one cross, the threading cross, since it is so short and there is no need for both a spreading cross and a threading cross. This one will serve both purposes.

Winding the warp on the loom

When I wind the warp onto the loom, I start by fastening the warp thread loop, which is nearest the cross, to the apron stick of the warp beam. I insert the lease sticks in the cross and spread the warp in a raddle, checking that the width is right when I am through. I also spread the threads on the apron stick to the same width. I center the warp in the loom and secure the raddle so it does not move during the winding. The lease sticks ride along in the warp and have to be moved from the

back beam towards the raddle continuously. Or, the lease sticks can be tied to the castle or the sides of the loom to keep them stationary so I don't have to remember to move them constantly. I just keep an eye on them to make sure the threads run smoothly and don't get stuck.

When winding the warp on, hold it back as far as possible from the raddle so that the outside threads don't angle in sharply.

I prefer to have a helper when winding a warp onto the loom, especially a rug warp, because the warp has to be very taut and tightly wound. As soon as the warp touches the warp beam, sticks are laid in about an inch apart, or whenever there is a flat surface on the beam, in order to keep the beam smooth and even. One complete turn of sticks is laid in, then one or two turns of warp are wound on, then another layer of sticks and so on. For each layer, the sticks should be placed on top of each other, not in the space between sticks. If there are not enough sticks, a thick paper can be used every other stick turn. The first turn on the beam should always be a stick layer, though.

The one who holds the warp has to stand as far as possible from the loom holding the warp, thus eliminating the sharp angles of the outer threads that otherwise occur. The further away one holds the warp, the less angle there is and the more even the threads. It is very important, always, to keep the warp threads at the same tension, both in making the warp and in winding it on to the loom. In winding, I check the tension every so often by feeling across the warp with my hand. At the end of the warp, the holder automatically comes near the loom thus creating a sharp angle in the outer threads; but at this point it is of no great importance since the tension will be adjusted when the warp is tied to the apron stick of the cloth beam after the threading and the sleying.

When the warp is wound on, the lease sticks are tied to the back beam, the end loop is cut and the warp ends pulled out of the raddle, which is taken away and the warp ends are temporarily tied in groups in overhand knots to secure the cross.

Threading

The threading comes next, and I always do it from the right towards the left since I am right-handed. It is easy in this weave, being tabby, just 1, 2, 3, 4 and repeat, with one thread per heddle, except in the two first and two last heddles, where the threads are doubled. This is to reinforce the strength of the selvedge threads which are exposed to extra handling in the weaving when the wefts are turned and manipulated to look neat and nice.

Sleying

After the threading comes the sleying of the reed and again I do this from the right to the left, one thread per dent except the two first and the two last dents, where the threads are doubled. When I am finished I check that the width is right and no threads forgotten anywhere. I make sure that the warp is centered in the reed, and more important, that it is centered in the loom.

Tying the warp

When I tie the warp to the apron stick of the cloth beam, I always start with one knot in the middle of the warp, making sure I tie it to the center of the apron stick. Then I tie one knot in each

selvedge and alternate tying knots on each side, either going from the sides in towards the middle or from the middle and out. I comb the threads between my fingers to straighten them out and to get the same tension on all of them. This is the only time a warp is allowed to be combed. I check every so often that the threads are straight behind the harnesses and not tangled or stuck in the lease sticks.

I tie small groups of threads, hardly more than an inch, all across except for the selvedge groups, where I take very few threads, the fewest possible. This is to help hold out the full width when starting to weave. It is important that the warp has an even tension all across when the tying is finished and all knots tightly tied. The knot should be a square bow knot, which is easy to untie when the weave is finished and is being taken off the loom. The bows are the warp ends that will be used for the fringe.

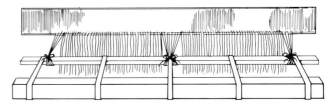

Very few threads in the selvedge groups.

Tying the harnesses

The next step is to tie up the harnesses if the loom so requires. Mine does, since it is a Swedish counterbalance loom with heddle bars and string heddles. It is vital to do the tying with equal measurements on both sides and with the same height on both sides, so the harnesses will balance well in action.

Tying the treadles

The tie-up for the treadles is easy since it is a tabby: harnesses 1 and 3 are tied up to one treadle and 2 and 4 to the other treadle, whether the loom is a counterbalance or a jack-type loom. The result will still be tabby.

Checking the set-up

Now comes the big test to see if the weave is properly set up and works well. I try the treadles to see if they operate the harnesses correctly and evenly, check so there are no crossed threads behind the reed, see if the position of the warp is of the right height in the reed so the beater will work properly, watch out for double threads indicating threading mistakes or errors in the sleying, and check all kinds of things that could possibly have gone wrong.

When everything is checked and found correct — or is corrected — the weaving begins by closing the gaps between the ties to the apron stick. A very good way to do this swiftly is to open the first shed, make a weft with a rag strip or a heavy scrap yarn, do *not* beat, change sheds, make a second weft, close the shed and, now, beat. It is amazing how much the warp gaps close right away. Repeat this procedure several times until all the gaps are closed and all the threads nicely together.

There is another way of preventing the weave from drawing in besides tying slim knots at the selvedges. When one of the first wefts is made, make the selvedge loop very long and fasten it around the end of the apron stick, stretch the weft (which is allowed here *only*), beat, do the same thing the next weft at the other selvedge and beat. Then continue to make the two wefts without beating in between to close the gaps. The sooner the long selvedge loops are made, the more effective they are.

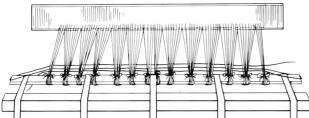

With the first picks of filler weft, make loops around the ends of the apron rod to keep the weaving from drawing in.

Testing rag strips for width

Now the routine work is done, the loom is ready for weaving and the warp looks straight and centered and tight and neat in the loom. Or doesn't it?

I have told how to cut the rags and how to join the strips, but I did not mention in specific measurements how wide to cut them. That is what has to be found out now.

Different qualities of rag rugs demand different widths of strips to make the weight wanted. It can be a waste of both time and rags if the strips are cut beforehand and found not suitable for the result expected. Of course after having done a great number of rag rugs and more or less specialized in one kind, I know how wide the strips should be cut.

Nevertheless, it is practical to have the weave set up first, then to try out the best widths for the strips, then to cut them all accordingly.

The best way to test the width is to cut some strips of the same rag fabric in two or three different widths, weave a few wefts with each width, and see and feel how they appear in the weave. Which is the best one in width for the particular rag weave you are making? When you have decided that, you have the width for your "test" strip and the quality for your weave is established.

The next step is to determine how wide you have to cut the rest of your rags, which might be thinner or thicker fabrics than in the "test" strip. To accomplish this, roll the test strip between your thumb and fingers to feel its thickness, cut strips from the other rags, feel them the same way and match the thickness with the test strip. Then cut all the rest of the rags accordingly.

For this quality rug I am making — with 12/6 cotton carpet warp set 6 e.p.i. and using double strips in the weft — I cut thinner fabrics, like shirt material, about ¾" to 1" wide. Heavier fabric, like well worn jeans or denim material, I cut ½" to ⅝" wide. A stiff and less worn jeans material I cut even narrower and I do not use two strips together, but blend one strip with one of softer material in order to pack them together better in the weave.

Naturally I do not have only shirt and jeans material, but all kinds of cotton and cotton/polyester fabrics in my rag pile; and they all have to be cut in widths that correspond with the thickness established in my test weaving.

It is satisfying to know that the cutting does not take a very long time anymore. Before I learned this revolutionary way of cutting rags with a knife, it was frustrating to have the loom set up and ready to go, wanting so badly to weave and then having to wait — for weeks, it seemed — before all the strips were cut and ready to weave with. All the wonderful ideas and the inspiration faded while I sat there with a pair of scissors hurting my fingers and cut and cut.

Now I can have this great idea for my rug in the morning, and at noon time I am all set to start weaving. It seems cutting the rags is done more incidentally. It takes even less time if the garments are trimmed ahead of time leaving the pieces flat and ready for rolling. They can even be rolled in advance, for that matter.

Of course the joining of the strips adds some time to the preparation before the actual weaving can begin, but even that does not take too long. And, practice makes perfect — or quick at least. Gluing, or sewing, goes faster after a little practice. Or maybe you have very long strips and do not have to glue, or you choose to glue the strips as you weave along. I do that most of the time.

Testing rag strips for color

After testing how wide my strips should be cut, I do another kind of test weaving, which is sheer fun and pleasure, a pleasure united with frustration, disappointment, despair, lack of self-confidence as well as struggle, patience and persistence, but nevertheless a full-scale pleasure. I am trying out different rags for colors and color combinations to see how they appear in the weave.

Most of the time I do my designing of a rug or a tapestry directly in the loom. I might have an idea in my head or a vision of the finished piece after having gone through my rags and discovered all the treasures in colors, or seen a new color combination when two rags accidentally met, or found a large amount of one rag that will go far enough for the basic color in a rug.

Once in a while I have made a sketch that has to be translated into rags, and that is more difficult. The colors of the rags never appear in the weave the way I anticipated when I picked them out. Rags are very unpredictable and absolutely have a will of their own.

Therefore I have to try and try again. I test different colors in the same weft, or beside each other. I try two different shades together to make a third, I weave with combinations unthought of and may discover that they give a glorious effect, and above all I try to combine colors to a pleasing result which matches my vision.

It takes a lot of backwards weaving before I am pleased and can go ahead. Sometimes I am happy for 10", then I take it all out; it is discouraging to undo what I labored over yesterday or an hour ago, but very satisfying in the long run. Sometimes I hit the "mother lode" at once.

With all this test weaving I do of all kinds of different rags, it would be dumb to cut them all in advance. Therefore I usually cut just a few strips of the rag I am testing, and not until I really know that I am going to use them do I cut the full amount.

Weaving

At last the actual weaving can begin. When making rugs I usually start, and also end, the rugs with four wefts of the same material as the warp to stop the rags from floating out or unravelling when the rug is cut down and taken out of the loom. When making the fringes I can choose to take out the four wefts or keep them. I believe that they strengthen the edge though, so I always keep them.

The yarn wefts have to be very generously laid in little arches before beating so they do not draw in the weave in any way.

Sometimes there is a demand for a hem on the rug. Then I can either sew on a special binding, or I can weave a wide hem in the same material and the same way as the four wefts. The wider the hem is made, the more careful one has to be not to draw in. Be very generous with the weft. The hem can also be woven with rags, if desired.

Joining strips in the weave

In starting weaving with the actual rags, and using double strips wound together on one shuttle, the strips have to be trimmed off at an angle to be joined smoothly. Cut one strip shorter than the other, pull them through the shed so the shorter end stops a couple of inches from the selvedge and the longer one 3" to 4" outside the weave, turn the longer end around the outer warp thread and tuck it back in the shed overlapping the shorter one. Thus you eliminate a clumsy or bulky start and you get a very smooth join, which is not thicker than the rest of the rug will be.

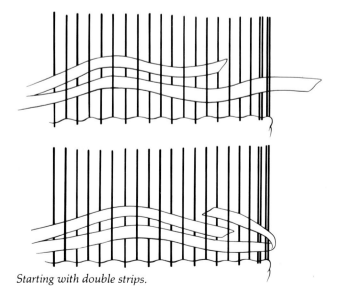

Starting with double strips.

*"Double binding" is essentially a double-faced block weave which makes a thick, reversible rug.
See Appendix IV for threading and treadling information.*

The same procedure is done when finishing with double strips at the very end or when there is a color change.

In weaving or beginning with a single strip, the strip should be trimmed off at a very low and long angle, the end sticking out of the shed in the first weft then turned around the last warp thread and tucked back in the same shed. The trimming makes this a very smooth way to start or end a single rag weft.

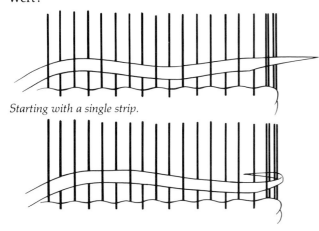

Starting with a single strip.

When you suddenly run out of strips in the middle of a shed, the joins are made the same way as when you are gluing strips together; overlap the slanted end of the strip in the shed with the new strip, also slanted, and glue, if desired.

When there is a color change in my rugs, I finish the old color with a full weft, then I add the new color in the next weft in the ways described above. If I were to glue the new color to the old one where it stops, I might get a small piece of the old color showing in the new weft. I am not in favor of that look in precisely striped rugs. Sometimes, though, this way of joining can be planned as part of the design and give very attractive results. I have used it many times in table mats and runners and vest material, where there was not a call for solid, evenly finished stripes. It is fun to do and makes the weaving much easier since one does not have to be overly precise and careful.

Selvedge control

To make the selvedges smooth and neat looking in my weaves, I take extra precaution. When I make a weft, I pull it through the shed until there is a little loop of the weft sticking out at the selvedge. I twist the two wefts in the loop with my fingers, then tighten the weft only at the selvedge so the turn pulls in, and secure the twist I just made. I

make sure the rest of the weft is loose and generously laid and then I beat. I do the same thing weaving with a single strip.

It is now, in making the selvedges good looking, that the double warp threads at the sides are useful. Yet I try not to handle the selvedge threads more than absolutely necessary to prevent them from stretching. Wavy edges are very bad looking.

Beating

Often the question comes up whether to beat with an open or closed shed. There are times when one way or the other is necessary, and I know that many books say to beat with the shed closed in rag rug weaving. I am not of the same opinion and I do not do it myself. I feel that when a weft is made and the strips placed generously in the shed and it closes, the warp threads lock the weft in a position that is unchangeable. For instance, if an arch has been made and is a little too high, it has nowhere to go except out through the warp threads and end up being a "mouse ear". I have the opinion that if the weft is beaten in an open shed, it has a chance to stretch out and partly rearrange itself before the beat hits. This is all a matter of every weaver's special touch and way of doing things, and I think you should please yourself.

When I have beaten in my open shed, I change sheds and beat again. The first beat sets the weft in place, and the second beat is the one that packs it together. And I beat with emphatic and strong beats, really swinging the beater. It is of no use to beat short, staccato beats without any strength or to just press the wefts together with the beater. That way is harder on the weaver than the really long, forceful beats, where the beater is the tool that makes the effort.

Tension

Again I will emphasize the need of having the warp taut. You can feel when you beat which is the best tension; if the warp is not tight enough the beater bounces when you beat, but if it is tightened hard and good, you can feel how the beat "takes".

Handling the weft

The wefts have to be laid in generously, as I have said. Sometimes it is difficult to make arches with rags, but the main idea is to feed the weave with enough weft so it does not draw in, and whether you make arches or place the weft at an angle or are generous in general does not matter. One thing though, do not lock the weft at the last selvedge by pulling it down to the very corner. Leave it to go straight out of the shed or even at an angle upwards and do not pull on it. The weft should be flowing in the shed and not in any way stretched.

Weaving with a temple

A good help to avoid draw-in is to use a temple or a stretcher bar. I always do when I am weaving with rags.

It is important to attach the stretcher bar to the weave as soon as there is enough material woven to fasten it to. If you wait too long and there is already a draw-in in your weave, it can be difficult to ease it out to the full width. And if you are able to do it, you will end up with an uneven weave anyway, where the first part is drawn in and the rest is full width. On the other hand, if you attach the bar without stretching the weave to its full width, the bar will do no good.

When attaching the stretcher bar to the weave, adjust it to the length necessary, which is the measurement of the width of the weave in the reed; fasten both sides with the teeth about ¼" from the edge of the weave and then close the bar carefully. There will be a little resistance, but if it is extreme, do not force the bar to close. Then the stretcher bar might be set too long after all, so make it shorter and try again. Never make the bar longer than the width measures in the reed, or you might tear the selvedges or break threads in forcing it to close. Besides, there is no use of trying to make the weave wider than planned for. When you have woven 2" or 3", it is time to move the stretcher bar.

Checking measurements

In rag weaving it is easy to get carried away by all the intriguing colors and patterns and forget to measure the weave now and then. It is important to remember, however, especially if the rug has to be a definite length. It is also important to add enough for shrinkage.

I learned it the hard way once when I made a long rug for a friend of mine. The rug was going to be placed in a hallway and had to be exactly five meters long. I wove the rug about two feet longer, but when it was taken out of the loom and had been lying on the floor to relax for a couple of days, it had shrunk about a foot under the five meters. I know I had not measured wrong in the loom.

The explanation of this shrinkage is that the cotton fiber is being so stretched in the weave that when the tension is relaxed, the fibers contract and pull the wefts together even more than in the weaving. The twist of the double twisted carpet warp might have something to do with this contraction also.

So from experience I know that I have to count on about 6% shrinkage when using this warp. A rug woven with linen warp shrinks very little. The linen fiber is rigid, and does not contract when the tension is released. It has not allowed much stretching in the first place.

When I check the measurements in the weave, I always loosen the tension and take away the stretcher bar before I measure.

Following a sketch

When I have a sketch to follow, I often count the number of wefts instead of using the tape measure. When I have woven one repeat — if it is a design with repeats! — with the shrinkage added, I measure it, count the wefts of the different colors, write them down on a paper with the respective measurements beside, and use that as my guide.

Another way of measuring when the sketch has repeats is to mark a band with the different measurements of one repeat and then let the band ride along, pinned to the weave, as the rug proceeds. When one repeat is woven, the band is moved to the next one, etc.

Several times when I have woven irregular or abstract designs I have used a working drawing attached underneath the warp, following it by looking at the contours between the warp threads, as in tapestry weaving.

Whatever trick you use, be sure to follow your sketch, or your "vision", and check your measurements so the rug will end up with the length you planned on.

Placing beaming sticks

When two or more rugs are woven in a row, you must not forget to leave warp for fringes — if wanted — between the rugs. To leave the warp bare is not very practical; something substantial is needed to beat against when the next rug is started. A clever solution is to weave in beaming sticks, as many as needed to make the length of the fringes, one for the rug finished and one for the following rug. If there is a shortage of sticks, heavy folded paper can be used to the same effect. If the warp is nevertheless left unwoven, sticks or paper are still needed when the bare warp comes down on the cloth beam to prevent the threads at the sides to slide outside the roll on the beam.

In connection to this, I would like to mention the necessity of placing beaming sticks on the cloth beam as the woven material gradually winds on. Cloth beams, as well as warp beams, are always uneven on account of cords, grooves for the apron bands, slots for the apron stick, etc., not to mention the row of bumps that will appear when the apron stick with its knots reaches the beam. It is just as important to even out the cloth beam with sticks to prevent the woven material (especially thin and delicate fabrics) from being distorted as it is to care for the warp in that respect. Place the sticks on the cloth beam the same way as on the warp beam, with the difference that only one turn of sticks is needed. After that, the weave itself keeps the beam flat and even.

Cutting down the rug

At last, after so many hours or days of weaving, the rug is completed and we have come to the most exciting part of the project: cutting down the rug, taking it off the loom and placing it on the floor to see it — see it for the first time, it seems.

It is a completely new experience to see the rug in full size as opposed to the few inches you have in front of your eyes on the loom when weaving it. It never ceases to amaze me how different the rug looks when I take this "first" look at it: "Oh, is this what I have been struggling with and had so many worries about? Is this what it looks like?"

Critique

I look at the rug with critical eyes regarding the look as well as the execution, asking myself: Is the design well balanced? Are the colors beautiful together? Are the proportions pleasing? Did I get a good result for the purpose I intended for the rug? Is it well woven? Are the selvedges straight and nice looking? Is the rug flat and does it lie well on the floor? If all these questions are answered in a positive way, I have a treasure.

Since I have woven a vast number of rag rugs and have so many years of practice, I do not have to worry so much about the execution anymore — mostly the rugs meet the standard in that respect

— but it is the look of the rug that is my greatest concern. It is seldom I am 100% satisfied with the result. Sometimes the rug lacks a lot in the design elements or in the colors or color combinations, but once in a great while the result is even more attractive than I expected. Anyway, it is always a surprise and again I come to the conclusion that rags have a will and a life of their own.

Finishing

After having had this exhausting experience of critiquing my creation, it is time to go back to work and do the finishing of the rug.

First the sides where the warp ends are hanging have to be taken care of — you did not forget to allow for fringes when you cut the weave off the loom, did you? There are different ways to make fringes; they can be knotted, they can be twisted or they can be braided, all of which can be done in several ways and with variations.

The fringe I like best and use in 99 cases out of 100 is the twisted fringe. It looks good and is very durable. In the rug on page 86, with its open sett, I had to add extra threads to the fringe to make it look full enough. It is not nice looking if the fringes are too sparse and cry out after each other. It is just as bad looking if they are too dense, by the way. In adding threads, I use the same yarn as in the warp. I cut ends — a whole bunch of them at once — a little more than double the length of the fringe, take two of them and lay them loosely in between the two pairs of warp ends which I am going to twist. The two pairs from the rug I tie around the middle of the two extra threads with half a square knot, tight but not so it distorts the edge. Now I have eight threads together for the first fringe. I take four of them in each hand and twist each handful in the same direction as the thread is twisted, in this case towards the right. When ½" or ¾" is twisted tightly, I twist the right twisted bunches together in the opposite direction, towards the left, and change hands. I repeat and repeat the same thing until I have the length of fringe I want. Then I take one individual end from the fringe, no matter which one, and make a half hitch around the whole fringe where the twisting stopped, tightening it hard. I take another individual end and make another half hitch just under the first one, pulling it tight. Thus I have secured the twist so it will not come undone and it will last for a long time.

The same procedure is done for all the fringes,

making all of them the same length. This is easiest to accomplish if a paper measure is used. It is almost impossible to get an even length on all of the fringes by comparing the just finished one with its neighbor. Somehow the even line you strive for will go more and more on a slant that way.

After all the fringes are made, I trim off the ends to an even line about ½" from the half hitches. When you get used to this twisting and can keep track of all your fingers and know where to place them, it is a very easy and relaxing way to spend an evening.

If you choose to braid the fringes, I would suggest you use the braid with four strands (in Appendix I) which is flat and rich looking. Extra threads can be added the same way as for twisted fringes, if necessary. The braids can be finished off the same way with half hitches, and then trimmed off evenly.

For weavers who have trouble with their hands in twisting or braiding, the knotted fringe is less strenuous. Choose an appropriate amount of warp ends and tie them together with an overhand knot, which is pushed up close to the edge of the rug and tightened hard. Then cut the length wanted as evenly as possible.

If you are fond of knots and like to tie them, a variation of the look can be made by tying an overhand knot at the very end of each individual thread in addition to the big knot.

If you wish to have a hem on your rug and you have woven a few inches for the purpose, it is a good idea to first whip stitch the cut edge for security before folding and stitching it. If you have not woven the hem, but want to bind the edge with another material, such as a cut bias strip of a suitable fabric or storebought binding bands, you have to secure the wefts first so they do not unravel. This is best done by tying square knots or overhand knots on the warp ends, pair by pair or four by four on closer setts, all along the edge, cut the ends and then apply the binding. A rag woven edge can also be folded and used for the hem, but it makes the hem very thick and bulky, even clumsy sometimes.

Blocking

A rug that comes directly from the loom and has been handled in the fringing or hemming process can be in need of pressing or blocking. Many times it is enough to place the rug on the floor — where

Soft, faded cotton calico stripes give a sweet, traditional look in this small rug.

else! — and leave it "set" for a couple of days. Sometimes it is good to put weights on it to press it. The weights have to be evenly distributed all over the rug and left on for a couple of days or overnight, depending on the need.

I saw a clever way to press rugs at a weaving studio where I worked many years ago. Big sheets of masonite were placed on the fresh-out-of-the-loom rug, covering it completely, and here and there pieces of railroad ties a foot or two long were placed. It was a very adequate way to press rugs, but who has railroad ties?

If pressing is not enough to get the rug nice looking, or if it is uneven or bubbling, you have to block it. Needed for this is a good blocking board or, even better, a wooden floor. A wooden floor you can hammer nails into is about as easy to come by as railroad ties! However, if there is a will, there might be a way.

Draw the size of the rug on the blocking board with right angles. If the rug is crooked and in places a couple of inches wider, draw a line on the average width, the same for the length. When nailing, you consequently have to pull on some parts to stretch and push on other parts to keep the excess inside the drawn lines. Place the rug on the blocking board inside the drawn lines, nail it with a hammer and rustproof nails in the four corners first, then in the middle of the length and the middle of the width, then part each section in halves and nail. Continue this way until all four sides of the rug are nailed closely and evenly, following the drawn lines.

When the nailing is completed, cover the rug with moist towels or cloth, cover that with paper — newspapers are fine — and then place weights, evenly distributed again, on top and leave overnight. In the absence of railroad ties, boxes, suitcases, books or other flat, heavy objects can be used as weights. The next day, take away everything on top of the rug, but leave it nailed until it is absolutely dry, then take away the nails. The result is a completely straight and flat rug and it looks ten times better than it did before the blocking.

This is, by the way, the same kind of blocking you can use for any kind of weave that needs it, especially tapestries. It can transform a disaster into a beauty. The importance of a proper finish, including blocking, cannot be emphasized enough.

Care

The day-to-day care of rag rugs is effortless. The rugs are easy to vacuum clean or to sweep with a broom; it is painless to take out a stain or mop up something that has spilled on a rag rug; and they are easy to manage in smaller sizes, when taken out to shake or air outdoors. A wonderful thing to do if you live in an area where it snows in the winter is to take the rugs out in the snow, which has to be dry, and brush them on both sides with the snow. It is a delight to see how clear the colors become and how clean and new the rugs look. Plus the wonderful, fresh air that comes in with them!

When finally the rug has become soiled and no snow in the world can help, it has to be washed. (For the first time! There is no need to wash a rug first thing when it comes off the loom. We did use clean rags, didn't we?) If it is a smaller rug, it can be washed in the washing machine in not more

than lukewarm water on a gentle cycle. It should not be centrifuged, to avoid heavy creases, and tumble dried only lightly. When the rug is still damp, hang it with clothes pins on a line along the selvedge without bending the edge, or lay it down flat to dry.

If the rug is too large for the washing machine, maybe you can proceed as people do in Sweden. I know many Swedes, including myself, who take their dirty rag rugs down to the basement or out in the patio where they soak the rugs with the garden hose, scrub them with a hard brush and soap — real soap, no detergent — rinse them thoroughly with the garden hose again, and hang them or lay them flat to dry. Many people have access to a lake or a river, or even the coast, where they scrub their rug. Can't you just feel the freshness and the good scent that this brings!

In transportation of rugs and storing rugs for a length of time, it is best to roll, not fold them. Keeping a rug folded might cause creases or wrinkles that are hard to get rid of unless the rug is blocked.

When rag rugs are getting old and worn and not in their prime anymore, they are often used for other purposes. I know a family that always took an old rag rug along to sit on when they went on picnics or camping trips out in the woods. A friend of mine happened to have a rag rug in his car once when he got stuck in the snow. He placed the rug under the tires and was soon driving out of the snow drifts. And I remember from my childhood, the use of old rag rugs in muffling sounds and the demolishing effect of blasts when a water main was dug. Often rag rugs are being used as tarpaulins and rain covers. The list of ingenious ways of using rag rugs is indeed long.

Conclusion

Weaving with rags is a process which is not needed today in order to stretch our means or to save resources. We see rag weaving as a new and charming way of decorating our homes or adding fashion to our clothes. Yet it gives such a satisfaction to many of us to recycle waste into a product of utility and beauty.

To me, rag weaving is not only that, it represents a whole culture and a way of life. It links me with weavers of past times and I feel related to that first rag weaver in the little village somewhere on earth.

Weaving Warp-Faced Rugs

Lynne Giles

Warp-faced rugs have been largely neglected by handweavers. Only a few examples come to mind: the striped druggets of 19th century America, plain and patterned Bedouin rugs, and rep weave rugs from Canada and Scandinavia. This almost uncharted territory, in fact, offers a multitude of possibilities for the weaver who is willing to explore. Twill patterns that are well known in weft-faced and balanced weaves look fresh, almost exotic, when turned around 90°. Warp-faced summer and winter features spiky transitions between blocks that make ordinary designs look dynamic. Unlimited large or small scale designs are available to the experienced weaver who chooses to work with one-weft double cloth pick-up. Crackle weave gains an appealing simplicity when converted to warp-face. The list could go on indefinitely. Berta Frey in *Designing and Drafting for Handweavers* gives excellent directions for making conversions from weft-face to warp-face when working with block weaves, explaining that the threading and treadling drafts trade places. Certainly no one interested in warp-face should feel limited to plain, vertical stripes.

Warp-faced rugs offer a number of advantages in addition to the pleasures of exploration. They are exceptionally durable and are definitely indicated where hard use, even abuse, is expected. A high grade canvas, with its hundreds of warp/weft intersections, is perhaps the most rugged of all textiles. In colonial America it was, in fact, used to cover floors. Canvas rugs, also known as floor cloths, painted to imitate Oriental carpets, proved especially practical in hallways and on staircases. Floor cloths, however, have disappeared and thick, soft carpets are popular. The weaver today who works with unbalanced structures (warp- or weft-faced) must find a satisfactory compromise between weight (thickness) and durability. The terms of this compromise should be dictated by use. Obviously rugs have varying purposes. A bedside carpet has a different role from a rug needed in an entryway. A rug that can survive the assaults of muddy shoes must be tough indeed, and it is here that warp-face shines. A rug made with 8/4 cotton carpet warp set at 36 e.p.i. — a true warp-face would be set even closer — can be woven at 5 p.p.i. with a weft having a ¼" cross-section. The result is 180 intersections to the square inch. A typical weft-faced rug, set at 4 e.p.i. with 24 p.p.i., runs to only 96 intersections. Furthermore, the firm, tightly spun yarns that make good warps do not serve well as wefts in weft-faced rugs since they do not pack in easily. Clearly the advantage lies with warp-face when durability is the weaver's primary consideration.

It follows from the above that warp-faced rugs, having few picks per inch, are much faster to weave than weft-faced rugs, despite longer warping time. More important, perhaps, is the fact that the weaving time is likely to be far less stressful. Tension inequalities seem to be minimized by the large number of ends per inch. With true warp-face, the weft requires no bubbling, and even when the sett is fairly open in warp-dominant rugs the laying in of weft is quick and straight selvedges are easy to maintain. One has the feeling that the rigidly rectilinear warps discipline the wefts, forbidding any aimless meandering. An even beat is also rather simple to establish, since one usually beats as firmly as the loom allows. A pleasantly flexible rug is the normal result, since it is virtually impossible to over-beat a warp-faced rug. A word of warning is, however, in order at this point. The warp-faced rug does make heavy demands on the loom. The ideal loom for this kind of weaving should be heavily built, counterbalance or countermarch, with treadles hinged at the back, a generous distance between the front and back beam and a weighted beater (I have attached a 25-pound steel bar to mine). A loom that has few or none of these features should not be expected to function with a dense, wide warp. For example, a typical jack loom will not make a shed with a 42" wide warp of 8/2 cotton set at 48 e.p.i. If the warp width is reduced to 36", the same rug is possible, if difficult, to weave.

The strong vertical influence of the warp on the structure of warp-faced rugs has its corollary in terms of design. Multicolor warp-way stripes with clean edges are easily produced in any size, including delicate, two-thread lines. Since weft-way stripes tend to look heavy and crude except in very narrow widths, the designer to whom stripes

appeal will find warp-face an ideal medium. The stripe width, of course, cannot be altered once the weaving is under way, but if one uses a block weave threading, horizontal lines can be treadled in order to interrupt the verticals and ideas can be worked out at the loom as well as on paper. Summer and winter and crackle are block weaves that might be used. This chapter will explore four harness rep weave, also called rib weave or *ripsmatta*, which resembles both crackle and the familiar log cabin.

Rep weave, in its simplest warp-face form, is produced by the alternation of thick and thin wefts. End-on-end color changes in the warp, traditionally light and dark, can be used to emphasize this alternation. Rep weave is an excellent structure for rugs since the combination of thick and thin wefts increases the number of warp/weft intersections. A thick weft, for example, that weaves at 5 p.p.i. by itself weaves at 7 p.p.i with a thin partner, without, it should be noted, sacrificing thickness, since the rug simply acquires deeper channels than normally appear between rows of thick wefts. Furthermore, rep weave makes use of what are, in effect, two warp systems; one set is elevated to the surface of the rug by the thick weft while the other set is held below the surface by the thin weft. This means that in any given area of wear, alternate threads will escape abrasion and will remain intact. Rep weave also combines the structural advantages of plain weave with the thickness of twill and double-face fabrics.

Sett is an important variable in rep weave design. Warp-face, in the strictest sense, allows no choice. One simply finds the number of ends per inch that completely covers the warp. The recommended method for determining this number involves winding the warp yarn around a ruler, then multiplying by two the threads that cover one inch. I use this method only as a very rough guide, because I believe that more interesting results are likely when some of the weft is allowed to show between the warps. This weft spot can range in size from near zero to ⅛" in a warp-dominant rug. At the latter spacing, the weft has a powerful influence on the warps and the weaver gains considerable design freedom, since decisions about the weft can be made as the rug is woven. This sett, of course, sacrifices some of the durability that is the hallmark of warp-face, and a rug of this type will be thinner and softer than a rug of the same materials set more densely. But rugs have different purposes,

Because the warp is set in such a way that the weft shows a little, color interactions between warp and weft give this simple block pattern great visual interest.

looms have varying capabilities, and weavers have personal preferences. A rug that is reassuringly firm to one weaver may be board-like to another. What seems flimsy to one may be pleasantly soft to another. In any case, a rug need not be thick nor beaten ferociously to wear well. An early rug that has proven one of my sturdiest has been on the floor for more than ten years. It is thin and soft rather than firm. Its materials are undistinguished: the warp is 8/4 cotton, the wefts are Aunt Lydia's rug yarn and a wool of comparable weight. The secret of this rug surely lies in its warp/weft arithmetic: 12 e.p.i. $\times$ 14 p.p.i. or 168 intersections per square inch.

The aesthetic benefits of the thick-thin sequence are numerous. The ridges and channels formed by the two wefts give textural complexity to the rug surface. This effect is especially pleasing when the fat weft assumes a tubular shape as it is packed in. The fine horizontal lines formed by the thin weft add delicacy to rugs, especially rag rugs, that might otherwise appear coarse and heavy. The serried effect of rep weave also gives an orderly, clean look to textiles. Again this is valuable for rag rugs whose bulky, sometimes uneven wefts tend to push warps out of alignment, creating a somewhat sloppy surface.

In addition to the contrast supplied by two different wefts, the weaver can add further textural contrast by alternating dissimilar warp materials—for instance thick and thin or dull and shiny or rough and smooth yarns. In block designs this can have considerable interest, justifying such special measures as winding onto two warp beams or weighting one set of warps separately in order to compensate for unequal stretch factors.

Color blending is another interesting feature of rep weave. It is the automatic consequence of alternating two colors, end-on-end, in the warp. Each color presents itself as a horizontal line, corresponding to the weft, thick or thin, beneath it. The color that encloses the thick weft, of course, is dominant, but it is modified by the color that encloses the thin weft. One has to handle this design element with some care when working with high contrasts, as there is a danger of busyness or even optical dazzle that some people find disagreeable. But used sparingly, there is real excitement offered by these lines. Low contrast lines are safer and they add a richness of color not unlike the pointillism that enlivens balanced weaves.

Rep weave gives two-block designs with two harnesses and four-block designs with four harnesses. Block arrangements include checkerboard, twill lines, i.e., zigzags and diamonds, window frames, trees and endless variations of square and rectangular figures on a ground. A good way to gain understanding of these possibilities is to set up a sample with a twill arrangement of blocks and then to play at the loom with treadling combinations, remembering that each block always weaves with a block adjacent to it, either to the left or to the right.

One should always keep in mind with block threaded rep weave that both vertical and horizontal design emphases are available. Horizontal lines appear automatically as texture and color elements and horizontal blocks can be threaded and treadled. Vertical lines may appear as stripes, created during the warping process, or as warp-way blocks. When planning stripes, it is useful to think in terms of the two warp systems discussed earlier. Different treatments can be given to each set. One set may be striped, while the other remains monochrome. Or both sets may be striped, either in or out of phase with each other. The addition of blocks is a further complication.

I have chosen a variation on window frames in the rug I designed for this chapter. It features solid stripes in the warp, used to frame and to spread out design motifs, and a block arrangement that offers an alternation of positive and negative space in the motifs themselves (next page).

For this project I used a 12/6 cotton seine twine that yields 1400 yards to the pound. This is an ideal yarn for warp-faced rugs since it is smooth, strong, and very tightly spun. It is the easiest warp yarn I have ever worked with and it is a pleasure to handle. The color range is limited, but endless variation can be achieved by the use of different weft colors if the sett allows weft influence. My thick wefts are strips of shirt weight cotton-polyester fabric. Thin wefts are 10/2 cotton and variegated crochet cotton.

Calculating the warp

Sett is best determined by making samples. A shortcut is possible here. Sley and tie up the central 3" of your sample (which should be at least 8" wide, unless your warp is precious or in short supply). If

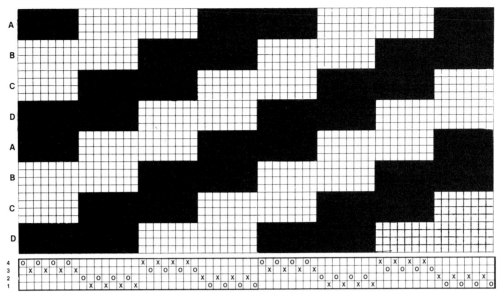

X = Dark
O = Light
A = 2 3 Thick Weft, 1 4 Thin Weft
B = 2 4 Thick Weft, 1 3 Thin Weft
C = 1 4 Thick Weft, 2 3 Thin Weft
D = 1 3 Thick Weft, 2 4 Thin Weft

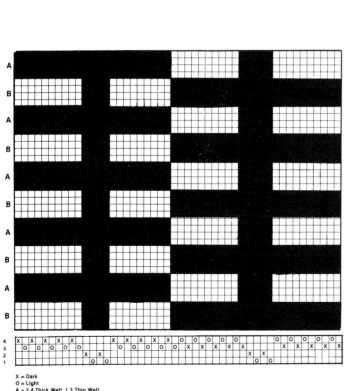

X = Dark
O = Light
A = 2 4 Thick Weft, 1 3 Thin Weft
B = 2 3 Thick Weft, 1 4 Thin Weft

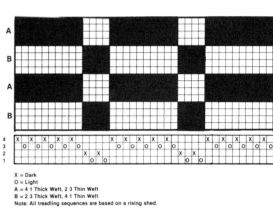

X = Dark
O = Light
A = 4 1 Thick Weft, 2 3 Thin Weft
B = 2 3 Thick Weft, 4 1 Thin Weft
Note: All treadling sequences are based on a rising shed.

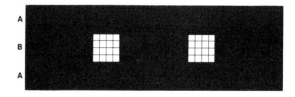

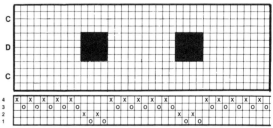

X = Dark
O = Light
A = 2 4 Thick Weft, 1 3 Thin Weft
B = 1 4 Thick Weft, 2 3 Thin Weft
C = 1 3 Thick Weft, 2 4 Thin Weft
D = 2 3 Thick Weft, 1 4 Thin Weft

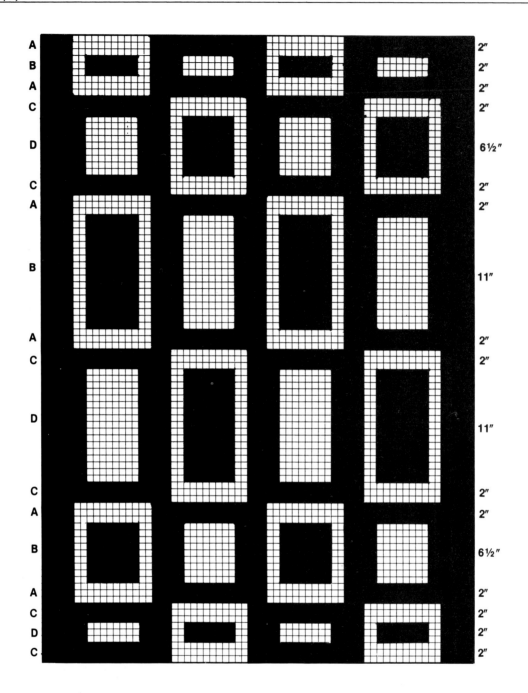

Row labels (top to bottom) with dimensions at right:

A	2″
B	2″
A	2″
C	2″
D	6½″
C	2″
A	2″
B	11″
A	2″
C	2″
D	11″
C	2″
A	2″
B	6½″
A	2″
C	2″
D	2″
C	2″

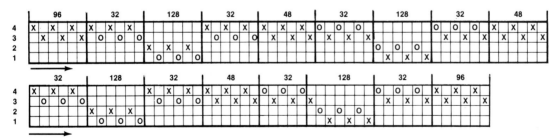

X = Dark
O = Light
A = 1 3 Thick Weft, 2 4 Thin Weft
B = 2 3 Thick Weft, 1 4 Thin Weft
C = 2 4 Thick Weft, 1 3 Thin Weft
D = 1 4 Thick Weft, 2 3 Thin Weft

NOTE: The numbers above the threading diagram represent the total number of warp threads (dark and light) in each design unit. The drawdown does not include beginning and ending borders.

The strong graphic quality of this rug yields to tiny color surprises in the thin weft — see the detail on page 110.

the sett is obviously wrong, you can try again with the same 3″ section. When it looks right, you can quickly sley and tie on the remaining warp.

Thirty-two e.p.i. is a good sett for seine twine in a rug that features strong graphic qualities in its design. Blocks will read very clearly.

For a 3′×5′ rug I usually plan on a three yard warp, (on my reel this is actually 116″). This allows a generous 20% take-up plus a yard for loom waste. This last figure is variable; some weavers who abhor waste will wind the warp nearly to the heddles. The price of materials or the nature of the warp are other factors to consider. Easy warps can be woven closer to the end. Extra length may be necessary if you want to experiment, since not all warps respond well to ripping out.

The window frame design, when set up for a 34″×58″ rug, requires two 1550 yard spools of black and one spool of gray seine twine. There are 24″ of alternate black and gray warp and 10½″ of solid black. 24″×16 e.p.i. (half of 32 e.p.i.)×3 yards=1152 yards of gray and black each. 10½″× 32 e.p.i.×3 yards=1008 yards of black. Total black is 1152+1008=2160 yards. After weaving my rug and a 4″×36″ sample, I had one ounce of gray and seven ounces of black left over. You may not want to come this close to running out of the gray if it is not available locally. You can either buy an extra spool or reduce the length of the rug slightly.

Calculating the weft

Again a sample is invaluable. You can try out different sizes of rag strips and different weights for your thin weft. I generally use two strands of a fine weft. When you have found a combination that gives as many picks per inch as possible with a weight that you consider satisfactory, count the number of thick picks. Multiply the width of the rug by the p.p.i. (thick only) by the total length of the rug to compute the running length of the strips you will need. A piece of yardage 45″ wide will yield roughly 40 1″ strips. If you divide the running length by 40, you will have an approximate figure for the required yardage.

If you are using strips from an assortment of pieces, you might prefer to have an estimate of the weight of weft required. In this case, weigh your sample, calculate its square footage and using the ratio of its weight to size, compute the weight needed for your rug. The total weight of cotton-polyester strips in the window frame rug was 1¾

pounds. Supply yourself with more than you need. It is frustrating to search for materials in the middle of a project.

When weaving with purchased fabric for weft, I like to work with a piece that measures a few inches longer or shorter than three or five times the width of my rug. I cut a continuous strip by the following method.

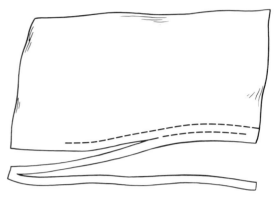

A strip cut in this manner will form small "ears" at the turns (which you should round off with scissors), and if the ears appear at intervals unequal to the rug width, then the slight lump they form will cycle uniformly throughout the rug.

Winding the warp

A spool rack is invaluable for this process. Dowels stuck through a weighted cardboard box will do while you are waiting for the real thing. Conveniently, my seine twine was put up on tubes, but if you should be working with a yarn that comes in another form, I urge you to buy or make large spools and transfer your yarn to them. I have found that spools are a necessity when working with multiple strands. The yarns feed smoothly, at an even tension, with little or no inclination to snarl. Wind each color that you plan to use on a separate spool. The cardboard spools used for sectional warping are cheap and can be enlarged for heavy warp yarns. You will probably have to devise shims in order to seat them firmly on your bobbin winder. Three bamboo skewers work with my winder.

The warping order for the rug is as follows:
1. 3″ of black.
2. 6″ of end-on-end black and gray.
3. 1½″ of black.
4. 6″ of end-on-end black and gray.
5. ¾″ of black.

This is the mid-point. Repeat in reverse order, i.e., repeat step 5, and work back through step 1.

It is sensible to make a cross at both ends of the warp as an insurance against disaster. Weavers have been known to lose their crosses, (if not their chains).

I prefer at all times to wind two warp ends simultaneously. Not only does this cut winding time in half, but I find that threading is easier when pairs of warps appear at the cross. It is important when winding two or more strands to prevent them from twisting around each other as you work. Use your fingers as guides to keep them in order. With a pair you can let one warp travel over the index finger while its mate travels under.

One inch sections of warp should be separated from each other with a chain. Although raddles often have ½" division, I prefer to minimize interruptions to the warping rhythm. It is a simple matter to divide 1" bunches later.

As the warp builds up on the reel, the risk of winding unequal lengths increases. I recommend that you warp sections no wider than 8" at a time; smaller warp bundles are fine if you don't mind the extra handling. Tie loops of thick cotton twine at the beginning and ending loops of the warp. Tie all four layers of the principal cross with separate loops of twine. You can be more cavalier with the second cross, tying it with a single loop. Make choke ties at half-yard intervals. Remove the warp from the reel and insert the lease sticks in the cross, being careful to observe the correct orientation of your design if it has a right-to-left direction. Putting the warp bundles aside in order to insert the lease sticks in one step simply invites confusion.

Although we will not be using this method, I would like to mention a warping trick used by Lillian Elliott to make complicated striping sequences. It avoids the tedium of counting yet offers the balance of repetition. If you make your warp twice the required length and half the width, with crosses at both ends, you can fold the warp in half and treat each loop as the back beam end of the warp. After beaming, the mid-point of each warp bundle must be cut. There are four different ways to arrange the warp loops. Because every color appears at least twice, this technique lends itself beautifully to warps that use up odds and ends of color. If fuchsia runs out, you will be undismayed since you know that it will reappear in another area of the rug.

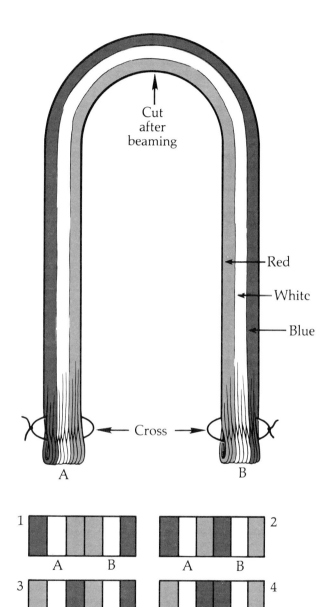

Measuring half the warp ends at twice the needed length, then doubling it over, reduces warping time substantially.

Beaming the warp

When the entire warp has been arranged on the lease sticks, they must be tied to the loom. I prefer to place them in front of the harnesses.

Spreading the warp is easier if the raddle can be tied to the front rather than the back beam. (If you are working full width and cannot remove the harnesses or heddles, this will not be possible since the heddles will squeeze the warp and prevent it from winding on at the proper width.) Match the center of the raddle with the center of the front beam and attach it firmly to the beam.

Carefully insert a heavy bar (mine measures ¾″×1¾″) through the loops behind the cross. Attach this bar loosely to the back bar of the loom. Ideally both bars should be only a few inches wider than the rug.

Find the mid-point of the warp. Drop warp bundles into the raddle from the center to the sides. Remove the counting chain. Further divide the warp bundles if you are using a raddle with ½″ spacing. With heavy rubber bands or a length of twine, trap the warps inside the raddle.

Spread the warp evenly on its bar. It helps to have someone else tug on sections of warp to provide some tension as you do this. (Weights tied to sections of warp can replace a helper; I use one gallon plastic bottles filled with water.) Measure a length of heavy twine four times the width of your

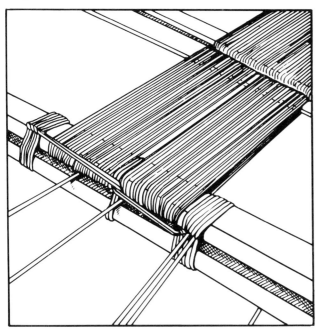

Tie your warp rod to the apron rod firmly with larks' heads and half-hitches.

rug. Use it, doubled over, to tie the two back bars together, first using a lark's head followed by half-hitches spaced evenly across the warp. Use at least three half-hitches to begin and end and be sure to pull hard on the twine as you make each knot so that slack cannot develop in the course of your weaving. Finish with a firm square knot.

You are now ready to wind on. To prevent uneven warp build-up, you must insert either sticks (¼″ thick and a few inches longer than your rug is wide) or corrugated cardboard or a combination of the two. Because I do not have a friction brake, I use sticks for the first full turn and cardboard for the rest of the warp. Sticks have a maddening habit of sliding into a heap if, in a careless moment, you allow slack to reach the back beam.

It is nice but not essential to have a helper hold the warp under some tension as you wind. The water bottles mentioned above are handy for the first turn or two if you are working alone. At intervals determined by the size of your warp beam, you must grasp 4″ sections of warp and, leaning away from the loom, use your weight to tighten the warp. Work from the sides to the center and back. My warp beam is a 6″ cylinder. I repeat this procedure two or three times for a three yard warp.

Threading

When only 18″ of warp remain in front of the lease sticks, you have completed beaming and are ready to thread. Attach your threading plan to the loom for easy reference. If your lease sticks are sitting in front of the harnesses, you must transfer them to the back of the loom.

At this point it is wise to count heddles in order to be sure that your harnesses do not end up with heavy clumps of extras on one side. Shove all the heddles on each harness to one side; find the midpoint (I measure) and move half to the other side. After consulting your block scheme and computing the total warps for each harness, divide by two and push this number of heddles to the appropriate side of the loom. Some weavers work from the left, some from the right.

Rib weave is exceptionally easy to thread. Calculate the number of heddles you will need for each block and push them to your working area. Repeat as needed. Errors are unlikely since the blocks are easily distinguished and counted. It is possible to transpose the two colors on a given pair of harnesses, but you can check this as you thread.

Make a direct tie-up with your treadles: harness one to treadle one and so on. After 3" or 4" of threading, raise harnesses one and three, holding the warps taut in order to create a shed. Threading errors will show at once as rogue color, a black warp, for example, in a gray block. As you thread, make slip knots with 1" bundles of warp, 32 ends for this rug.

Sleying

A dense warp requires a wide spaced reed sleyed with several warps per dent. This reduces the abrasion inevitably inflicted on the warp as the rug is beaten. With 32 e.p.i. an obvious choice would be an eight-dent reed carrying four ends per dent. I have chosen instead a six-dent reed holding a three-step sequence of six warps, five warps, five warps. This has the effect of creating a slight irregularity of spacing. The warps that show above any given thick weft appear as two groups of three followed by a pair. The weft spot on either side of the pair is noticeably larger than elsewhere, a small but pleasant effect.

I would like to add a note here about irregular denting. With warps that show a fair amount of weft, this technique, which normally would be used only out of necessity, may be chosen deliberately as a way to introduce interesting vertical streaks. An irregularity of spacing (in this case larger weft spots) that offends the eye in the lightweight fabric can give pleasing variation in a heavier textile. The use of blocks enhances this effect because a streak that appears in one block will not be visible in its opposite. A line running the entire length of the rug might not have the same appeal. Since the eye most easily perceives vacancy, one should choose a multiple of ends per dent that requires that some dents be filled with fewer ends than the average. For example, with 36 e.p.i. and a ten-dent reed, most dents in a 1" section would carry four ends. Four of the ten will carry only three in the following sequence: 4, 3, 4, 4, 3, 4, 3, 4, 4, 3. The placement of the irregular dents within 1" sections can be a repeating pattern or can itself be irregular. There is room for much experiment here. One interesting consequence of irregular denting is that the weft spots that rep weave always exhibits in the transitions between certain blocks, as a result of unavoidable "flats" (sinking pairs of warps in an otherwise over-one, under-one sequence), can be echoed and enriched as a design element.

Install the reed and tie the beater so that it sits midway between the harnesses and the front beam.

With the warp arranged in 1" bundles, it is a simple matter to center the warp in the reed. Count the total inches, taking note of the incomplete bundles and adding them as fractions. Use this number to center your warp. It is best not to rely on the number of inches you thought you warped on the reel. Inaccuracies are more likely during this count. Because I do not trust myself with a tape measure, I usually find the midpoint of my warp and reed (the center of my beater is permanently marked) and sley from the center out, although this is doubtless slower than working in one direction only.

Once again it is possible to check for errors as you work. After sleying a 1" section, pull it taut. Treadle 1 and 3 to make a shed. Sleying errors should show up behind the reed (crossed threads) or at the reed (empty dents). Treadle 2 and 4 and check again at the reed. Irregularities are easy to detect, unless, of course you have put them in as a matter of policy. Checking for errors is more complicated in this case. Again make slip knots with 1" bundles of warp.

Sley more densely at the selvedges. 8,6,6 for instance gives a solid band of black at the selvedge.

Tying on

Pick up a central warp bundle and pull it taut. While maintaining tension on the entire group, tug firmly on the ends from each dent, one dent at a time, to further remove slack. Separate each bundle into two equal parts and tie them in a half knot around the front bar. There is a trick to maintaining tension throughout this operation. Try different positions with your hands until you find a series of motions that feels natural. It is important to keep all warps equally taut.

After tying the center, move to the selvedges. Tie them. Fill in the remaining spaces by dividing them in half successively. This prevents the cumulative slackening that occurs when you work away from a fixed point. Make sure that the front bar is parallel to the front beam as you tie.

When the entire warp has been tied to the front bar, use the ratchet and pawl to increase tension on the warp. Check for inequalities. A strumming motion is useful. You may need to re-tie some knots. When you are satisfied that the tension is even across the warp, complete the half knots, turning them into square knots. Pull hard on each one.

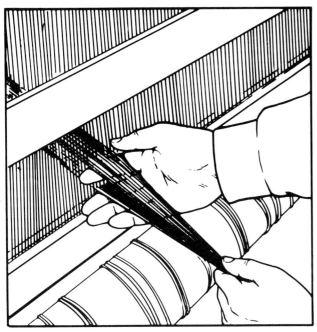

After sleying an inch of warp, raise each harness in turn to check for errors.

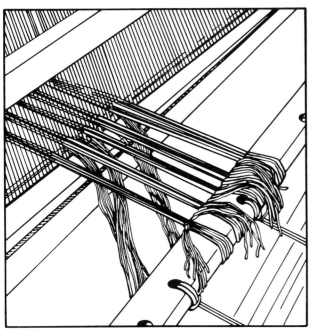

Tie on the center and the selvedges, then the remaining warp in alternate bundles side to side.

Tie-up

Directions for this vary, of course, from loom to loom. With some designs a direct tie-up will prove most practical; with others a twill is best. I have used a direct tie-up, since the treadling sequence of my window frame rug is quite simple and it is easier to break the shed if you have individual control over the harnesses.

Weaving a heading

A few picks of heavy rag will efficiently reduce the gaps created by the tie-on knots. A 2" to 3" sample of the rug should follow. This will help establish the natural distance from selvedge to selvedge and it will dispose of minor tension inequalities. Examine the sample for errors that may have escaped your notice earlier. If you must untie knots to make corrections, insert a steel crochet hook into each knot and pull.

It is important to establish a fell that is parallel to the front beam. Check this as you weave the heading.

If you have chosen to finish your rug with a hem, you may now weave 3" of tabby. The weft should be a single strand of the yarn you have chosen for the fine weft of your rug. As you weave each pick, arrange the weft at a 45° angle. This will help to minimize the tendency of the hem to draw in relative to the body of the rug.

An ornamental edge can be added to the rug when the hem or the heading is complete. Two rows of twining will form a raised ridge that can echo a card-woven selvedge and serve as a reinforcement of the fold at the hem. Because my seine twine was rather fine, I felt these edge treatments would show too little to justify the extra effort.

Using pick-up to create a border

This is optional, of course, but it is satisfying to frame the design, to give it breathing room. If you examine the draft and drawdown on page 102, you will see that it is not possible to treadle all the blacks or all the grays at once because the two colors have traded places in the alternating frames and windows. For instance, in the first motif, bottom left C block, harness four raises black while in the second it raises gray.

You can, however, carry a large butterfly of rag weft (one 2" strip or two 1" strips), by hand through an all-black shed which you create by raising successive blocks.

1. Raise 4-2. Working left to right, insert weft to the point where the gray block begins. Bring the weft out of the shed and onto the top surface of the rug.

2. Raise 3-1. Re-insert the weft into this black-on-top shed and again exit where the next gray block begins.

3. Continue this procedure until the rag weft has traveled from selvedge to selvedge. Repeat the same steps with the fine wefts wound onto one bobbin, using the opposite treadles. The fine wefts can be carried on a boat shuttle, which it rather easily dives in and out of the shed.

4. Do not be alarmed by the "flats" that appear at block transitions. These are unavoidable.

5. After 14 rows of this pick-up, seven thick and seven thin, you will be ready for normal treadling. The border should take about a half an hour.

Weaving your rug

The thick weft must be wound on a ski shuttle. If you plan to work with a single thick weft, you may wish to use a second ski shuttle for the thin weft also. If, however, you wish to insert two wefts in each thick pick, hence throwing two ski shuttles one after the other, you will probably find a boat shuttle more convenient for the thin weft. This will simplify shuttle order and placement.

The placement of shuttles can be a fairly complicated matter with rep weave. The two wefts (thick and thin) must wrap around each other if floats at the selvedge are to be avoided. This can mean that shuttle A must sit behind shuttle B on the right side of the rug, while on the left side, the order is reversed. A sequence that works for one treadling of blocks will not necessarily work for another. Because I used four shuttles, two ski shuttles carrying rag and two boat shuttles, one carrying 10/2 and the other crochet cotton, the sequence was unvarying: the working shuttle was last in line (farthest from the fell) when I picked it up and went to the head of the line (nearest the fell) when I put it down.

If you have woven a hem, your rug will be slightly drawn in at this point. Make a generous arc with your initial picks. Watch the reed as it presses against the fell. It should deflect the warps no more than ¼" from their straight path across the loom. When you check the width of your rug, it is best to measure just after you wind forward, so that the fell is a constant distance from the front beam.

Fabric tends to spread as it approaches the reed and to contract as it travels over the front beam. As your weaving proceeds, the rug will require less weft. Rugs that are entirely warp-faced need no bubble, since the weft lies in a straight path between warps that are deflected by it. Our sett of 32 e.p.i. will allow some weft take-up. The rag weft should be laid in at a shallow angle. If you decide to work with a still more open sett, you must add even more weft to compensate for the movement it is thus freer to make.

If you are working with a single thick rag strip, the weft will wear and look better at the selvedges if you give it a special treatment with each pick. After throwing the shuttle, leave a loop of weft at the edge, pinch it about an inch above the point where it emerges from the last pick and give it several firm twists (counter-clockwise seems easiest), insert the loop and press it firmly into the fell, thus locking in the twist you have added. Working with two 1" strips carried on separate shuttles, I found that the edge looked better without the added twist, because the weft bumps were almost in invisible. Extra twist forced them to sit away from the selvedge.

Leave a similar loop of fine weft and tug it where it emerges from the rug in order to remove any slack at the edge of the previous pick. Before beating be sure that it fits snugly around the selvedge.

I like to beat three times; first on the open shed my weft has just entered, then twice after changing sheds. With some dense, sticky warps you will have no choice about beating on an open shed, since the resistance to the reed will be obviously excessive when the shed is closed. In any case, it is clearly easier on your warp to have half the threads raised as the beater moves past them. The speed of the beater as it reaches the fell affects the force of its impact. For this reason it is wise to wind forward frequently, since the beater will have less momentum as the distance between it and the rug diminishes. Measure the picks per inch at regular intervals. I tend to relax as the rug grows. The consequence is a lighter beat that I need to guard against.

If you find that your rug is sleazy even though you have weighted the beater and are using all your force to press the weft in, there is a remedy worth trying. If you can locate or make a sword longer than the width of your rug, insert it between the reed and the fell just before you beat. The wedge shape of the sword will increase pressure on the fell.

It is important to measure, occasionally, the distance from each side of the fell to the front beam in order to be sure that the two are parallel. You can unconsciously favor one side of your body as you beat, giving a slight twist to the beater which then translates as a slanted fell and non-rectangular rug. If this problem arises, concentrate on centering your hands as you beat and watch the beater closely for twist. A warp with side-to-side tension inequality is another possible culprit when the fell is crooked. This is more difficult to correct. If the misalignment measures less than ½", it is best to delay tampering with your warps in the hope that the problem will not be progressive. A gross tension inequality can be remedied by c-clamping to the back beam a stick which you have inserted under the loose warps. This stick can be made into a wedge if necessary by supporting it at intervals with shims of diminishing size.

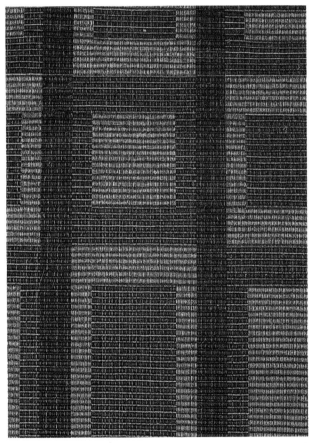

The large, clean blocks of this rug (shown on page 103) gain close viewing interest through the use of a colorful variegated fine weft that peeks unexpectedly out in the channels between heavy rag wefts.

There are numerous solutions to the problem of joining rag wefts. I prefer to eliminate sewing by simply overlapping 2" sections of tapered weft. These joins are essentially invisible and they offer complete freedom of choice if you are striping the weft. Even short lengths of rag can be wound on the shuttle if you lap as you wind. Join the fine wefts by overlapping them.

At this point you should have some feeling for the final product. It is still possible to alter your design to fit better the textile that is appearing before you. Is the total effect livelier than you expected? Perhaps you should treadle larger blocks than planned in order to create some calm. The reverse may be true; in this case smaller blocks may be called for. If the surface of your rug seems lacklustre and if your wefts show through at all, try using a weft that frays, creating a halo of tiny threads (unless, of course, you are among those who consider this a defect of rag rugs). Try adding an occasional pick of brilliant, or of dark or light color. I have machine embroidered corduroy before cutting it, in order to embellish, very subtly, the surface of my rug. Wefts can be space-dyed to give them more life. And you can, even now, completely redesign the rug. I have unwoven and rethreaded my warp in order to escape an inappropriate block design. If you must take this desperate measure, do not forget to reinsert the lease sticks so that you will have a cross again. This is a painful solution, but it is probably better than weaving a rug you don't like.

If you are concerned about weaving an exact length, you should take measurements before releasing tension and after the rug has rested overnight off tension. This will enable you to estimate the warp take-up which must be part of your arithmetic as you decide on the length to weave. The take-up with seine twine is surprisingly high. My rug shrank from 62" to 54". You can add 4" to the total on page 102 by using the picked up border or by altering the motif measurements.

When you reach the end, repeat, in reverse order, the steps you followed at the beginning. A 4" sample heading is unnecessary, but you will want an inch or two to protect your hem.

When you cut the rug from the loom, do not, in the excitement of the moment, forget to leave ends long enough to braid, knot or twist should you decide that a fringe is the finish this rug needs. And

Very soft and subtle color changes are the hallmark of this large wool rug. Slentre braids make a handsome finish.
SETTING: LAW OFFICES OF JOHN O. WALKER

for the same reason, do not cut the tie-on knots. Patiently untie them.

Finishing

I have found that fringes are fragile. They have proven more vulnerable than either the selvedges or surfaces of my rugs. Daily vacuuming can reduce them to wispy stumps, making a binding necessary for the continued life of the rug. Weaving a hem is a satisfying solution to this problem because one can have confidence that a hem will last as long as the rug itself. A hem has the added advantage of being a quick and easy finish, which is a pleasant exception to the rule "slower is better" that seems to govern most weaving processes.

Put two rows of machine stitching at the end of your hem (if you pull out a weft or two it will be easy to keep this line straight). Cut away the heading. Fold the hem over twice, using pins and a steam iron to flatten it. Pin it to the wrong side of your rug and whip stitch it in place with linen thread.

A hem, unfortunately, is not always possible. Bulky yarns do not lend themselves to this treatment, nor do certain designs. Perhaps your rug looks amputated without a fringe. Take some time with this decision. If you wove a hem, fold it under and spend a day or two looking at your rug. An initially negative response may change as you become accustomed to the absence of the familiar fringe.

If you decide that a hem simply will not work, you can extend the life of a fringe with warp protecting braids and knots. Bulky warps should be divided into two layers of braids. Use the final pick of plain weave to separate the layers. A stick inserted between the layers will simplify matters. You can c-clamp it to your work surface where it will simultaneously hold the rug in place and preserve a shed.

The Scandinavian technique called slentre (see Appendix I), or walking fingers, produces braids of exceptional beauty. Wool warps treated this way are especially handsome.

Hair fringes are surprisingly delicate. It is best to work with small units of warp, since large over-hand knots made with this yarn are not very stable.

Care

I generally shake rugs to remove dust and debris Vacuum cleaners abrade and pull out fibers. You can brighten color with the following mini-wash: Spray the right side of the rug with water. Lay it wrong side up on a large towel and steam iron the entire surface.

Other warp and weft materials

As I have indicated earlier, the ideal yarn for a warp-faced rug is smooth, tightly spun and strong. In fact, in the interest of working with good colors, special textures or simply what is available, these requirements can be stretched considerably. The following list is not exhaustive; however, should you wish to use a yarn I have omitted, do not fail to make a large sample.

1. **8/4 cotton rug warp.** This humble workhorse can achieve a surprising elegance when densely set. Thirty-six e.p.i. works well with a cotton rag weft (1½" to 2" wide). The color range is not inspiring, but you can successfully over-dye this yarn with the widely available fiber-reactive dyes. The low price helps to justify the extra time required. Nice color harmonies can be produced by winding, then over-dyeing, a striped warp. But dyeing is not essential. The commercial colors lack subtlety, but they can have a cheerful, forthright charm.

2. **8/2, 10/2 mercerized cottons.** These are yarns for the colorist. They are available in a wide range of beautiful tints and shades. Canadian rug weavers set 8/2 cotton at 48 e.p.i., but it is also possible to warp with multiple strands in the heddles. Three 10/2's per heddle, set at 20 e.p.i., make a handsome warp with an intriguing color blend when two or more colors appear in each heddle. Perle cottons also come in jewel tones, but some that I have used are very susceptible to abrasion: they might be best used in designs that feature small areas of brilliant color, thus limiting their exposure to wear.

3. **8/8 cotton.** I have examined a lovely old Amish rag rug woven with this warp. It is set at 16 e.p.i. and the spaces between the warps are approximately equal to the warps. Woven at 5 p.p.i., it is a perfect weight, solid yet flexible. The color range of this yarn is narrow, so dyeing is probably in order.

4. **Hair: goat, camel and mohair.** This is a first-class warp yarn, an import from Multiple Fabrics in England. It is tightly spun, intrinsically hard and tough, and oily. These qualities combine

to make a surface that defies dirt and wear and tear. It exhibits the pleasing halo effect typical of hair yarns (hairs that rise above the surface), and its numerous shades of gray have the gentle beauty of natural color. The camel hair, when dyed with chemicals, gives the soft, rich colors one associates with vegetal dyes. The only drawbacks are high price and a certain intransigence that comes from its prickly, inelastic nature. It should never be warped from the front, through the reed and heddles, to the back beam, because, given half a chance, it will twist on itself, creating havoc at the reed. The sett for an initial project should be no closer than 18 or 20 e.p.i., since a sticky shed is likely with this yarn. Knots will require extra attention. Do not be discouraged by these warnings; this yarn is worth special effort.

5. **Frisé wool.** This is an over-spun medium weight (600-800 yards per pound) that is exceptionally tough yet easy to work with because it is smoother than goat and camel hair. When set at 12-18 e.p.i., it combines well with a multiple strand wool weft. It is less interesting but still handsome when set closer. Like carpet warp, it is a good choice for first projects because it is inexpensive but sound.

6. **Singles rug wool.** This yarn, about 600 yards per pound, is typically Scandinavian — beautiful, durable (and expensive). Some companies offer a breathtaking range of colors. It can be a rather hairy and matte-surfaced or smooth and high lustre yarn. Set at 18 e.p.i., it neither sticks nor breaks.

7. **Thick, plied rug wool,** (400 yards to the pound). The loftiness of this yarn makes it a good choice for a bedside rug. It is easy to work with and can be set to cover the weft completely. The examples of this yarn that have come my way have proven remarkably resistant to pilling.

Weft yarns play a minor role in true warp-faced rugs since they may be visible only as small bumps at the selvedges. At a more open sett as in the window frame rug they may contribute an effect not unlike the water color wash, influencing but not determining hue and value. In the warp-dominant rug the weft almost rivals the warp in importance.

1. **Cotton rags — including corduroy.** I have great faith in the durability of cotton rags. Because of their high thread count, they can be cut or torn into very fine strips. This means that two rag shuttles can be thrown in the same shed from opposite sides. This practice insures smooth selvedges with unobtrusive weft bumps. It also allows, in the warp-dominant rug, a blending of weft colors. This blending has practical as well as aesthetic advantages. One is often faced with a collection of disparate rag colors; for this reason rag rugs sometimes look fairly chaotic. If, however, one rag in each shed remains constant while its partners change color, the effect can be interesting, even mysterious. The wefts can be manipulated in the shed to give dominance to one or the other.

Corduroy is particularly satisfying as a rag weft. If it is torn or cut along the wales, it packs in most compliantly; cut across the wales, it resists beating and tends to show through the warps more insistently. One can use this effect for textural contrast, at a price unfortunately, since wales that present themselves vertically, or parallel to the warp, wear away sooner than wales that are, in effect, tied down by the warps.

2. **Wool rag wefts** are normally heavier than cotton ones, because most wools pull apart when cut into narrow (½″ to ¾″) strips. This means that only one shuttle can be thrown in each pick and lumps at the selvedge cannot be avoided. Army blankets are an exception. They can be cut into ½″ strips which have ample tensile strength and pack beautifully. If wool can be torn rather than cut, it will be easier to beat. As with any rag material, tearing gives a frayed look to the rug surface that some people value and others dislike.

3. **Synthetic knit rags.** The purist may skip this discussion. Of course, one cannot expect to find treasures at the remnant table of the dime store. What I did find once, during an emergency search for extra weft, was a yard of polyester knit that curled into lovely, fat tubes of weft when cut into strips. The dull color of the fabric showed only as a dark background for the vivid warps, while the ugly synthetic shine could not be detected at all. Synthetic wefts make sense for rugs in the bathroom and kitchen where a non-absorbent, quick drying material is eminently practical.

4. **Multiple strands of wool.** With a wool warp set wide enough to allow ⅛″ spaces between warps, this weft deserves as much attention as the warps themselves. One can combine weights and

colors with a freedom that seems almost unweaver-ly. High quality yarns, when mixed with pedestrian fillers, add lustre, rich color, strength. Color combinations that would be crude in weft-face, due to excessive contrast in values, are tamed by the warps, looking lively rather than busy, brilliant rather than gaudy. Dividing the wefts into two high contrast elements, a light group and a dark group, gives a tie-dyed effect that can be carefully controlled when each group is carried on a separate shuttle. A vast array of color and design effects is available to the weaver who is willing to space-dye these multiple wefts.

Rya

Carol Thilenius

ya rugs have a lushness that delights the eye and invites the touch. Long before I started weaving, I wanted to make a rya rug. I collected catalogues and studied the designs. It was a good way to begin. The earliest known rug to use the rya or Ghiordes knot is the Pazyryk rug which is now in the Hermitage Museum in Leningrad. It was found in a south Siberian tomb, preserved in ice, and is believed to date from 500 B.C. The design is complex and detailed. With an overall size of 6'6" × 6', a thickness of 1/10" and 230 knots per square inch, it shows a high degree of skill in both design and craftsmanship. Pictures of this rug can be seen in Held's *Weaving, A Handbook for Fiber Craftsmen* and Reed's *Oriental Rugs and Carpets.*

Early Scandinavian ryas were used as bedcoverings. With the pile inside they made warm blankets which wore better than skins. Boat ryas were used for warmth in open fishing boats. They were better than fur for warmth and resistance to salt water. The early ryas had uncut loops of a single color or stripes. In time, the thick, widely spaced, utilitarian ryas gradually gave way to finer, shorter pile ornamental ryas for bedcoverings, tapestries and sometimes rugs. In recent times the longer pile has again become popular for its rich texture and color.

Contemporary Scandinavian pile rugs are of two main types: the rya with a long pile and the flossa with a short pile. The line between the two is indefinite, but the categories are still useful.

Rya has pile lengths of ¾" to 2" or more in rows that may be as much as an inch or more apart. This allows the pile to lie down in various directions and may have a shingled look because of the widely spaced rows. The most appealing rya designs are those that benefit from the intermingling of the long pile between color areas. Definite shapes or outlines and fine details would be lost in the tousled lie of the pile.

Flossa has shorter pile lengths, usually less than ¾". The rows of knots are closely spaced so the pile stands upright. With less intermingling of the pile, flossa can be used effectively for more detailed designs. Oriental rugs with hundreds of knots per square inch, detailed designs, and smoothly sheared upright pile are at the opposite end of the scale from the shaggy rya.

I like the shaggy ryas. Several years ago, before I began to weave, I ordered a kit to do a large, 2 × 3 meter rug for my family room. It taught me a lot! When I opened the box, the colors leaped out at me. I had thought from the picture there might be seven or eight colors. There were 12 color combinations involving 17 different colors of yarn. Each color combination had two or three different colors. The background area, which looked black in the picture, was made up of alternating knots of two color combinations with a total of four different colors.

The rug pattern was printed on graph paper that had 12 spaces per square across equal to seven spaces per square vertically. This gave proportions that would be repeated in the rug. Areas were outlined and numbered to correspond with the color combination numbers. The color combinations were tied along the edge of the pattern for easy reference.

The backing into which I was to tie the pile had a linen warp and wool weft. The ends had 1½" of plain weft-face weave and the warp fringe was tied in overhand knots. The narrow gaps into which the pile was to be tied were separated by ⅜" of weft-face weave. The gaps ran to the selvedge and the knots were tied in a continuous row from selvedge to selvedge. After every seventh row, a gray stripe was woven into the weft-face divider to correspond to the heavy lines on the graph.

Making the rug began as a lap project, but soon graduated to the dining room table. Fuzz became a part of our lives. Pushing the needles through the narrow gaps in the backing was not easy. When the rug was finished, I had a callus on my index finger almost as hard as the fingernail. There had to be a better way.

My interest in fiber crafts turned to weaving and led me to Convergence '74 in San Francisco. One of the marvelous programs featured Stennet Heaton, who showed his microscopic photographs of insects, many of them butterflies. The butterflies' scaled wings looked like rya! Some scales were frayed on the ends, others hair-like, and some tab-ular. The patterns were fascinating, the colors, rich—just like rya! The seed was planted.

While working on the Handweaver's Guild of America Certificate of Excellence requirements, the seed germinated. An unwary moth stayed too long on the bedroom screen and ended up under the microscope. (I was once a biologist and am still hauling around the impedimentia; microscopes, nets, samples, books, etc.) The edge of the moth's wing had an interesting pattern that became the pile sample for the Certificate requirements (see picture on page 53, *Shuttle, Spindle and Dyepot*, Fall 1981). I used a variety of knots and some variation in pile length. Tying the knots was easy on the open warp—no more calloused finger! The weaving between the rows of knots was reduced to give a thick mattress-like rug. When it was finished, I put it on the floor in the living room for the family critique. My ten year old lay down on it, ran his fingers through the pile, rolled around and demanded "place-backs" if he had to leave the room. Whatever the artistic merit, it was a textural success.

After the Certificate of Excellence work was completed, I needed a new project. The idea of a series of rya rugs based on butterfly designs began to grow. My boys were in need of summer entertainment. A Ranger Rick club seemed to be the answer, so we gathered their neighborhood friends for an afternoon a week. We built butterfly nets, took hikes, collected insects, flowers and rocks to study with the microscopes. We took the butterfly nets along on family outings as well, and the collection grew.

The big showy butterflies were often less interesting under the microscope than their duller relatives. Some had sections that were attractive designs in themselves while others had bits of border design that could be repeated to make a bordered rug.

Once the designs for the series were done, I calculated the yarn requirements and ordered the yarn. The amount of rya yarn needed to make one 8½' × 11' and five 3' × 5' rugs was beyond the stock locally available. The yarn store ordered it all from Europe and in six months it all arrived and I was ready to weave.

The length of time that had elapsed between the designing and the weaving made some of the designs seem like total strangers. The one that made me most uneasy during the weaving has turned out to be one of my favorites. I was glad I trusted my

The inspiration for this vivid rug was a wing segment from a Baltimore butterfly.
SETTING: TIMBERLINE HOMES, FORT COLLINS, COLORADO

design and did not try to second guess myself by making changes.

Each small rug took about two weeks to weave; the large one, about three months. My weaving is frequently interrupted by household chores, family demands and goofing off, but I try to accomplish a given amount each day. If I get ahead of schedule, I feel so virtuous it encourages me to work even longer. Any prolonged absence from the loom seems to make the job bigger and harder to get started on again.

Designing a rya rug

To sit down with a blank piece of paper and "design" something can be intimidating for lots of us. At the same time we know what we like and can recognize a good design when we see it. We respond to pleasing patterns and colors even if we do not know why they are successful. To make use of these designs, we need to develop techniques for abstracting the desired design and color scheme.

Nature had already designed the butterflies. All I had to do was pick the part I wanted, put it on graph paper and reproduce it with yarn. In looking at the butterflies under the microscope, I tried various magnifications and tried mentally to superimpose a rectangular frame on what I saw. This gave me some idea of how it would look in a rug. If you are working from a picture or other source, try framing the parts you want with rulers or "L" shaped pieces of paper. The elimination of surrounding areas makes the design easier to evaluate. In some cases the design I wanted from the butterfly was there in total while in other cases, a small section might be repeated to form a border or an all over design.

A rectangle was drawn on a large piece of graph paper. The size was determined by the size of the rug desired; one square across equalled one knot, one square vertically equalled one row of knots. Since I was getting three knots per inch and five rows per 2", the proportions on the graph paper did not quite correspond to the resulting rug. To allow for this, I tried to make the design a bit squatty. Circles were flattened into ovals about five units high by six units across. If graph paper can be found that is ruled in a 5 × 6 grid, this adjustment would not be necessary. If you want your rows farther apart or find that your spacing is not 5 × 6, adjust your design accordingly. Be sure that the

squares on the graph paper are big enough to be easily read. Ten squares per inch seems to be about as fine as most people can see readily.

I sketched the major areas of the design within the rectangle. Ignoring details, I worked to get the proportions and placement right. If you have difficulty sketching what you see, it may help to divide the rectangle into quarters and mentally divide what you are trying to sketch. The placement of major lines or shapes within one quarter can be more easily estimated than when the whole blank rectangle is considered.

After the sketch of major areas is satisfying, redraw the lines on the lines of the graph paper. Diagonals become stair steps; verticals may need to be moved a bit so they fall on a line. This makes it clear whether a knot is within a color area or not. Add the details and be sure to mark each area with a letter or number to indicate the color it is to be.

There are many other design sources in nature, art and science, just begging to be used in some kind of fiber art. These may be easier to use than butterflies under a microscope. One of my students liked the idea of using butterflies but found Alaska in the winter is a poor place for collecting them. She used a segment of a photograph in an entomology book. Pictures of solar flares, galaxies, rock formations, tree bark, etc. can all provide striking designs and rich color combinations. The field of medicine is another rich source. I saw a photo of the inside of an intestine that looked like it already was a rya rug. The villi made it look like velvety shag and the red-orange-yellow colors were wonderful—what a piece for a doctor's office!

Look at scenic pictures that you find pleasing; blur your eyes slightly and look for the color blends and arrangement of color areas. Sunsets can give marvelous colors and patterns.

Again, if working from a picture, divide it into smaller rectangles or squares to help in getting it transferred to the graph paper. If you are working from a slide, project the slide on the graph paper. Move the projector closer or farther back till the desired portion fits the rectangular outline and sketch in the major areas. Placement of details and final color decisions may need to be made with a small viewer. It is often difficult to see the details and make color decisions in the dark.

Remember the design will be elongated if the graph is used as is. One solution is to eliminate every sixth row. If you do this, make the initial rectangle on the graph paper accordingly and

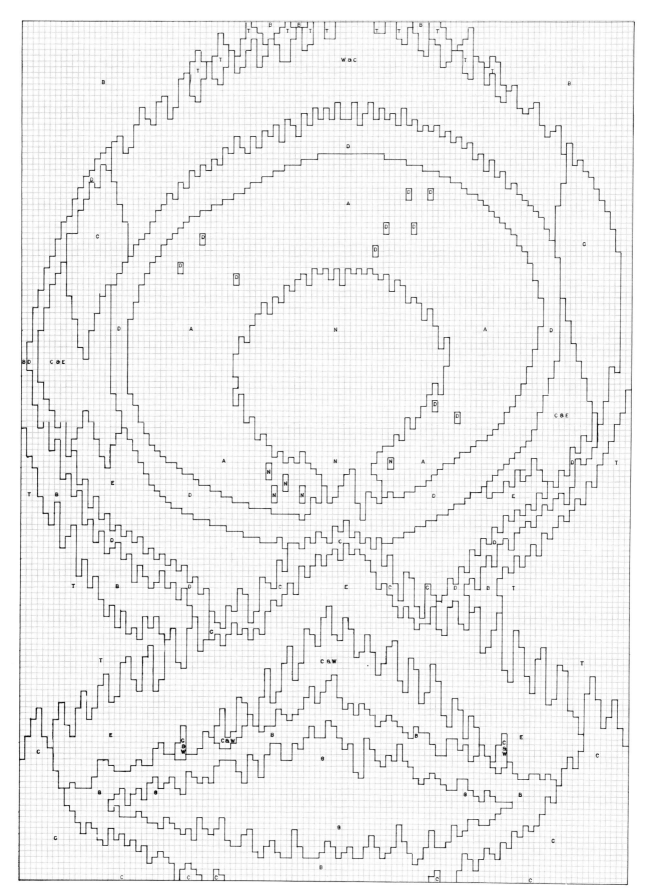

This chart was prepared by the author for the rug on the next page (shown about half size).

COLOR KEY: *W=White (white, off-white, cream)*   *C=Cream (off-white, beige, cream)*   *E=Ecru (beige, cream, ecru)*   *T=Tan (ecru, lt. ecru, tan)*   *B=Brown (med. brown 2×, taupe)*   *D=Dark Brown (dk. warm brown, dk. cool brown, chocolate)*   *A=Azure (powder blue, French blue, pale turquoise)*   *N=Navy (wedgewood, prussian, dark turquoise)*   *G=Gray Blue (taupe, pale turquoise, powder blue)*

A Blue-eyed Painted Lady wing detail provided the design for this rug.

This rug derives from a Golden Painted Lady.

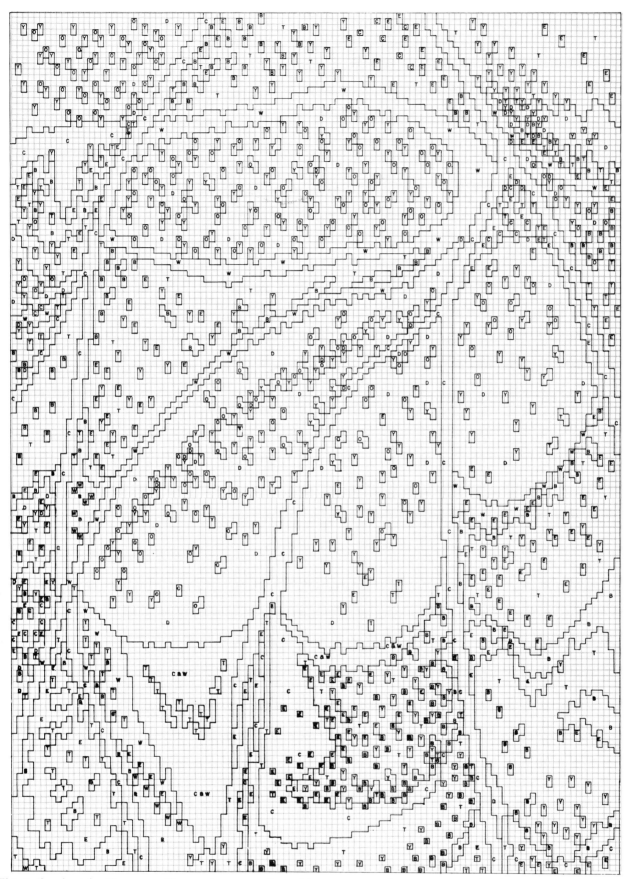

This is the chart for the rug on the previous page. In making your own chart, you can color-key areas with colored pencils.

COLOR KEY: *O=Orange (cream, med. gold, bright gold)*   *Y=Yellow-Orange (med. gold, lemon, ivory)*   *D=Dark Brown (dk. warm brown, dk. cool brown, dk. rust)*   *B=Brown (med. brown, golden brown, lt. taupe)*   *T=Tan (ecru, lt. ecru, tan)*   *E=Ecru (off-white, cream, tan)*   *C=Cream (beige, off-white, cream)*   *W=White (white, beige, off-white)* beware of small color areas or shapes that may be lost or distorted when rows are eliminated.

In another method, the design is drawn full scale on heavy paper and pinned under the weaving, just as cartoons are used in tapestry weaving. This would work best on large scale designs with few color combinations. More complex designs would be difficult to follow when viewed through the warp. Yarn requirements would have to be estimated, since the number of knots of each color combination would be unknown.

Another option in developing your design is to use graph paper with each square across representing a knot, then put the rows in as needed. This would be a good solution for widely spaced rows where a definitely shingled look is desired. The warp width and number of knots across is set by the warping, but the spacing of the rows can be determined by the width of the weft-face band woven between rows. A line drawn across the design at the place a row of knots is to occur intersects the color areas, and numbers of knots can be counted along the line.

Choose the method that best suits your situation and design.

Selecting the colors

The rich, vibrant color of rya rugs is one of their most appealing features. To achieve such richness, the colors are blended by using several different colored strands of yarn together. In the kit that I began with, most of the color combinations were made up of closely related hues, values and/or intensities. One combination was high intensity red, red-orange and cerise; another was all very dark — olive-green, red-brown and blue-violet. Although most of the combinataions were blends, one was not; it sparkled. A combination of contrasting hues, values and/or intensities gives a sparkling or stippled effect. A pepper and salt black and white would be an example of contrasting values. In this rya kit, the sparkler was a combination of chartreuse with orange and yellow-orange. The values were similar, but the contrast in hue of the chartreuse with orange and yellow-orange added a surprising scintillation to the small areas where it was used.

Studying the colors of the butterflies gave some startling insights. The old "tried and true" color schemes were not there; it was time for some new combinations. In many areas the scales proved to be blends of closely related colors. Some scales may be translucent and the colors are further blended by mixing with the underlying color. By combining three colors of yarn, similar rich blends can be produced. Sparkle and iridescence can also be achieved if a close look is taken at the component bits of color. Choose yarns that have these colors and twist them together to see if the combination produces the desired effect.

Blend and sparkle combinations within individual knots can be combined with different combinations for further blend or sparkle effects. Alternate knots of a dark blend and a light one would give a sparkle effect. Two or more closely related blends can be combined to add further richness. Several blends with one or more common color components can be arranged to give subtle shadings from one area to another.

The butterflies had some color surprises for me. One looked green as it flew but turned out to be covered with scales of yellow, black and white — just as mixing yellow and black paint gives olive green shades. Another ugly white butterfly had a small dramatic pattern of red and black. The scales were solid color and so the rug was made with knots of solid color. Some areas were alternately black and white for a stippled salt and pepper effect, just as the scales were arranged in a stippled pattern. Most of the butterflies lent themselves to designs made up of blended colors, so blends were used in all the other rugs.

Selecting the colors for the rug needs to be done as the design is being developed. As an area is sketched on the graph paper, the colors need to be at least tentatively selected so the color combination can be labeled and used elsewhere in the design.

To make a blend, choose the color that matches best for one of the three colors. Then look for two that are near that color. If you want to keep the value the same, pick adjacent hues of similar value; for example, if red is the best match, add a red-violet and red-orange. If a sparkle or stippled look is more appropriate, pick lighter and darker values of the same hue, such as red with wine and pink. A sparkle combination may have contrasting hues such as red, blue and green and give a confetti effect. Sometimes variations in intensity are desirable — for instance a bright red with a dark red-brown and maroon.

Alpine and Copper butterflies provided the designs for this pair of small rugs.
SETTING: TIMBERPEG HOMES, FORT COLLINS, COLORADO

If you wish to give the entire piece a unified glow of one particular color, try to find a dark, medium and light shade of that color to use in the various combinations that will make up the rug. Reduced intensities are probably best in these yarns since they should blend in as background, not stand out or contrast sharply.

If you have whole skeins of yarn, you can lift a strand from the side of each and twist them together to see the combined effect. Sample cards are less easy to handle, but selections can be made from them with care. Lift the color on the sample card away from the other colors and view it against a neutral background to evaluate its desirability. Then bend the card and twist one color with the other colors selected to check the combination.

When all the selections have been made, look at them all as a group, either by piling the skeins together or by separating the colors on the card so they can be viewed together. If the group looks pleasing, the colors will probably be pleasing in the rug. A color that jumps out at you and seems discordant may need to be changed. Go back to the design to see where that color was used, what it was combined with, what it was adjacent to and whether it is necessary for the desired effect. If another less discordant color can be found you may wish to use it instead.

Evaluating the colors to be used is further complicated by seeing the yarn in a skein or sample where you see the sides of the fibers, not the ends. In the rug, the cut ends of the yarn are seen and the colors are much darker since you see the shadows between the cut ends, not the highly reflective sides. With use the rug pile begins to lie down and you see more of the reflective quality of the yarns. The effect is the same as when we stroke velveteen and look at it from different directions — sometimes we see ends of fibers and it looks dark; sometimes we see the sides and it shines.

Making a sample

Make a sample to check that your plans will give the desired density of pile. The pile length should extend to cover half or more of the previous row. If the pile seems sparse, either make the rows closer together or make the pile longer.

I like a pile length of about 1½". With five rows every 2", the overlap is considerable and the pile tends to stand upright.

Record the number of knots you tie from each three-strand combination and how many strands each skein contains. These figures are needed to calculate the quantity needed.

Your sample can be used and enjoyed as a pillow top or chair seat pad.

Selecting materials

Three kinds of materials are used in rya rugs: the pile, the warp and the weft.

The pile yarn is what shows, and is usually rya yarn. It is spun of lustrous long-fiber wool. The yarn is two-ply and well set so there is little tendency for the cut ends to un-spin. Even after years of heavy traffic and vacuuming, only about ¼" of the cut ends fray. Softer, less tightly spun yarns can be used in decorative pieces, but will mat and fray if used in a rug. The dyes should be fast and fade resistant. Most are moth proofed.

Rya rugs use a lot of pile yarn, and it is relatively expensive. Cheap yarns and a less dense pile will make a shabby rug; I know, I have tried it and the results were disastrous. Careful calculations can help make efficient use of the yarn and assure that there will be enough to finish the rug. When the design is complete and the colors selected, count the number of knots of each color combination. Graph paper that has heavy lines every five or ten squares is helpful in the counting. When you have totals for all color combinations, list all the colors involved. Each knot is made up of three "bits" of yarn which may all be different. Under each color of yarn, list the totals of all the color combinations in which it is used. If it is used more than once in a knot, that is if two strands are the same color, list it twice under that color. Total each color to get the number of "bits" needed.

To convert "bits" to skeins of yarn, first count the strands in several skeins of yarn. The rya yarn I used had 70-75 strands per skein. I used 70 in the calculations to be on the conservative side. Each three strands made 15 to 17 knots, so I figured 15 "bits" per strand.

Fifteen "bits" per strand × 70 strands per skein = 1050 "bits" per skein. Divide 1050 "bits" into the total "bits" needed for each color to get the number of skeins needed.

There were leftovers, but not an unreasonable amount. A design with many colors will have more partial skeins left over than one with fewer colors.

If all this counting and calculating is not for you and you do not mind a larger volume of left-overs, try estimating the areas involved. Since I was getting 1050 "bits" per skein and three "bits" per knot, three skeins would make 1050 knots. I was tying three knots per inch across (or 36 knots per foot) and have five rows of knots per 2" (or 30 rows per foot).

Thirty-six knots × 30 rows = 1080 knots per square foot. That is a few more than the 1050 knots I was getting from three skeins, so estimating three skeins per square foot would be close. Add some excess to be on the safe side and be sure you know your yarn. I found another brand of rya yarn was coarser and yielded only about 900 knots per three skeins.

Warp for a rya rug needs to be strong since it carries the knots of the pile. The kit backing had two linen warps used as one. For weaving, I used 8/4 linen rug warp at 6 e.p.i. A slightly heavier warp would have worked as well. If a finer size is used, it may need to be doubled. Just be sure it will weave with the weft to produce a tight, firm weft-face weave.

The weft does not show in the finished rug. It needs to be strong enough to bind the warps together and resist abrasion on the edges. Mill ends can be used, but be sure there is enough for the whole rug. I used 1½ pounds in a 3' × 5' rug with closely spaced rows. Color is not usually important, but a light colored rug may look grubby if a dark tabby shows through. A weight similar to the rya yarn is suitable.

Choosing equipment

Since a rya rug is woven with a two-harness weft-face plain weave, any sturdy loom will do. If you have a four-harness or eight-harness loom, thread as for a plain weave on all harnesses (1-2-3-4 or 1-2-3-4-5-6-7-8) to equalize the stress on the loom.

The loom should be rigid when in use to maintain good tension. I have used a folding loom and found it more difficult to keep the tension even than with a non-folding loom.

The tensioning mechanism, whether a ratchet, friction-brake, or combination, needs to be sturdy and dependable. As the rug is wound on the cloth beam, the stress increases and the tensioning becomes more difficult.

Rugs of two yards or less in length can be wound on most looms without difficulty. Longer rugs build up on the cloth beam and may make it difficult or impossible to use the beater.

I use a 12-dent reed sleyed alternately to give 6 e.p.i. If the warp is heavy or rough enough to spread the dents or resist beating, use a 6-dent reed sleyed one per dent.

Some way of storing the pile color combinations where they can be reached from the loom is needed. A needlepoint stand worked well for me. A clothes drying rack would work, or even a couple of chairs.

Large-eyed blunt needles, about 2¾" long, are needed to handle the pile yarn in making the knots. The eyes should be large enough for easy threading. Each color combination needs its own needle so that changes from one color combination to another will not require rethreading a needle; you'll just pick up the next color off the storage rack.

The length of the pile can be controlled with the fingers or a gauge can be used if consistency is important. Use whatever width of gauge will give you the desired pile length. The gauge should be strong enough not to collapse, and smooth enough so it can be slid along without catching on the yarn. Wooden moldings or dowels can be used with a little sanding. Plastic or wooden rulers of the desired width can also be used.

Sharp scissors to cut the pile and a shuttle to carry the weft complete the necessary equipment. A tapestry beater may be helpful in packing the weft-face bands between the rows of knots.

Warping

Warping for a rya rug presents no special problems. I warp from front to back on a jack loom, first sleying, then threading. Each inch of threaded warps (six warps, in this case) is held with the ends even and tied together with an overhand knot. The overhand knot is attached with a lark's head knot to a tie-on cord which is attached to the tie bar on the warp beam. When all warps are tied on, open the shed and insert a lease stick behind the harnesses, then open the opposite shed and insert another lease stick. Change the shed again and begin to wind on. The lease sticks are wound on with the warp and serve to untwist the warp groups and spread the warp more evenly as it starts over the back beam. One-sided corrugated cardboard (smooth side out) is wound on with the warp to provide a smooth, even surface. If you cannot find this kind of cardboard, you might try Flex-o-Pane, a plastic window material. It is more expensive than cardboard but less bulky when winding long warps. Heavy paper is a less satisfactory alternative. With widely spaced warps under high tension, some warps may crease the paper and become loose.

The warp is wound onto the warp beam a turn at a time, then tightened by pulling on small bunches from the front. Work across the width of the warp and back. The shed is open and is changed periodically as the warp is wound to help keep the warp from twisting when not under tension. A couple of shuttles can be inserted between the harnesses to keep the shed open.

When the warp is wound, tie to the front tie bar. The warp groups should be an inch or less in width. Be sure all groups are equally tight. Argatch, or edge warps, are wound on with the rest. If these warps become slack during the weaving process, hang a weight on them between the warp beam and the back beam.

I have used a sectional beam with 1" sections for rya rugs. If six warps are wound in each 1" section, the warps tend to build up in spots and slip down into the roll in others. Winding 12 warps in alternate sections made the warp wind more evenly, but was still not as satisfactory as the non-sectional beam with cardboard.

Weaving the rug

Weave a heading with rag strips or heavy yarn to spread the warps to an even spacing and then weave the 1½" to 2" weft-face heading for the rug. Both the heading and bands between rows of knots should be tightly woven and firmly beaten. Be sure the edges are firm but do not draw in. The bulk of the knots that follow will keep the warp spread to a consistent width. The heading folds back under the rug and will not show.

In making up the color blends, a major hurdle for me was getting up the courage to cut a whole skein of yarn. I cut the skein near the knot that ties the ends together, then separated it into individual strands. (If only part of a skein is used, the tie with label attached can be left with the unused portion for future reference.) I laid the strands out on tables, benches, couch, chairs and whatever else was available; a pool table is ideal. I cut another skein and laid the strands out with those of the first skein; then a third skein, to make up the three

strands needed for a particular color combination. As I picked up the three strand combinations, I tied a slip knot in each so it could be easily separated from the others when needed. I hung these bunches of knotted strands on a needlepoint stand and threaded a needle for each combination.

To argatch or not to argatch is open for debate. The argatch is a selvedge which carries no knots. The kit that I began with had no argatch; the knots ran from selvedge to selvedge, so I made my first small rugs that way. No particular problems have resulted, but they have been used as hangings or in low traffic areas. The bulk of the pile running to the edge gives the rug a slight tendency to curl to the back, which helps it lie flat or hang close to the wall. I had seen rya rugs with wide argatches that showed beyond the pile and had a tendency to ruffle. I did not want that, but the large rug needed the support; so I wove an inch wide argatch on the sides. This was hemmed back under the rug so it does not show, but has added to the strength and durability of the edge. In addition it helps compensate for the reduced thickness of the pile at the edge of the rug. Since the edge pile can lie down beyond the edge of the rug, it is less upright than the pile in the central part of the rug. Sometimes this is compensated for by knotting the pile closer together on the edges. This is not a problem to lose sleep over; if it lies flatter at the edge, it is less likely to get scuffed up by the traffic. I used a narrow argatch of two doubled warps in the last two small rugs. To weave the argatch, make additional shots back and forth with the weft yarn to compensate for the bulk of the knots (see figures on the next page). Beat these shots down well with the beater or tapestry beater if necessary. If the argatch seems to ruffle, add weight to these warps in back of the loom. The warps that carry the knots may have more take-up than the argatch warps and leave them loose. Do not try to pull them forward as this can add to the ruffling. Other methods of weaving the argatch are given in Collingwood's *Techniques of Rug Weaving*.

Knotting the pile

The pile is knotted using the rya, Ghiordes, Smyrna or Turkish knot. It is a most secure knot since it tightens when pulled. For a right handed person, it is easier to sew with the needle moving right to left. The knots are sewn in a series of backstitches beginning at the left side of the warp. With

Making the argatch:

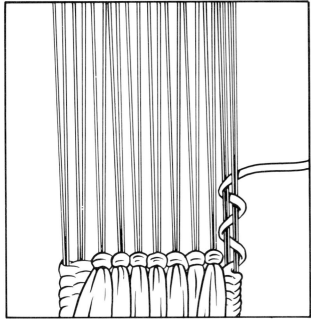

Argatch shots on the right selvedge compensate for the bulk of the rya knots.

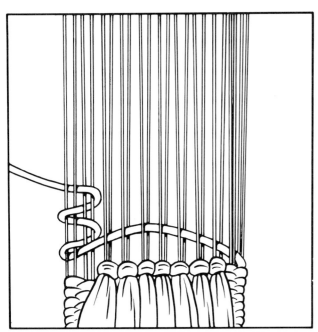

Argatch shots on the left selvedge are woven after the first shot of the weft-face band.

the needle to carry the three strands of yarn, stitch right to left under the left-most warp that is to carry a knot of that color. Hang onto the ends of the yarn with the left hand and pull the needle away from you with the right till the length of yarn held by the left hand is the length desired for the pile. Lay the yarn away from you and hold between the left middle and ring fingers as the next stitch with the needle goes right to left under the next warp to the right and comes up on the near side of the loop from the last stitch. Pull toward you till the knot tightens. Hold the yarn toward you with the left index finger to make the desired length loop to be cut for the pile, and proceed as before. When the desired number of knots have been tied, cut the remaining yarn and loops between the knots to the desired length. With practice the loops will be even, no trimming should be necessary, and the waste is very small.

If you use a gauge to keep the pile even, the yarn is held against the gauge for the first stitch, then looped around the gauge after the second stitch. This gives even sized loops between the knots. Slide the gauge along as you progress across the row and cut the loops when the row is complete or cut most of the loops on the gauge and slide it along with the few remaining loops holding it in place.

Other methods of making the rya knot can also be used. Some precut the yarn into "bits" of uniform length. The desired colors are selected and laid across the two warps, the ends are tucked under and come up between the warps. A tug on the ends tightens the knot. I use this method when I make a mistake and must pull out a knot. The yarn can be put in the next row in an appropriate place. The spot where it came out can be stitched in with a needle.

Precut bits can be looped around the two warps, the ends evened and then tucked under and up between the warps.

Finely knotted rugs use a single strand of yarn in each knot. The yarn comes from a ball or bobbin and is passed down between the warps, up around the right warp, left across both warps, down around the left and up between. The free end is held with the left hand while the strand leading to the ball (on the right) is pulled to tighten the knot, then cut with scissors or a knife held in the right hand. The knots are tied from right to left and cut as tied. See Collingwood's *Techniques of Rug*

Making the rya knot:

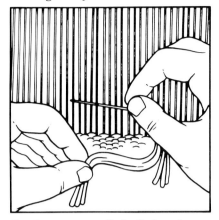

For finger-controlled pile length, begin with the needle carrying the pile yarns right to left under the left warp.

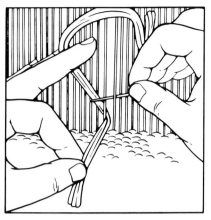

Holding the yarn as shown, pass the needle right to left under the next warp to the right.

Pull the pile yarn toward you until the knot tightens; hold the loop while starting the next knot.

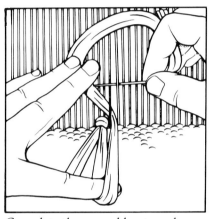

Complete the second knot, and proceed across the row in this fashion.

Cut the loops and remaining yarn ends to the desired pile length.

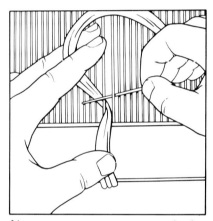

You can use a gauge to control pile length: hold the loose yarn end against the gauge as you start.

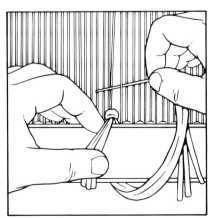

Take each loop around the gauge before beginning the next knot.

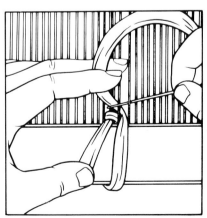

Complete the second knot, and proceed across the row.

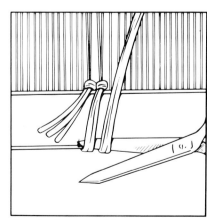

Cut the loops and loose yarn ends evenly.

The cut soumak knot:

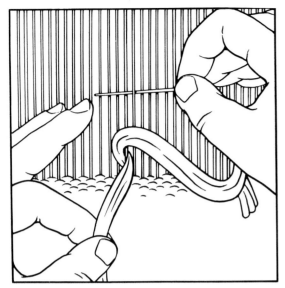

The first stitch is the same as a rya knot, but the second stitch comes up on the far side of the loop across the two warps.

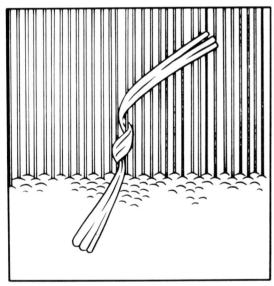

The pile ends tend to open out in opposite directions.

Weaving for illustrations and explanations of these other methods.

These alternative methods seem more complicated than using the needles when handling more than one strand of yarn. However, if you are handling thrums or scrap yarn they may be helpful. Try them and see what works best for you.

The rya or Ghiordes knot gives a direction or grain to the pile, like hair on a dog's back. This is not a problem until you reach the end of the rug; then the lay of the pile may expose the backing or heading at the far end. Whether the piece is to be used for a rug, hanging or pillow, it would be nice if the backing did not show and the pile looked the same at both ends. To remedy this, two variations of the knot can be used to alter the direction of the pile in the last few rows. I used a cut soumak knot every few knots in the fourth row from the end. The only difference between it and a rya knot is that the second stitch comes up on the far side of the loop across the two warps, instead of on the near side. The soumak knot does not tighten down as it is tied, but is almost as secure as the rya knot once the next weft-face band is woven. Leave the loops un-cut until after the weft-face band is woven to help hold the knots in place. The pile ends tend to open out in opposite directions. The frequency of this knot increases in the third row from the end and is used with reverse rya knots in the second row from the end. The reverse rya knot is just that, the ends come out toward the far end of the rug and the loop across the two warps is toward the weaver. It is a most unstable knot until the weft-face band is woven. The last row is all reverse rya knots so the pile at the end will lie outward and cover the edge.

Finishing the rug

Weave the final weft-face band and a few shots of rag strips or heavy yarn to hold the band in place, and the rug can be cut off the loom. Allow enough warp (4" to 6") to tie a Half Damascus edge (see Appendix I). Take out the rag strips as the edge is tied and be sure the ends fold toward the back of the rug. I either hem my rugs, or sew cotton twill rug tape to the weft-face heading with several rows of straight and zigzag stitching and hem it back. Rods can be inserted in the hem for hanging.

Special problems

I wove my 8½′ × 11′ rug (not shown here) in three sections and sewed it together afterward. The bulk of an 11′ rya strip was almost too much for the loom. The beater rubbed on the huge roll on the cloth beam. I had tried doing two of the small rugs, one after the other, so the problem was anticipated and I knew I was pushing the limits.

Edge warps tended to get mushy and loose as the weaving progressed. The pile near the edge lies down and out of the roll on the cloth beam so the roll gets spindle-shaped. Rolling corrugated cardboard or sticks with the woven rug helps maintain a cylindrical roll to some extent.

The three pieces of the 8½′ × 11′ rug were sewn together by hand using linen rug warp. Each stitch caught both the weft and the edge warp. Small discrepancies in size between the three pieces were reduced by holding the warps with pliers and sliding the pile and weft-face bands up the warp a bit. This is not a good solution. Careful measuring during the weaving to avoid size variation is needed. I finished the ends after the pieces were sewn together.

Living with a rya

Fuzz is a part of making a rya rug and when the construction is complete, the fuzz continues. Some brands of yarn may be fuzzier than others. Traffic across the rug picks up the fuzz which is then distributed throughout the house. A dry climate where static is a problem makes it worse, but a damp climate is no solution. After a year of heavy traffic and frequent vacuuming, the fuzz tapers off but never seems to end completely. I am admittedly not an enthusiastic housekeeper; I would rather spend the time weaving.

Regular cleaning can be done with a vacuum on a shag setting. My original kit rug presented no problem if I took care at the corners so the vacuum did not try to swallow the edge. Occasionally I took it outside, hung it over a fence, and shook it. Years of heavy traffic began to mat the pile. To remedy this, I ran a defunct ballpoint pen or crochet hook handle between the rows of knots. This lifted and separated the pile so trapped soil could be shaken and vacuumed out. The improvement in appearance was well worth the effort.

My big rug was less cooperative. The old vacuum choked on the deeper, denser pile so we

Reverse Rya Knot

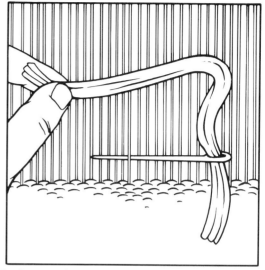

The first stitch comes up on the near side of the ends held in the left hand.

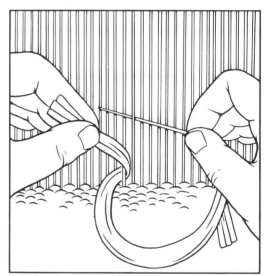

The loop across the two warps is on the near side of the second stitch.

The completed knot, with ends pointing away from the weaver.

had to get a new vacuum with a higher shag setting. The rug is almost too heavy to lift and requires four of us if it is to be shaken. I do occasionally drag it out to the porch rail, hang it over and shake a bit at a time.

A rya rug used as an area rug on top of wall-to-wall carpet had advantages and disadvantages. The rug and padding underneath add to the thickness and springiness, making it even deeper and lusher underfoot. For slumber parties the boys have insisted on sleeping on the rya.

At the same time, wall-to-wall carpet often has a direction or grain to the pile. The rya on top may creep in that direction as it is walked upon. My personal choice would be a dense, short pile wall-to-wall carpet with no pad to go under area rugs, whether rya or flat woven. Many prefer hardwood, vinyl, tile, etc. If that is your choice, a rya will lie pretty well by itself. If it tends to slide or rumple easily, a non-skid pad should help.

Small rya rugs make wonderful hangings. They are rich and colorful to look at and lush to touch. Hang them in places where they will be touched; they can take it. A light vacuuming with an upholstery brush to remove dust is the only care needed.

To prepare for hanging, insert a dowel or rod into the casing at the end of the rug. If hung by the ends of the dowel, the weight will bow and sag the dowel. I make two loops for hanging, 18" apart (or 9" either side of the center). This spacing distributes the weight on the rod so there is little tendency to sag. (I use this spacing on everything I hang so the same nails can be used to hang different pieces, rugs, tapestries or whatever.) With carpet warp or heavy thread, sew through the casing, under the dowel and out several times to make a loop. You may wish to buttonhole stitch the strands of the loop together to make them easier to handle.

Whether you choose to walk on it or hang it on the wall, a rya rug brings a lush warmth to any room. I know you will enjoy making and living with a rya.

The Challenge of Block Weaves

Bryn Pinchin

or those weavers with a technical bias, block weave rugs offer the challenge and pleasure of a good puzzle. For those of us who find designing an intimidating process, the rectangularity of block weaves allows the comfort of designing with a ruler on graph paper. For those of us who find finger manipulated weaves tedious, block weave rugs can be created relatively quickly because the patterning is loom controlled. And finally, for those of us who have to stretch an idea to its limits, the process of shaft switching blocks offers literally an endless variety of designs on one threading; and the crackle overshot, the challenge of literally turning one weave inside out to create another.

The block weave rugs to be presented here are flat, weft-faced structures. Generally, they are two-color rugs, characterized by strong, bold patterning. They are reversible, although it should be said that often one side will have a more pleasing design than the other. They are thick, well interlaced rugs with short, even floats. As a result, they are tough and springy.

The block weave rugs discussed here are created by bound weave treadling sequences. Unlike the patterning of a twill rug, which is most often created by changing the color sequence of weft, that of a block weave rug depends on a prearranged threading plan. In other words, the pattern arises out of its structure. Depending on the threading plan, blocks of any size can be woven and the delight of drafting a block weave rug lies in its large scale.

In sum then, by using unit weaves already familiar to many weavers, such as summer and winter, overshot and crackle, we can create boldly designed rugs which wear well, lie straight and flat and have sturdy loom controlled selvedges. I suggest that readers familiar with the concept of the block and comfortable with the challenges of designing block drafts, move directly to the rug suggestions presented here. For the rest, let's do some basic groundwork and establish what a block is, how it works—and for that matter, why you need more than one of them.

Building blocks

In twills it is the interplay of single warp and single weft threads that creates the design. In block (or pattern, or unit) weaves it is the interplay of groups of warp threads, and thus groups of weft threads, which make the design. Consider the checkerboard motif below. The first square on the right hand corner is black. It is labelled A. Note that blocks are labelled in capital letters to distinguish them from numbered harnesses. Note that the position and dimension of that A block does not change in the checkerboard. Any black square in that vertical rectangle is an A block. The same thing is true in the horizontal rectangle. Whatever color or pattern effect that is created in the corner A block with which we began occurs in all A blocks in that horizontal line. In other words, whatever we have done to the group of threads in the right hand corner Block A is repeated four times across the warp.

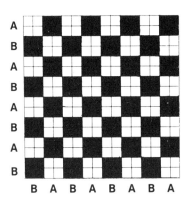

As can be seen from this simple checkerboard, all pattern blocks in any given vertical row are the same width and all pattern blocks in any given horizontal row are the same height. The width of a block, that is, its warp-way dimension, is a direct result of how it is threaded. Once threaded, it cannot change and so, logically, the blocks remain the same width. Again, logically, its weft-way dimension is the result of the build-up of the weft from selvedge to selvedge. Thus the dimension of the block cannot change horizontally; the A block in the right corner cannot be taller than the A block in the left corner of the same row.

The second space horizontally and vertically in the checkerboard is black. However, it is not in the same position as the A block. Therefore, it is not an A block. We will call it B. It conforms to the same constructions of warp and weft-way dimension as does block A. We label blocks in a diagonal

direction. Thus, the third, fifth and seventh black squares running horizontally, vertically or diagonally are A blocks. Only two blocks make up the checkerboard (mark that design for future consideration!).

The dimensions of our checkerboard can be changed. For example:

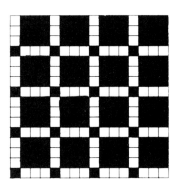

In this case, A is one unit smaller and B is one unit larger. Any or all blocks in a pattern may vary in height or width or both; but note that they do so consistently in that once a dimension of the block is graphed (i.e., threaded) it may never change vertically and once treadled, it may never change horizontally. An A block remains an A and a B a B! Sounds simple, and so it is.

In the designing of two-block patterns the most important factor is the variation of the size of the blocks. That is, in effect, the only design tool we have. One caution: I find it more difficult to design two-block motifs that are rectangular. Squares seem relatively easy to design, but a square is not the most pleasing shape for a rug. A rectangle imposes a direction on the design. On the floor, the rectangle will carry your eye; a square has no direction. Begin your designing by graphing out a rectangle proportional to the dimensions of our proposed rug, then fill in and manipulate the blocks within that space. A dark square on the first line of your graph paper is a B block. The light, unfilled, squares are A blocks. At this point, let me recommend Berta Frey's *Designing and Drafting for Handweavers* for those readers just stepping into designing with blocks. She is wonderfully clear and succinct.

One should note that it is, of course, possible to weave patterns containing four blocks on a four-harness loom and many more, according to the number of harnesses available to the weaver. Two-block designs are not limiting. Refer to the examples I have given as a start. You can achieve some very interesting effects with two blocks and two colors—not to speak of two blocks and more colors! We will stop at two since at the moment, on four harnesses we are limited to that number for the rugs in hand.

Filling in the blanks. . .

Remember that the block is an element of design and a graphed two-block pattern is just that—a design. At this point the design is like a lock that needs a key. We must substitute for the units of the design, units of threading which will weave us our rug. Each of the weaves which we can apply to the block draft has its own character. Overshot, for example, has lively patterning, a great deal of movement, long floats, areas of pattern background and "gray" areas which are a blend of both. Huck weaves could be substituted if one wanted lace, or summer and winter if one wanted a closely woven reversible fabric. In substituting we move from a purely pattern dimension to questions of texture, color, weight and the ultimate use of the piece.

In our case, we are aiming for rugs. We want to reproduce our blocks boldly on a large scale. We must have a thick flat weave, closely woven, without long floats to wear or catch a heel. At this point, let us say as well that we are using a four-harness loom. Immediately, it is obvious that overshot, for all its richness of pattern, is not available to us because of the problem of the long floats, which are unsuitable in a rug. We will find a way around this problem later, but for the moment the most useful block weave to use for rugs is the summer and winter weave. We will look at it in detail in this chapter both as a two-block weave and as the basis for shaft switching.

Let's go one step further in the preparation of two-block designs for rug weaves. Refer to the figure at right. As it stands it is a two-block pattern. We need to isolate the blocks in the pattern in order to substitute a threading draft. To do this, we derive a profile, or short draft, from the motif as follows. First, note that for the reason I have given above, the original square format has been modified into a rectangle. The two blocks that make up the image have been marked on the graph lines directly above the design. The blocks are named in capital letters and are drafted in the same way that harnesses would be, that is Block A is on the graph line closest to you, followed by B—and C and D if they were relevant. Thus, this two line

draft indicates we have two blocks, A and B, and that A is three units wide, B is one unit and so on across the design. This is the profile draft. A profile draft is also called a substitution draft because one substitutes a chosen unit of threading for each unit of design in the draft. A profile draft is much more concise and easy to work with than the threading draft which indicates the order of threading individual warp ends.

For example, one can take this to the loom,

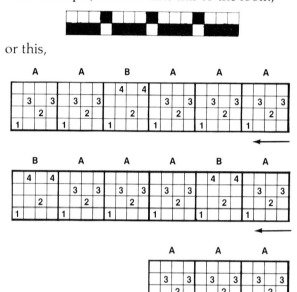

or this,

It is obvious that the profile is easier to deal with than the threading draft. One further note: as a rule, profile drafts and block designs are drafted with solid squares, whereas the thread-by-thread drafts use x's or numbers, as above.

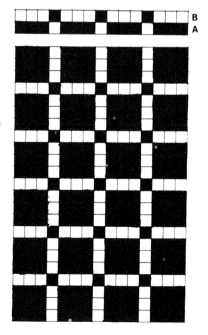

Some two-block designs with their profiles

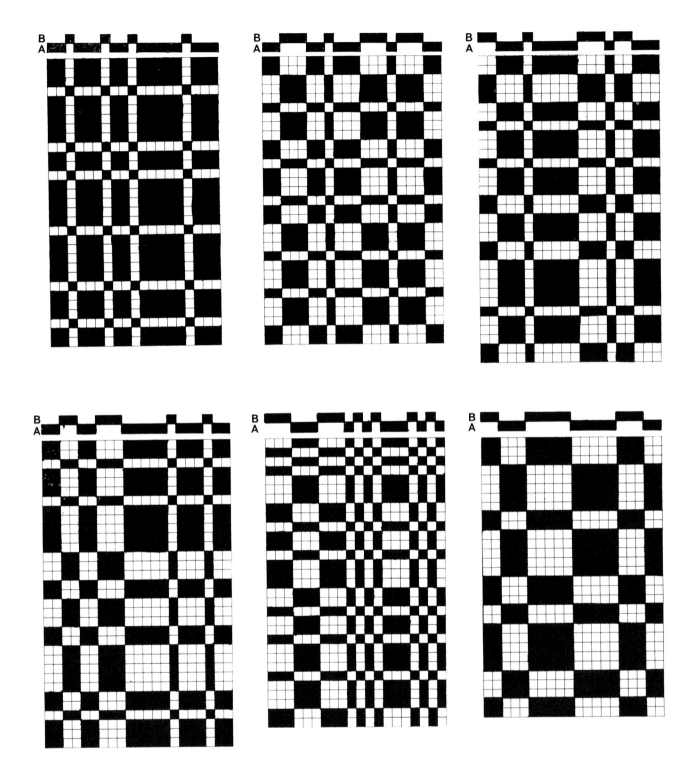

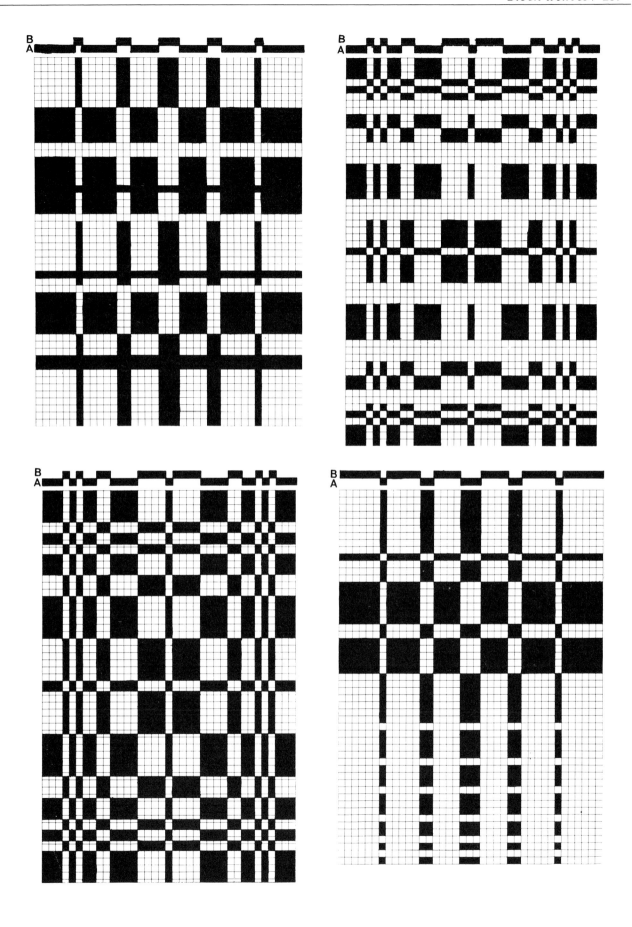

At this point, let us consider other terminology used in block weave rugs.

The naming of parts

Compare this design with the one on page 135. They share the same profile drafts, but they are quite different. The rug depicted there is designed to be woven *to square*, or *as drawn in*. Each block has been treadled that number of repeats which will make it as long as it is wide. The rug depicted here has been designed so that block A changes size while block B is treadled square.

All of the block weave rugs considered here are woven as bound weaves on opposites. *Bound weave*, as the term is used here, refers to a method of treadling which produces a flat weft-faced structure. While loom controlled, the patterns are formed by combinations of threading, treadling and weft color. Because the warps are relatively widely spaced, the weft beats down very closely and colors are covered and re-emerge to form the pattern. Because it is so firmly woven and a minimum of two, or more often four, weft shots are required for each row, the weave produces very thick rugs and requires relatively large amounts of yarn. Treadling to square in bound weave takes many more picks per inch than other types of textiles. There are two to four shots per row; thus

often it will take up to 24 shots to square 1" of a bound weave rug.

There are many treadling sequences which, used in combination with a widely spaced warp, will result in bound weave effects. For block weave rugs woven as bound weaves we often weave *on opposites* so that after every pattern shot, another shot of contrasting color is made on the opposite shed. This treadling sequence results in thick rugs with solid blocks of color. It is generally a two-color weave, although pleasing effects can be created by using three or more colors.

Bound weave rugs are widely sett — generally at four to five ends per inch. However, it is necessary often to increase the number of warp ends in the rug to provide strength and stability, and to avoid the problem of a sparse fringe. One cannot simply increase the number of ends per inch without making it impossible to beat the colors over one another properly. The solution is found in the concept of *working ends per inch* or *working e.p.i.* If a sett of four e.p.i. is desired, calculate the warp at six ends per inch and thread single, double, single every second dent in an eight-dent reed. The double thread is used as a single thread in the reed and in the heddle, and so works as a single while adding additional ends for fringing and stability. Likewise, a five working ends per inch sett wound as seven ends per inch in a ten-dent reed is satisfactory.

At this point we should perhaps discuss the problem of selvedges. The combination of a very thick weft and firm beating usually results in some draw-in. Although with care it should be able to be controlled and kept to 1" each side, there is still a great deal of friction on the selvedge threads. Therefore, special attention should be paid to the *argatch*, or side edges, of the rug. In all the rugs discussed here the argatch is threaded as follows:

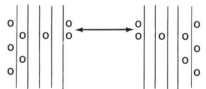

—tripled at the outside edge, no empty dent, doubled, then space, then single space, double and so on across the warp to the other selvedge where the arrangement is repeated. It is important to crowd the argatch in this manner. One of the joys in weaving block weave rugs is that the weft is properly caught in the selvedge as one weaves and so devices such as weft wrapping or, the ultimate annoyance, a floating selvedge, are not needed.

What's needed now

Bound weave rugs need little special equipment. However, the heavier the loom you can use, the more satisfactory will be the weaving process. One must have a loom that will withstand frequent hard beating. If possible, the loom should stand in a room where it will not skid around the floor as you beat. If the loom is not heavy enough, try weighting the back beam with sand bags for the duration of the project. I find it very helpful to weight my beater bar. On my 12-harness 60" loom I tape my husband's 5' long, 25 pound crowbar under the reed with *many rounds* of fiber tape. The additional weight is not hard to handle and makes an enormous difference to the rug. Lengths of lead pipe would also be suitable, but make sure they are well taped. Also, when beating with a weighted beater, use your body properly. Pull back by leaning back, not by whipping your elbows behind you. You can hurt your chest badly that way and it doesn't do as good a job.

You do not need special shuttles for block weave rugs, although small boat shuttles are unsatisfactory. Generally, I like to work with six to eight plies — that is to say three or four strands — of rug yarn, and that is impractical on a small bobbin. Stick shuttles are better; large ski shuttles are best. They combine the efficiency of the stick shuttle when winding the yarn with the smoothness of a boat shuttle when throwing a shot.

Many rug weavers better than I use temples when weaving rugs, so temples must be mentioned when discussing equipment, although I find them a nuisance to use. For those who have trouble controlling a straight edge a temple may prove very useful. Be careful when placing them into the selvedge that you do not fray the warp, and try to move them often.

One tool that I find useful when setting up a rug is a pair of soft, fine leather gloves. Linen is very hard on the hands and yet it must be knotted and pulled very tightly. I wear black kid gloves when knotting at the front beam and adjusting the tension. They work and I look so elegant!

The warp for these rugs needs special attention because of the heavy beating necessary. There are four choices: acrylic, wool, cotton and linen. Let's consider them. First the acrylics. Many are strong and inexpensive and some have low elasticity.

However, I have never seen an acrylic rug warp which didn't stretch with disastrous results. Also, the strongest acrylics have very coarse fibers which exert a great friction on the weft as it is beaten in. In short, they are an unsuitable rug warp. Don't use them.

A wool warp would have to be chosen carefully for strength and low elasticity. The best wool rug warp would be a hard twist yarn. A wool warp would make the rug softer and more flexible and would therefore be suitable for saddle blankets. It might not be able to withstand the tension and friction of a bound weave.

Cotton is the second choice as it is strong, durable, easily available and relatively inexpensive. It is possible to warp with 8/8 cotton. However the rug will be very soft and floppy on the floor. Cotton does have the advantage of coming in a wide variety of colors to complement the weft. If you do use it, consider mixing two tones of one color (for example, two shades of red, or a black and a navy) in the warp. It adds a dimension of richness in the braid or fringe. Structurally, the best cotton to use as warp is a seine twine, which has all of these characteristics; however, it's very slippery and I have found that it unplies in the fringe unless braided and tends to slip out of the rug with use when it is sewn in. It is difficult to knot as well. In short — use it as a last resort.

The best warp material, from my point of view, is linen. It is also the most expensive and often the most difficult to get. It is strong, not elastic and its neutral color allows you more options in the finishing. I recommend a number six wet spun linen for rug warps. Many rug linens are dry spun and have a rather fibrous look to them. They are strong and the right color but they fray easily — especially at the selvedges — or in the warp knots in the fringes. If you have no choice but to use a dry spun linen, make sure it is plied rather than a thick singles, and try to keep it moist with a spray bottle and/or a damp towel over the warp from the back beam to the harnesses. Be very careful with your draw-in!

Warping with linen makes many weavers nervous, although it should not. Warp from the front or the back with the same results, but be very careful that you have a tight, even tension. In this, linen allows no errors since it has absolutely no elasticity to forgive you. Warp quickly for any rug — or find a way to maintain tension in the warp if you must leave it. A linen warp left wound and untied on the back beam for a day will lose its tension and cause real problems as you weave, even if you tie and tension carefully at the front when you return. That's a note from bitter experience!

Weft yarns need a good twist, need to resist abrasion, and need to be somewhat elastic or supple or they will not move properly around the warp and pack in well. A coarser rather than a smooth yarn is best, as highly finished yarns do not seem to stand up to the wear of traffic over the rug. On the other hand, highly finished yarns have a special glow that may be suitable for a rug woven to hang on a wall. Obviously in choosing wefts, common sense applies. If you are preparing hand-spun for your weft, it should be spun worsted with a great deal of twist. Plied yarns are stronger and more resistant to wear but singles reflect the light off their surface better and can be more handsome. A beautiful but softer yarn can be closer sett so that the floats are as short as possible.

I find it more satisfactory to weave with three to five strands of a two-ply weft; I prefer the texture that multiple plies give me. I have the additional tool of blending colors or even textures in my bundle should I choose. It is often easier to weave to square with multiples of weft because you can add or subtract a ply when adjusting the weave to the profile. However, there are many five- or six-ply rug yarns which weave beautifully at a sett of four working ends per inch. My advice is this: if you are weaving a rug to be used in a high traffic area, *or* if you want the effect of a clean, hard, flat surface, use a five-ply rug yarn at four working ends per inch. If your rug is for a wall, or if the interplay of light on the surface is a design factor for you, experiment with multiple plies of yarn.

Having chosen the warp and weft, one is left with the problem of calculating amounts. According to Collingwood the following formula applies:

"A flat-woven rug uses about ½ pound of weft per square foot.
A pile rug uses ¾ pound upward of weft per square foot."

I use his figures as a guide. Thus a 3' × 5' rug needs approximately 7½ pounds of weft. A block weave rug needs two colors of weft. Therefore, we need about 3½ — perhaps 4 pounds of each color. I confess I always round up and have about a pound of each color left because Collingwood's formula is generous. However, I can't bring myself to order less!

The rugs

The most satisfactory unit weave for a two-block bound weave rug is summer and winter. The substitution, or threading draft reads as follows:

Block A			3		3	
				2		
		1				
Block B			4		4	
				2		
		1				

In other words, wherever you have drafted an A block in your profile draft, substitute 1-3-2-3, wherever you have a B, substitute 1-4-2-4. These threading units are constant and complete and you need no linking or joining threads between blocks. However, to weave the edges properly you must balance the threading by adding a 1 and a 2 (tie-downs) at the end. Thus the threading reads:

				4		4						
	3		3									
		2			2						2	
1			1					.	.	.	1	

We will not dwell in detail on the structure of the weave except to note that it has two elements. Harnesses 1 and 2, which alternate, are tie-down or structural harnesses, and 3 and 4 are the pattern harnesses. Harness 3 is the pattern harness of block A and harness 4 is the pattern harness of block B. A multi-harness summer and winter would see the pattern blocks continue on 5, 6, 7, 8 and so on. This arrangement allows the pattern shot to float over three and under one warp thread regularly. It is a particularly fine and versatile weave for our purposes.

It is a reversible weave. From this point, let us say that our proposed rug is black and white.

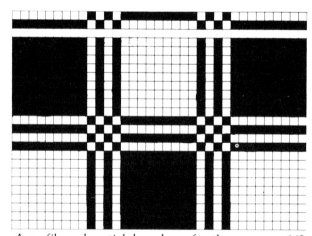

A profile and partial drawdown for the rug on p. 142.

Those areas black on the surface will be white underneath and vice versa. Again, to thread the rug, substitute the appropriate number of threading units of A where you have an A block, and threading units of B where you have a B block. Thus, the threading for the profile of this rug would read:

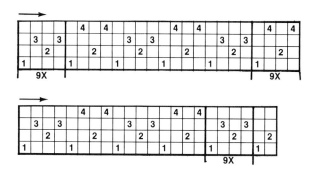

There is no adjustment necessary where the blocks adjoin.

The treadling of a summer and winter rug is very simple and *never* changes. I would like to work it through as for a jack loom, using for this purpose a portion of the design of the rug illustrated here.

In order to weave a black A block and a white B block:

1. Lift ½ of the tie-downs plus pattern harness 1&3 of A (3) and throw white.
2. Lift the same ½ of the tie-down plus pat- 1&4 tern harness of B (4) and throw black.
3. Lift second ½ of the tie-downs (2) and pat- 2&3 tern harness for A (3) and throw white.
4. Lift the same half of the tie-downs (2) and 2&4 pattern harness for B (4) and throw black.

Thus the treadling for bound weave on the summer and winter threading is:

1 & 3	white
1 & 4	black
2 & 3	white
2 & 4	black

This treadling is not varied. It is part of the engaging simplicity of the weave.

In order to change the color order so that block A is white and B is black as in section II of Figure 8, simply change the order in which the colors are thrown. *Do not* change the treadling order. Thus it becomes:

1 & 3	black
1 & 4	white
2 & 3	black
2 & 4	white

Note that you throw the two shuttles from opposite sides in order to properly catch the selvedges.

Should you wish to weave a solid band of one color in the design, keep the treadling order constant and *continue to use two shuttles* from opposite sides of the web.

1 & 3	black
1 & 4	black
2 & 3	black
2 & 4	black

Note that this treadling will result in a solid colored band *on both sides* of the rug.

Interesting color effects can be created within the blocks if you use two colors or two tones of a color for one block as follows:

1 & 3	black
1 & 4	white
2 & 3	black
2 & 4	cream

This way, block B would be black, but block A would have a pick-and-pick strip of cream and white. These strips can be reversed by alternating the order in which they are thrown. Carrying this concept even further, if you throw four colors in the same treadling sequence the rug loses its block character and has warp-way stripes. There are other variations with which one can experiment, within the same treadling order. Personally, I prefer the clean two-block effect of the two-color weave. Three or more colors tend to break down the bold impact of the images. Also, it is difficult to keep a tidy selvedge using more than two colors at a time.

Using a four-end threading draft at 4 e.p.i., each unit is an inch wide. This makes designing and weaving the rug much easier. If, when trying to weave to square, you find it is not possible using the yarns chosen to square a block in a multiple of the four shots, it is possible to make an adjustment. *Continue* the treadling sequences. However, after the second shot switch colors into the next block.

Thus:

1 & 3	black	previous block
1 & 4	white	
2 & 3	white	switch to new block
2 & 4	black	
continue		

This rug uses the block design on the previous page. The warp is #6 linen set at 4 working e.p.i.; weft is a five-ply rug wool in black and white.

There is a small sacrifice to be made at the corner edge of the block. It may seem a little unbalanced, at the corners but it is structurally sound and may be better than an unsquare block in an otherwise carefully designed image.

Shaft switching

We should subtitle this section "How do you get there from here?" Perhaps we'd all be more confident approaching this technique if it had been called "harness-hopping". Keep that in mind because that is really all there is to it!

Shaft-switching developed when someone wise (P. Collingwood) said "What would happen if. . .?" What would happen if we could free the pattern blocks from the restrictions imposed by the fact that their dimensions are fixed because they are threaded?

Consider the structure of the basic summer and winter weave. It has, you'll remember, two elements. Every second thread is either a 1 or a 2. These are tie-down threads. They are, in effect, the bones of the weave. Harnesses 3 and 4 are the pattern harnesses. They operate in groups, or units, corresponding to the blocks in the profile draft. What we have, in essence, is a solid infrastructure, with room to fiddle around with the pattern threads.

Now—what would happen if a pattern thread of A—3—became a 4? What would happen? Let's see:

Here we have a profile—four units of each block threaded as follows:

							4	4	4	4	4	4
3		3		3		3		3				
	2		2		2		2		2		2	
1		1		1		1		1		1		1

If we changed two units of the 3's to 4's and likewise, two units of the 4's to 3's, this would happen:

				4	4	4	4	4	4		
3		3		3	3					3	3
	2		2		2		2		2		2
1		1		1		1		1		1	

which would look like this in profile:

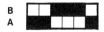

two units of A, three of B, and one of A. Totally different.

If the profile can change, then the design can change; and there we have the magic.

The only trouble is that these warp threads are threaded and therefore the dimension of the blocks cannot change. But "what would happen if" we could invent a way to change the action of those threads from behaving as pattern harness 3 and turning into pattern harness 4?

There have been innumerable articles about how to re-rig your loom in order to shaft switch—using everything from knots (which are guaranteed to drive you mad) to pins, which aren't much better, to paper clips. All are based on the principle of floating pattern threads which by some mechanism are attached and re-attached to the necessary heddle—either a 3 or a 4.

I have a friend who also said "What would happen if?". What if the warp threads were threaded through the heddles and the heddles floated? Thus was born the simplest, most ingenious shaft switching method and Crys Harse deserves the credit.

Here's her method. Take two heddles one size shorter than your loom uses. Attach them together through the loops on the bottom and on the top with 8/4 cotton. From the bottom loop of a pair attach and hang a 1 ounce lead fishing weight. Tie a cotton loop about 2" long to the top of the pair and pinch two lead sinker weights, one right close to the top of the pair of heddles, one right close to the end of a string loop. You will need one of these heddle combinations for every block unit in your design.

Now to the loom. Get a strip of wood (quarter-round works nicely) as long as your harness — so that it fits nicely on top of it. Measure it carefully at 1" intervals and nail ½" finishing nails *up* through the strip of wood. Attach the strip, with the nails pointing up, to harness 1, and another, *exactly* the same, to 1 and 2. (I'll explain why later!) These strips must not move or slip, so tape firmly. Clear these harness frames of conventionally attached heddles and hang your new ones *between* the two harnesses, slipping the loop with the shot at the end over the nails. Hang them all on one harness for easy warping. If you have a multi-harness loom place a harness frame in the first slot, leave the second empty and place the second harness frame in the third slot. The space between helps to prevent any tangling. Mount the appropriate number of heddles on harnesses 3 and 4 in the conventional manner.

Can you see what is going to happen? We will thread each unit as follows:

(3/4)   (3/4)

1   2

The numbers in brackets mean we would like those pattern threads to be either 3 or 4, that is block A or B, *black or white* as our pattern dictates — in other words, we want to be able to shift these shafts.

Let me clear up why I had you hang your new heddles on harnesses 1 and 2. Consider these two threading drafts:

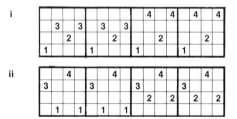

In (i) the pattern harnesses are 3 and 4 and the tie-downs (1 & 2) alternate. In (ii) the pattern harnesses are 1 and 2 and the tie-downs (3 & 4) alternate. It is the same draft re-arranged so that the pattern harnesses which have to be manipulated are closer to the weaver at the front of the loom. Obviously, if we have to manipulate our "portable" heddles, it is easier if they are on the harnesses closest to you. Thus, we use the reversed summer and winter threading draft.

As a result we have our new heddles arranged accordingly, hanging from the nails in the top of harness 1, suspended *between* frames 1 and 2. Harnesses 3 and 4 are strung normally. We thread as follows. Pass the first warp thread through harness 3, the second warp thread through the first heddle eye of our pair, hanging from harness 1, the third warp thread *between* the pair through the heddle eye of harness 4 and the last warp thread through the second heddle eye of the pair and so on across the warp where we add a 3 and a 4 tie-down to balance. Once threaded and tied, by simply switching the loop from the nail on harness 1 to the nail directly behind it on harness 2, the block changes from an A to a B block. It is quick and easy and accurate. It is also easy to read in that the position of lead weights on the nails corresponds exactly to the profile draft from which you are working. Remember to add the final 3,4 balance on the left selvedge so that both sides start with a tie-down thread.

In all other respects, a shaft switched rug is a summer and winter rug — a two-color bound weave. If you reposition the tie-down and pattern harnesses as above, the tie-up changes:

3 & 1	white
3 & 2	black
4 & 1	white
4 & 2	black

but the treadling order remains the same. Because you are no longer confined by the rules of block behavior discussed earlier, any design movement is possible. When designing on graph paper, I consider the black squares to be shaft-switched squares or B blocks. Remember not all the units in the rug need be shaft-switched. If you have border or striped areas which you do not intend to change, thread them through heddles strung normally on the front two harnesses.

Let's use the Maze rug shown opposite and on page 147 as an example and work through the process again. Consider that each graph square represents one block and at 4 e.p.i., a four end block is 1" wide. Thus, at each side there is a border, initially 4", wide which is not shaft switched. I find it better not to take the designs edge to edge because the draw-in — even 1" of draw-in — distorts a squared motif. This border is threaded normally. The shaft-switched heddles do not start until the fifth block.

40 39 38   36 35 34 33 32   30   28 27 26 25 24 23 22 21 20 19 18   16 15 14 13 12   10 9 8 7 6   4 3 2 1

Design for the shaft-switched portion of the Maze rug.

There is also a 4″ border at the top and bottom of the rug. In order to weave this border, I hang all the heddles on the first frame and weave the normal treadling sequence using two shuttles, caramel, white, because I want a white border on the front, but a caramel border on the back where the colors of the front of the rug will be reversed. Do remember that the rug is reversible so that any borders must be treated this way. It's easy to forget! Obviously, for the time being you will be raising an empty frame along with the rest—but that's all right.

Once the border is completed (keep track somewhere of the number of shots you needed to weave the border, because you won't remember at the top and they must be the same!) it is time to adjust the heddles. According to my design, calling the first solid square on the right, S/S block one, I move heddles 1 through 4, 6 through 10, 12 through 16, 18 through 28, 30, 32 through 36, 38 through 40 from the first harness frame to the second. These heddles will now behave as B blocks. Weaving with two colors, all the B blocks will appear caramel against a white ground. Weave whatever number of repetitions it takes to square these blocks (generally, from 4 to 6 depending on the yarn used), then switch again, following the pattern of the draft. Mark where you are carefully on your grid. If it is not possible to square the block and complete the four-treadle sequence, you can switch your block on the *third* treadle (4 and 1). Maintain your color sequence, however.

Shaft-switching done this way is absolutely painless and never boring as you move into the body of the rug, because there is always a change to be made—always something one can look forward to.

Shaft-switched rugs are like summer and winter rugs—essentially reversible two-color rugs. That does not mean that one cannot develop sophisticated color effects. It is possible, using bundles of weft as opposed to one five- or six-ply rug yarn, to shade the colors by controlling the mix of colors of the yarns used in each bundle. For example, the color could soften appreciably as you approach the design center of the rug, like a shaft of sunlight, then darken again as you approach the other border.

One can design a rug that moves from color pair to color pair. In simple terms one could:

Weave 4″ with A and B
　　　7″ with B and C
　　　11″ with C and D
　　　18″ with D and E,
all the while shifting the blocks to create a block design within the color changes. The weave is limitless in terms of block flexibility. Don't be limited unduly to weaving with two colors. This rug is 5′ × 7′; here's how it was woven.

Warp: 10/6 rug linen.
　　　Six e.p.i., four working e.p.i.
Weft: Three-ply medium rug yarn used four fold, white and caramel.
Threading: Summer and winter, shaft-switched. First four blocks are threaded:

```
    | 3 |   | 3 |
    |   | 2 |   |
| 1 |   |   |   |
```

40 blocks are threaded on portable heddles.
Last four blocks are threaded:

```
    | 3 |   | 3 |
    |   | 2 |   |
| 1 |   |   |   |
```

Balance 34 at end.
Treadling: Use two shuttles, one caramel, one white.
　　　Treadle　　13　　throughout
　　　　　　　　23
　　　　　　　　14
　　　　　　　　24
Finishing: Block and steam press. Damascus edge. Braided fringe. (See Appendix I)

Crackle Overshot

There is a third block rug technique which is rich in design possibilities, especially for those weavers with wider looms. It was developed in order to find a way to use the intricate patterning of four-block colonial overshot in a rug. I wanted to create a flat surfaced rug, without long floats and the need for a tabby binder, which at the same time, looked characteristically overshot. Weaving on opposites eliminated the problem of a binder, but more manipulation was needed to restructure the weave without distorting the pattern.

First, consider what other weave is similar to overshot in that it has four blocks and is twill based. The answer is crackle. Further analysis reveals that crackle is similar to the very useful

Some heddles were switched from one shaft to another after every weft block in this complex rug. It was woven as a commission, and the "maze" incorporates the initials of each member of the family for whom it was woven.
SETTING: TIMBERPEG HOMES, FORT COLLINS, COLORADO.

summer and winter weave. Crackle can be woven in a summer and winter texture, and under certain circumstances four summer and winter blocks can be woven on a crackle threading if they are treadled on opposites.

I'm skipping rapidly over endless draw-downs, but the delicious fact is that the combination weaves! In order to create a rug with an overshot motif without the floats, or a tabby binder, take a deep breath, and proceed as follows.

Step 1. Choose, or design, an appropriate draft. If you are creating an original, you now have four blocks to work with. If you are working with a colonial draft remember you have size limitations. An overshot block unit is two threads, whereas a crackle block has four plus the necessary incidentals. Your sett is 4, maximum 5 e.p.i., so you have to keep the motif small. Often, one section of a large pattern is useful, as shown in the rug woven here.

Consider the example of the "Patron de Couvre-pied" rug illustrated here. I wanted a rug for my kitchen that would measure 5' wide. At 5 e.p.i. that dimension gave me only 300 ends to work with. At four ends per block I have only 75 blocks to use — less when one considered there would have to be incidental threads included in the drafting. As a result, I was limited to choosing one motif that was part of an overall larger piece. To see the full design, refer to Davison's *A Handweaver's Source Book*, page 59. It will give you an idea of how you must limit your selection of traditional images because of the restrictions in the number of warp ends. The *Source Book* will provide an endless array of design ideas for this kind of rug.

Step 2. If you have chosen a colonial overshot pattern, derive the profile from the threading. This was my threading draft:

or, drafted as described earlier:

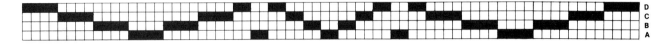

To review your block theory, now that we are dealing with four blocks instead of two, block A is on the graph line closest to you, block D is on the graph line farthest away. All of the wonderful patterns in the *Source Book* are drafted in numbers as above, in what Atwater describes as a "Southern" style. She suggests rewriting this style of notation before you go to the loom. The profile draft, I think gives you a clearer picture of your design. here is what my profile would look like expanded into the dimensions of my rug.

I should at this stage take a step back. It is easy to derive a profile draft from the *Source Book* because the drafts are given, however unusually, in blocks. It is necessary, for clarity only to substitute one form of block notation for another. Let us consider how one goes about deriving a profile from a conventional threading draft. Such was the process involved in weaving the smaller crackle overshot rug, "Whig Rose".

If your original draft is an overshot threading draft, as follows:

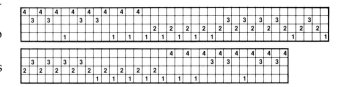

we have to work backwards — subtracting, so to speak, the threading units to derive the profile. The threading units for overshot are: A 1-2, B 2-3, C 3-4, D 4-1.

Return to the threading draft and circle all such combinations.

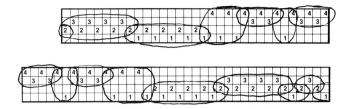

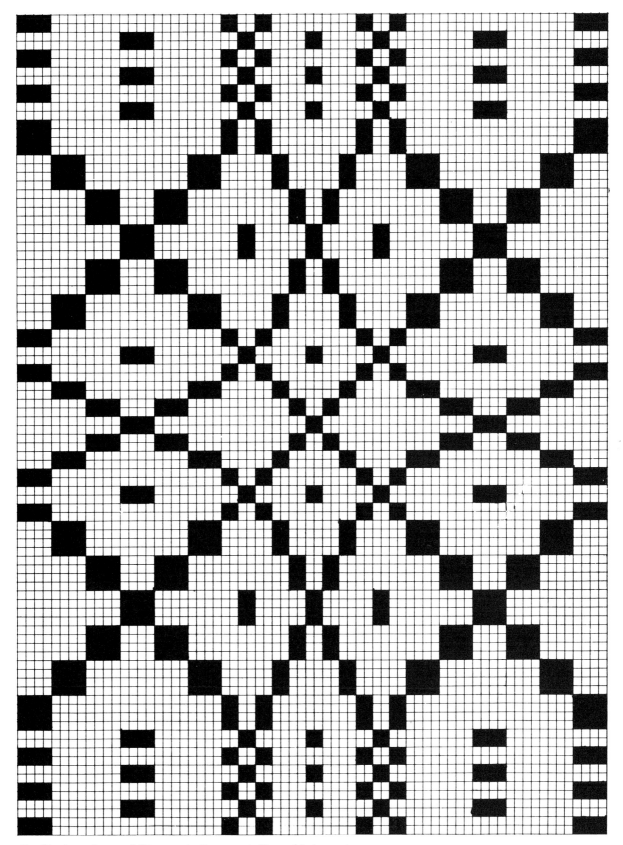

Profile drawdown of "Patron de Couvrepied" crackle/overshot rug.

Done correctly, you will notice that the blocks overlap, in that the first thread of one block is the last thread of the preceding block. Hence the name overshot!

At any rate, it is now easy to derive the profile design core. In this instance it would read:

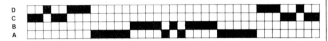

Step 3. Again, remember a profile is a design draft. We must now substitute the threading draft which will give us the texture we want. Redraft the profile to a *crackle threading*. In crackle, the substitution units are as follows:

Block A — 3 / 2 2 / 1

Block B — 4 / 3 3 / 2

Block C — 4 4 / 3 / 1

Block D — 4 / 2 / 1 1

You can see that each threading unit is a small point twill.

As you redraft, remember to maintain the even-odd sequence of the harnesses. This is often a problem where the blocks adjoin. Basically, balance the threading within each block and if necessary, add a warp end between two opposite blocks to maintain the sequence. If in doubt as to what "incidental" thread to add, *finish the point twill*. For example, below an "incidental" has been added between A & B to avoid two harness 2's from adjoining.

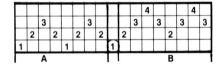

It is easier to deal with the crackle incidentals if you circle them as you go. It is sometimes necessary to add two incidentals at a time to maintain the odd-even sequence of harness.

It is also important to balance the threading from the mid-point of your profile. For this rug, I drafted from my middle block, working out to the right and then mirroring that development to the left.

Crackle overshot rug:
Patron de Couvrepied
Warp: 10/6 linen.

5 e.p.i. (I would have preferred 4 e.p.i. on an 8-dent reed, but that would have reduced the number of threads available to me.)

Weft: Singles handspun-style yarn in rust, used double, and Berber rug yarn used singly.

Threading: From right to left as follows:

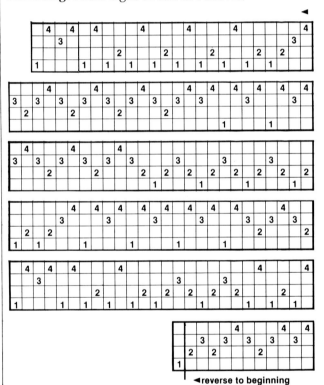

◄reverse to beginning

The strong, complex pattern of this rug clearly defines space in an interior. It is derived from the "Patron de Couverepied" draft in Davison's Handweaver's Source Book. SETTING: EARLE'S FLORIST, LOVELAND, COLORADO.

Step 4. Treadle your rug in in a summer and winter sequence, using two colors, thrown on opposites. These requirements result in the following treadling sequence for a jack loom:

To weave A black and C white (therefore B & D as half tones)

34	black
12	white
14	black
23	white

B black and D white

12	black
34	white
14	black
23	white

C black and A white

12	black
34	white
23	black
14	white

D black and B white

34	black
12	white
23	black
14	white

Throw your shuttles from opposite sides. Wrap one weft thread around the other as you weave to get a tidy selvedge.

The result is a rug which reproduces the overall design of the original overshot. The "gray" areas of the overshot become "pick and pick" halftones in the rug.

As always, it is not necessary to weave your rug in the traditional manner as drawn in. If you find the pick and pick areas discordant or distracting, play with your block treadling and introduce new colors as I suggested for the shaft-switch rugs. The blocks can be treadled as independent units in any order. We don't all have to be hide bound traditionalists! The drafting process may seem more time consuming or intimidating than our two-block summer and winter rugs, but the design sources are so rich in the colonial overshot patterns that it is well worth trying. Graph paper is cheap and this rug is a real challenge. It's a weave that deserves more attention.

The end — or is it?

These, then, are some suggestions for block weave rugs. Along with the recipes I've tried to give enough theory that you will feel encouraged to design on your own. The first thing is to forget being timid because of their scale. Rugs make you bold. Therein lies their satisfaction.

However, we aren't finished yet. Having designed and drafted, having warped with kid gloves and "tension", here are a few practical hints from experience. Most of you can add your own to my list. What great weavers we are cumulatively!

Leave a generous fringe when you knot at the front beam. Seven to 10" will be satisfactory. You will need this amount to prepare your fringe or edge. Start with a plain weave filler. I find it useful to throw four shots consecutively without beating, then beat them down all at once. It immediately draws the warp into place without inches of stuffing — useful when your warp has cost an arm and a leg. It will also immediately show you what areas need re-tightening because they will bubble. It simply must be perfect. Then weave a row or two of a contrasting color — at the end as well. When the rug comes off the loom the filler is discarded, but the contrasting holding weft should stay in place until you work your edge and then remove it only as you proceed along the edge.

To start the wefts in the rug, split the bundle — or the yarn — in half. Bring one half out between the warp ends 1" from the selvedge. Wrap the other twice around the outer warp and re-introduce it 3" into the shed. These can be sewn in later. When you run out of weft, again split the bundle (when working with four yarns I use each thread separately) or the ply and stagger out through several places in the warp. Re-introduce the new weft bundle, one ply at a time in the same warp spaces. Give yourself at least 6" to work with. Repair these ends as you go. I make it a point never to roll up without weaving in all the threads I have left. Using a blunt needle, sew them up at least 4" into the web. Always do this under tension.

If you want to warp more than one rug at a time, do so *but* cut each off as it is finished. Otherwise you will not be able to maintain your tension. Remember to add to your calculations the additional warp needed to tie on and fringe each rug. It's easy to forget this and leads to enormous frustration!

When weaving, throw the shuttles from opposite sides. Place the shuttle which carries the border color closest to you on the bench. If your bench isn't wide enough, place two small tables on either side of you. You'll be grateful to be able to place the large shuttles down in order as you adjust your yarns in the web. Thus it will always be in a position to wrap around the outside. The coverage isn't always perfect. Every few inches I clean "the selvedge coverage" by working and manipulating the loops with my blunt needle.

It is not possible to achieve a rhythm when weaving rugs with two shuttles — at least I can't. You must work carefully, and measure often to prevent drawing in. Throw the shuttle, then place the first 2" or 3" of weft where you want it by pushing it close to the fell with your fingers. Start the "hills and valleys" from this point. In other words, distribute the slack in the middle of the rug rather than the edges. Many ups and downs of the weft are better than one large loop. I run along the weft shot with my fingers spread in the spaces in the warp. I find "hills" of 3" to 4" and "valleys" about ½" from the fell the best. Then beat — with your body weight, not your elbows.

If you use a temple, the spikes would be placed between the argatch on either side and it should be moved every 2" — or as soon as you begin to draw in.

Keep a record as you weave. How many shots did you weave for the border? How many shots square the block? Mark off where you are on your design draft. What treadles were you using when you answered the phone? I've come to terms with the fact that I can't remember these details though I know I should and think I will. How many pounds of weft did you use — and of warp? Eventually, it's all handy reference material — when written down!

It is more satisfactory to resist even the most curious onlooker (yourself included) and not unwind your rug until you are done. You will never get it wound again exactly as it was — another good reason to write things down!

When the rug is finished and mended and checked and the edges done, you still aren't through. Most rugs will benefit from a thorough steaming. You may choose to have the rug steam pressed, or to do it yourself. Lay the rug on a clean surface — a nice piece of plywood is good, then nail or tack it to square. It will need a little push here and a pull there. Be sure your nails are *rust proof*. T-pins are, but ordinary thumb tacks aren't. Cover the surface with very wet (and colorfast) towels and cover the towels with an old sheet. Using a hot dry iron, press the whole thing firmly. Should I add — first make sure *your* yarns are colorfast? You may need to towel and press many times until the surface is satisfactory. Leave the towels on the surface until they dry. This gives a lovely finish to the surface of the rug.

Let me add — from bitter experience — that if you have country water be sure that its mineral content is such that when pressed it won't stain the surface of the rug. If your water has a high iron content, either don't weave a white rug *or* get a cleaner to steam press it for you. However, should such a disaster occur, the "weak tea" stains will come out by dry cleaning although the rug will soften. Take it to a good dry cleaner who will talk to you and appreciate the magnitude of your problem.

It is also possible to "felt" the surface of a rug with a linen warp should you wish to give the surface more substance. Submerge the rug in a tub of very hot, soapy water. Work it with your hands, (you should have to wear gloves), rinse in very cold water and block as above.

The choice of edge finishing must be taken very seriously. The warp forms the skeleton of the rug and it must be firmly and properly secured. Simple fringe knotting won't do. You must keep in mind three things when making your choice of finish. First, the nature of the warp itself. For example, is its color such that in a fringe or braided it will detract from the body of the rug? Or is the material such that it will fray, or unply if left loose? Second, whatever you do must be tough and tight and able to remain in place under wear. Third, it must relate in a design sense to the body of the rug. For example, I personally do not like a braided fringe. I think it interferes with the pleasing tightness and tidiness of a rug because the braids never lie straight or flat.

However, whatever the choice, there are two elements to consider. The edge finish should protect both the weft and the warp. First you must provide a firm edge to prevent the weft from sagging and then a firm finish to protect the warp from shifting and unravelling and from wear. Here are some guidelines.

Consider the scale of the fringe. How many warp ends do you have that would make a braid or fringe look skimpy? Is the warp coarse and dry so that the fringe would look too heavy or will it cause it to fray and ultimately disintegrate? The length of the fringe must be compatible with the size of the rug, and the thickness must not be greater than that of the rug or it will be more vulnerable to wear. The weft protector should be worked fairly tightly and evenly. Some warp fibers such as camel or goat hair do not hold a knot well,

The intricate patterning of crackle overshot is softened in this small rug by using tweedy yarns in close values.
SETTING: EARLE'S FLORIST, LOVELAND, COLORADO.

so the type of warp fiber must be taken into consideration when making a choice.

Essentially, the more complicated or successful the rug design is, the more discreet the edge technique should be.

The technique I find most useful is the Damascus edge (see Appendix I). This can be followed by braiding or knotting the fringe. If you choose to weave your warp threads back into the body of the rug, first work a full Damascus edge from right to left, then turn the rug backside up and work a Maori edge from left to right (Appendix I also).

That's it — a block weave rug designed, warped, woven and finished. It's obvious from all of this that block weave rugs can be more technically challenging and intricate than many techniques available, but to me therein lies the satisfaction of working with them. Happy Weaving.

APPENDIX I
Some Finishing Techniques

Overhand Knot

This is one of the simplest weft-protectors, but it has the disadvantages of lumpy knots and no protection for the warp ends. If you use it, be sure to cross the edge threads of each group over those of the next for a firmer edge. And keep your groups small.

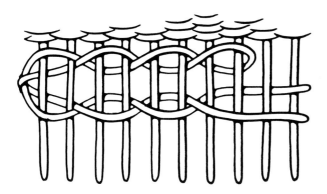

Twining

One or two (or more) rows of twining make an effective weft protector, and can be done on the loom. Twine around single warps or small groups. A twined edge is a good base for further finishing techniques.

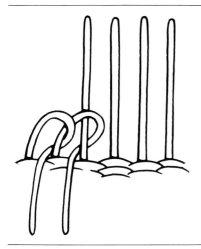

Half-Damascus

The Damascus edge is worked twice: across and back; or across, turn the rug over and across again. If you work only the first row, call it half-Damascus; it's a good foundation for other finishes.

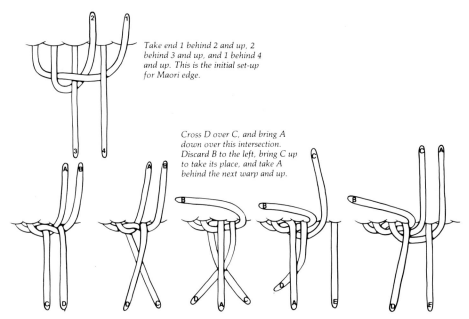

Take end 1 behind 2 and up, 2 behind 3 and up, and 1 behind 4 and up. This is the initial set-up for Maori edge.

Cross D over C, and bring A down over this intersection. Discard B to the left, bring C up to take its place, and take A behind the next warp and up.

Maori edge

This neat, firm, flat edge is used on Maori weft-twined fabrics. It is described and shown in more detail in Collingwood, from which this diagram is derived. Essentially, warp ends are plied together along the edge of the rug, old ones being dropped as new ones are added.

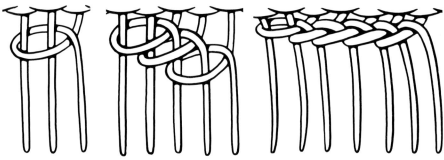

Philippine edge

This an easy and quick edge that makes a neat braided edge. You may elaborate it by working more than one row, either from side to side or by reversing the fabric in each row.

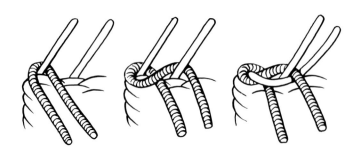

Four-strand sennit

Use a foundation yarn more than twice the width of your rug to work across, adding a new warp as you abandon the first one. Collingwood shows a variation in which each warp is used for four wraps instead of two, forming a firmer edge.

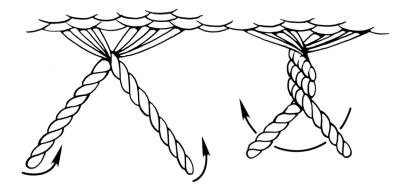

Plied fringe

This is a simple (though not quick!) fringe especially suitable for cotton warps. As all the fringes and braids shown here, it's best worked after a firm weft protector like a half-Damascus or Philippine edge. Extra threads can be added to each group if your warp seems too thin.

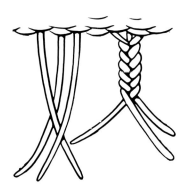

Three-strand braid

This is the ubiquitous braid of pigtail fame. It's easy to work, but tends to be less flat than the four-strand braid below.

Four-strand braid

This braid or sennit is worked by bringing the outside pair of a group of four across the inner two. The crossing pair must always cross in the same sequence (right over left *or* left over right) in order to form a flat braid.

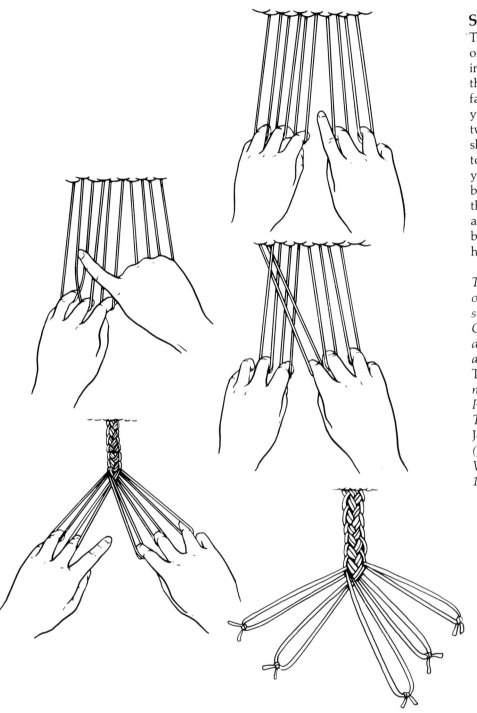

Slentre

There are many variations on this Scandinavian "walking fingers" braid, but this is the simplest. You must have fairly long fringes, which you knot in pairs and intertwine as shown. Worked as shown, the braid is flat on top and round on the back; you can work it from the back of the rug if you want the round side up, or work alternately from front and back, as Lynn Giles did in her rug on page 000.

These are only a very few of the documented finishes suitable for rugs. See Collingwood for a thorough discussion of many others; also Finishes in the Ethnic Tradition *(Suzanne Baizerman and Karen Searle, St. Paul, Minnesota: Los Tejedoras, 1978) and* Joinings, Edges and Trims *(Jean Wilson, New York: Van Nostrand Reinhold, 1983).*

APPENDIX II
A Cardwoven Selvedge for Weft-Faced Rugs

by Martha Stanley

This Appendix deals with some primary principles and specific how-to instructions for executing a card-woven selvedge for weft-faced rugs. Understanding the background principles isn't essential, but is helpful if one wants to experiment. There is a good deal of technical information here which may require more than one reading to comprehend.

The selvedge of any rug is subjected to more rigorous stress than the interior; the warp threads need to be strengthened here. The kneading action which can happen when a rug is walked on causes the warp and weft to move with respect to each other inside the rug structure, with resultant abrading of the softer of the two yarns by the harsher. Close sett, dense packing in of the weft, and non-slippery warp yarn generally minimize this phenomenon in rug weaving. But because the selvedge is more vulnerable, these additional two steps are often taken.

1. The warp threads at the selvedge are usually two-or-more-fold through the heddles.

2. These are usually spaced closer together in the reed. Consequently the weave structure is much denser at the edge and the weft is pretty well unable to move about on the selvedge warps. Because the edge of the rug is higher than the adjacent floor the weft there can wear more quickly when being walked on.

The Indians of the American Southwest introduced an alternate treatment of the selvedges in their work to help keep the weft immobile on the warp threads. Usually called the Navajo selvedge, it consists of two or three supplementary warp threads which twist around each other as they take turns being encompassed as final selvedge thread in the cloth. The thread(s) not being caught by the weft will float on the edge of the rug for a short distance before being caught again. This twining of the supplementary warp threads greatly diminishes the potential movement of the weft at the selvedge because the twining warps lock it in place with every twist. If this is not clear to you now, read on. As we delve further into the cardwoven selvedge it will become so.

About eight years ago I wanted to incorporate Navajo selvedge in a rug I was about to weave. One complication presented itself: the Navajos used a sword (or shedstick) to open the shed for the passage of the weft. The same tool is used to separate the twining warp

The material presented here first appeared in Weaver's Journal, *Summer, 1982, pp. 48-52.*

threads of the selvedge and to keep them lined up so that they can in turn be encompassed by the weft. The floor loom with its foot-treadled sheds begged for a solution which was suitable for its particular shedding system. Because cardweaving is a way of executing warp twining (and also maintains an open shed), it was selected as a technique to weave selvedges. You will need the following to try this:

- four 4-hole cardweaving cards;
- two 1" long "S" hooks;
- two weights of about 20-24 oz (570-680g) each (jugs with handles and filled with water are excellent); and
- a loom with a sample warp suitable for weft-faced weaving (sett of about 4-6 e.p.i. or 15-25/10cm); plain weave threading will be easiest to begin with. If possible your reed should be a 4-, 5-, 6- or 8-dent one; finer than 8-dent may present problems.

Weave in sticks (which I prefer) or rags to space out your warp evenly. Now measure off 16 separate strands, each about 2 yards (1.83m) long, of a plied weft yarn which has a lot of twist in it. This will be for your cardwoven selvedge warps. In this sample you may elect to use a yarn contrasting in color with the surface weft so that you can easily see and evaluate what you are doing. In a rug the edge is best done in the same color and yarn as the rug so that any irregularities are camouflaged until you have thoroughly mastered this.

You now have 16 strands and four cards, each with four holes. Thread each strand through one hole of one card. *But be sure the threads in the holes of one card are all threaded in the same direction;* that is, with the short ends on the same side of the card (see Photo 1). Two cards (eight threads) will be attached at each selvedge.

1. A threaded card.

Take the four short ends from one card and sley them from *behind* the reed through the dent adjacent to the regular outer selvedge warp thread. Sley the threads from the second card in the next dent. *All threads from one card must be in the same dent of the reed.* Now advance these warps far enough through the cards and reed so you can tie them to the front tie-on rod (*not the breast beam, please!*) immediately next to your regular warp selvedge.

Now go around to the side of the loom. On each side of the regular warp bring the eight warp threads through the shaft frames but *not* through heddles. The cards will float behind the reed (Photo 2). It will be easiest to manipulate the cards if you allow a 2" (50mm) wide space (free of empty heddles) on either side of the regular warp to accommodate the cardweaving warps and cards. If there are extra empty heddles on the loom beyond this, you may want to tie them out of the way.

2. *The cards for one selvedge attached and ready to weave. The top of the beater has been removed for clearer viewing.*

Take the cardweaving warp back over the back beam and comb the threads to even out tension irregularities. Tie the eight warp threads in a knot close to the end but at least 18" (46cm) off the ground. (I prefer to use a slip knot here, with the short ends stationary and the slippage occurring on the long end of the warp.) *Please note* that you neither tie them to the back beam nor beam them onto a warp beam. You are putting a warp-faced (twining) weave next to a weft-faced weave. Not only will the two weaves take up differently in the warp direction, but the twining will also build up twists behind the cards which need to be shaken out from time to time. Hence the preference for a slip knot which is easily untied.

Now, to tension the warp, take this dandy little "S" hook and put one end of the "S" through the loop of the slip knot, thread it through the handle of the bottle, and hook the other end of the "S" back around the warp just above the jug.

The cards at each edge should be positioned fairly close behind the beater; the closer the cards are to the weaving area the greater the shed depth. Naturally if they are in front of the reed they will interfere with the action of the beater. Both cards at one edge should be exactly next to each other, with their top and bottom edges parallel to the regular warp threads. Play with their positioning until you get all four top layer threads in one plane.

The cardwoven selvedge will be woven in a similar fashion to the traditional floating selvedge. Let me briefly explain how the latter works. The final regular selvedge warp unit is not threaded through a heddle but heads straight from the reed to the back beam. When the shed is open this floating selvedge bisects the center of it, blocking clear passage of the shuttle (see Figure 1).

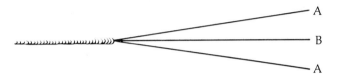

The shuttle enters the shed *over* this obstruction and exits *under* its counterpart at the other selvedge. It is this concept of the shuttle's passage consistently one way as it enters and in a different position with respect to the floating selvedge when it exits which will help you with what we are about to do. We might say that the cardwoven selvedge functions as a more intricate floating selvedge. Our rule is slightly trickier than the one I have just cited for the traditional floating selvedge.

In weaving the warp-faced cardwoven selvedge right next to a weft-faced cloth we are not able to change the shed of the cards as often as in the weft-faced area; there are far fewer picks per inch in warp-faced weaving than in weft-faced. Our cardwoven edge would become, at best, a ruffle if we attempted to change card sheds with every pick of weft. On the other hand if we simply throw the shuttle through the cardwoven shed every pick and don't turn the cards the weft will unweave itself in the cardwoven area just as it would if we threw the shuttle back and forth without changing the shed in regular weaving. The weft must have something to loop around at the edge to hold it in place.

Our solution is to alternate weaving a pick through the shed of the cards with a pick in which the shed is bypassed, thus looping around one layer of the card shed. That means that the shuttle will pass both above and below one layer of the cardweaving warps, *always* encompassing the threads which are in that layer and *always* ignoring the threads in the other layer, which then float. The card shed is changed approximately every quarter inch, so the threads all take turns being encompassed and floating and there is a pleasant angular twining stitch created on the edge by the floaters.

Proceed as follows: open the shed on your loom and

examine the relationship of the cardweaving (cw) shed to it. Often the cw shed is slightly out of alignment with respect to the regular warp so that passage of the shuttle both above and below one layer of the cw shed would be easier than above and below the other layer (Photo 3). Based on the relationship of the two open sheds (cw

3. The shuttle can clearly maneuver more readily both above and below the top layer of the cardwoven warp shed than the bottom layer.

and regular) you need to determine which cw layer will be easier to encompass, that is, easier for the shuttle to maneuver both above and below. Let us define the three possible places for the shuttle to pass with respect to the cw shed layers as over, through and under (see Figure 2). Once you have selected your layer, proceed to weave using the rule which seems most comfortable for encompassing that layer.

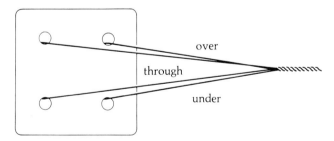

For the top layer:
1. Enter the shed with the shuttle in the *over* position and exit *through*, or
2. Enter the shed with the shuttle in the *through* position and exit *over.*

For the bottom layer:
3. Enter the shed with the shuttle in the *through* position and exit *under*, or
4. Enter the shed with the shuttle in the *under* position and exit *through*.

Photo 4 illustrates weaving with rule #1.

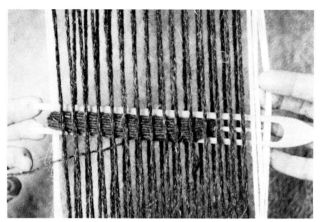

4. The shuttle entering the shed over the top layer of the cards and exiting through the card shed (rule 1).

Once a rule has been chosen, you will be using it *exclusively* with every weft pick of that project.

Don't forget to pull the weft taut at the edge so the cw selvedge is tightly against the regular warp.

When the fell of the cloth has advanced about a quarter inch you need to change the shed of the cards at both selvedges. After you have beaten in this last pick of weft leave the beater resting at the fell of the cloth. Lean over the beater and rotate the edge of the cards which is closest to you up to the top position (a 90° or quarter turn away from the cloth). All cards are turned the same amount after the same number of picks. After a bit of familiarity with this operation you'll be able to turn both selvedges at the same time.

To maintain a clear shed keep both cards of the same edge in exactly the same plane. Now put your fingers in the shed directly in front of the cards and bring the shed change forward to assure that the new shed is transferred through the reed. Return the beater to its resting position, and with your fingers transfer this shed change down to the fell of the cloth. This must be done with the fingers and is necessary only after turning the cards. Note that you will have to have woven four turns of the cards or 1″ of cloth before this edge twining looks like anything, since only then will you have completed one repeat.

As the shuttle manipulation is mastered you need to focus on fine tuning how often to turn the cards. Two factors are involved here. One is the amount of twist in the cw warp threads. Over-twist yarns will greatly enhance the appearance of the edge and also increase the durability during wear. Also, the more often the cards are turned (usually four to six times per inch), the handsomer the edge will be. Note that there is a fine line between turning the cards often enough and turning them too often. If turned too often the edge will flute slightly. Check for this by monitoring whether the fell of the cloth is straight across or slightly closer to the beater at the edges. (Too much weight on these warps might also cause a distortion at the edge.) Remember that for other projects the frequency with which you turn the cards may change because of different sett and weave, and different weight of weft, different weight of yarn for the cw selvedge warps.

You are guaranteed a rapid path to madness if you don't rely on mnemonic aids to help determine how often to turn the cards. For example, if you are doing plain weave with a single shuttle, turn the cards after an even number (2, 4, 6 . . .) of picks, or so that the shuttle is always at the same edge. Or if you are weaving a three-pick repeat as in Krokbragd, turn the cards after 3, 6 . . .picks.

The edge will be most durable and handsome if the cards are always turned at the same frequency and always in the same direction. Reversing the direction of turning the cards produces longer floats at the point of change; these are awkward. Reversals also compromise the durability which this edge treatment gives the selvedges.

As the weaving progresses twist (in the opposite direction to that occuring in the twining) builds up in the warp threads behind the cards at the same rate with which it is woven into the rug. This can become somewhat pesky after a bit. It exerts a certain torque on the cards and tends to create a twist which counteracts the opening of the shed of the cw warp and perhaps also causes tangling in the regular warp. Sometimes the cards will flip-flop over 180° so that the shed coming from them will become doubled (Figure 3). Straighten the

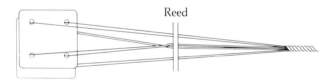

Reed

cards and shake out the accumulated twist before proceeding. It is probably a good idea to shake out this twist every 6"-12" (15-30cm) of weaving. This twist is in the opposite direction to that occurring in the twining and if allowed to accumulate too considerably will actually alter the spin of the cw warp threads. To shake out the twist untie the (slip) knot at the weighted end of the warp. Run your fingers *between* the groups of four threads emanating from each card to the end of the warp. These groups tend to counter-twist around each other, locking in the twists of the four threads. Once separated it is easy to untwist the threads of each card. Let each warp drop free of contact with its neighbors for a moment so that it may relax. This last is particularly important if the rug is a long one.

The layer of cw warps which floats comes from either the top or bottom shed of the cards. Consequently it is quite natural for those threads to float more toward the corresponding surface of the rug than right on the edge. If a rug is to be reversible it is quite annoying not to have it right on the edge. Two methods of attack may

be utilized to encourage its placement crisply on the edge.

The first and easier involves human persistence, and is easier to execute while you are learning this technique. Every time you turn the cards and beat down the new card shed, grasp the new shed of floating warp threads and pull them firmly to the opposite surface of the rug. Thus, for example, if the edge is creeping toward the underside of the rug's edge, hook your fingers around the lower layer of cw warps (which are the floating threads) and as you bring the new shed change down to the fell of the cloth pull these hooked threads up to the top surface. This will encourage the twined shed just completed to remain more on the edge. This method will help to rectify the problem but does not respond to the structural dynmaics at work here.

A better solution involves relating the twist of the floats to the layer of threads that is floating. Look closely at the twined stitches on the edge of the sample in Photo 5. The slant of the floats is down toward the

5. *A sample with about 1½" woven.*

underside in the direction of the cards. Note that the camera's view in the photo is with your eye nearly in the same horizontal plane as the cloth. You should view your own cardwoven selvedge at each edge from this angle to make the observation in Figure 4. The follow-

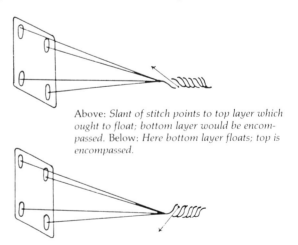

Above: *Slant of stitch points to top layer which ought to float; bottom layer would be encompassed.* Below: *Here bottom layer floats; top is encompassed.*

ing principle seems to wed the interacting components of this technique into a harmonious solution — right on the edge! *The slant of the floats ought to point toward the cardwoven shed layer which floats on the edge. The other layer is encompassed by the weft.* We may either change our rule to encompass the correct layer or we can flip the cards, reversing the slant of the stitch.

Flipping the cards involves rotating each card separately on its vertical axis. Let me elaborate. When you examine the cards on the tensioned warp threads you will note that the straight line of the warps causes the cards to angle slightly when viewed from above. This angle of the card represents the direction of slant the twined stitch will take in the cloth if the cards are turned *away* from the cloth when changing sheds. To change this from one angle to the other, that is to flip the card, hold the card near its top edge and increase the degree of the angle until it can no longer move freely (Figure 5). Now the card is angled in the opposite position and the stitch will slant in the opposite direction in the cloth.

When you first set up your cw selvedges on the loom for a project, examine the angle of each card and flip it if necessary so that all cards represent the angle of the twining you might desire. Having the two cards at one edge angled in opposite directions — or countered — will also help to keep the twining on the edge, but it is not always as handsome in appearance.

In a rug the cardwoven selvedge warp will need to be longer than the length of the regular warp. There will be some take-up in its weaving because it is warp-face. You want at least 2' (61cm) of warp length extending behind the cards to absorb the twist back there. You may also desire some extra at each end to be incorporated in any fringe treatment. Making your cw warps 2 yards (1.8m) longer than the length of your rug will meet all these criteria.

The number of cards at the edge depends on the thickness of the body of the rug and the thickness of the yarn used for the cw warps. You do not want this edge any more than slightly thicker than the body of the rug or it will be more vulnerable to wear. Two cards are generally easier to work with than just one at the edge. Three afford some design possibilities but might be too thick.

You will get durable results at the selvedges if your regular warp is strengthened by doubling in the following way. Assuming your regular warp threads are single through heddle and reed across the center of the rug, double them for the two warp units just prior to the cw selvedge. Then have a single strand encompassed with the cw selvedge (Figure 6).

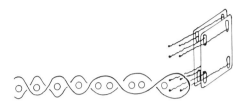

For those of you who know and love cardweaving there may be pleasure to see it utilized in this way. You may choose to push the cardwoven selvedge much further than I have by experimenting with others of the myriad of games cardweaving has suggested over the centuries.

After eight years of experimenting with a cardwoven selvedge on nearly every rug woven since I first used it, I think the edge's benefit can be stated thusly: well woven, with the twining occurring at the proper frequency, it becomes a sure deterrent to any movement of wefts on the selvedge warps. Its twining floats will provide a bit of further protection for the weft surface at the rug's edge. Additionally it can be — indeed, ought to be — an attractive and non-competitive decoration. Once mastered it is smoothly and speedily executed.

For some of the weaves in which a floating selvedge is recommended to produce a firm and reasonably satisfying edge, the cardwoven edge may produce more attractive results. With some of the pattern threadings, particularly double-faced weaves, its *visual* results are not as satisfactory as might be obtained in other ways. I have not experimented much with it for them, though, and would be interested in feedback on experimentation by others in this area. Most of my rug weaving for the past few years has been based on plain weave structures, where it is eminently appropriate.

The cardwoven selvedge is no "weaver's wonder drug". There is a fine line between its protecting the edge of a rug and its being so much thicker than the surface of the rug that it invites premature wear in that area. Its use should involve sensitivity and a critical eye for what it is and is not doing for you. Used carefully it offers structural strength and interest. Its visual appearance contributes an elegant, yet understated sense of finish to a rug; rather like a well chosen picture frame.

By no means is its use restricted to rugs. In fact it can become a far bolder and more decorative element where some of the rigorous restrictions of rug weaving do not apply. I hope this Appendix will encourage you to try the edge and join with me in a spirit of adventure as we further explore its potential.

APPENDIX III
Avoiding Draw-In
With a Bubbler

by Martha Stanley

The problem of draw-in in weaving, particularly weft faced weaving, is not always accurately understood. It is often presumed to be caused by pulling the weft too tight at the selvedge. Not only is this not accurate, it leads to solutions which make the rug's selvedge both loose and sloppy and quick to wear out.

In a weft faced weave, only the weft takes a meandering path in its interlacement with the warp. The warp moves straight through the cloth. The weft must traverse above and below each succeeding warp thread. Its path is thus a crooked one, and longer than simply the width of the weaving. If the weaver does not work in enough extra weft with each throw of the shuttle, the weft will exert pressure on *all* the warp threads to move closer together, narrowing the piece. Of course this phenomenon is apparent at the selvedges. But it actually is occurring across the entire cloth. To see this, bring your beater forward to within 1" of the fell of the cloth. You see the selvedge warps spaced at a different width at the fell of the cloth than in their dents in the reed. Obviously draw-in is occurring here at the selvedge. Now follow the line of warp threads in from the selvedge a few inches. Look at these warps where they emerge from their dents in the reed. When there is draw-in you will note that each warp is bearing hard on the inner edge of its dent; you may note a deflection or draw-in of these warps also. The symptom of draw-in is usually perceptible everywhere but the few inches in the very center. To correct it we must work in extra inches of weft evenly waved or bubbled clear across the fell of the cloth. There are many ways of executing this. One such method is using a "bubbler".

The bubbler in its simplest form is made from a dowel ⅝" (16mm) in diameter or thicker. My 60" (152cm) one is 1¼" (32mm) thick. It should be light weight but not flex as it performs its job. The bubbler must be as long as the width of the rug you will weave, and not longer than the width of the loom. Every 2" (50mm) in a straight line the length of the dowel, a ¹⁄₁₆" (1.6mm) hole is drilled, then a 1¼"-1½" (32-38mm) finishing nail is pounded in until the point penetrates the dowel but doesn't protrude from the other side. So much for the carpentry.

The bubbler is most efficiently located hanging loosely from the front side of the beater, but suspended high enough that the nails do not interfere with the pas-

sage of the shuttle in the open shed. A practical and simple way to attach it is with a chain of rubber bands larksheaded together with an overhand knot near the end of the last one. Put the small loop by the overhand knot over the bubbler, encompassing it and the final finishing nail at one end. Attach the other end of this rubber band chain to some convenient protrusion on the top at the end of your beater. Often a bolt and wing nut holding the top of the beater over the reed serve this function. Attach a similar length of elastic from the other end of the bubbler to the opposite end of the beater. You may have to add or subtract some rubber bands until the bubbler hangs high enough not to tangle in the shed, yet with enough elasticity to be pulled close to the fell of the cloth. You may prefer a heavier elastic if your dowel is thicker and longer. My large bubbler is attached with short bungee cords to cup hooks near the ends of my bubbler.

Now, to weave. Throw the shuttle from right to left. Grasp the final right hand warp with the right thumb and forefinger just above the weft and hold this warp so it won't move to the right. Now take the weft a few inches beyond the left selvedge with the left hand and tug firmly so that there is NO excess weft looped around the final right warp thread.

Maintain this tautness of the weft with the left hand, and with the right forefinger move to the center of the warp and bring up the weft to make a triangle.

Close the shed. Bring the bubbler down into the weft and pull forward toward the fell of the cloth so that it transforms the triangle into a series of uniform small 2" waves or bubbles. Don't bring the bubbler closer than ½"-1" to the cloth. Change to the opposite shed and beat in this pick of weft.

The height of the triangle, that is, the distance from the fell of the cloth to the peak of the triangle, determines the amount of extra weft length you are bubbling in. The correct amount varies with the coarseness of the weft, the coarseness and sett of the warp, and the weave structure. Plain weave would require more than a twill, for example. For any given project you will need to experiment for 2"-3" (50-75mm) of weaving to establish the correct amount. Once you determine this you will need to repeat accurately the same triangle size and shape with each pick. This size is a constant distance from the fell of the cloth, not from the beater. As you weave an inch or two closer to the beater, the peak of the triangle accordingly works its way toward the beater. In addition to making the right sized triangle, the bubbles need to be of uniform size across the cloth.

Learn to read the cloth; let its appearance tell you how you are progressing. Bring the beater forward and check to see there is no draw-in. The rug surface should appear smooth, even, sleek. Symptoms of some problems you may encounter:

• *Draw-in:* your triangle needs to be higher.

This article first appeared in the Summer, 1982 Weaver's Journal *under the title "Rug Weaving: How To Avoid Drawing-In of the Warp".*

- *Weft not covering warp:* 1) you are not bubbling enough; make the triangle higher. 2) Your warp sett may be too dense for 2″ (50mm) bubbles. I have found a 1″ (25mm) bubble does a better job on 8 e.p.i. (30/10cm) and so have added extra nails to one of my bubblers. 3) Your weft may be too coarse for the size space between warp threads. Use a finer weft or resley the warp somewhat further apart.
- *One selvedge fine, the other drawn in:* you are not making the triangle in the center of the warps. Consequently one side of the warp is getting more weft than the other. Glue a tape measure to the front vertical face of the beater's shuttle race. For each new warp locate the exact center of your warp and note the reading on the tape measure. Always make the point of the triangle between the appropriate warp threads.
- *Lumpiness or roughness on the surface of the cloth at 2″ intervals:* you are bringing the bubbler too close to the fell of the cloth. There is too much weft at these points and correspondingly too little by comparison in between. You may also be bubbling too much.
- *Bubbles not of uniform size:* 1)the nails may not be in a straight line. If so, try bending some to correct this. 2) Your triangle is not shaped properly; either "mesa-like" with no point at the top, giving larger bubbles toward the edges, smaller in the middle; or the sides of the triangle are almost concave, forming an "alp". The latter will give large bubbles in the center, small ones further out.

There is a limitation on how wide one can weave a rug making just one triangle to provide the necessary amount of extra weft. This limitation is best expressed as the width of the cloth compared to the depth of the weaving area. The beater can travel only so far toward the breast beam before it loses its effectiveness as a weft packer. With the fell of the cloth advanced close to this critical point on a wider rug you still might not have enough depth between the fell of the cloth and the beater to make a high enough triangle. You shall have to make two smaller triangles. (This occurs above about 36″ [91cm] width on my looms.) It is a bit trickier to make more than one triangle and keep the bubbles a uniform size across the cloth. Modify the spacing and shape of these two peaks and the valley between them until the bubbles are uniform. Refer to the tape measure on the beater to maintain the constancy of your solution.

At this point you may well ask "Why bother with the bubbler? Why not just make the triangle, change shed and beat?" If that works well for you, indeed, why not? My experience has been that to avoid draw-in and use one or several large triangles, I either had to weave in too much excess weft and the surface did not look as sleek, or I had to resort to a temple stretching the cloth out at the selvedges just below the fell. The latter must be advanced every inch or so and does not allow the weaver uninterrupted vision of the woven area. It is also difficult to use if the shuttle is not weaving selvedge to selvedge.

There are always both intimacy and distance existing between the weaver and the cloth being woven. Tools are introduced to make the work more efficient, easier. We must use these tools to help bridge the distance, to understand better what we are doing and improve our rapport with it. If after having tried the bubbler for a bit it does not function as a close ally, strike out for other solutions. It may not be your tool.

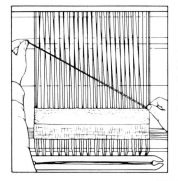

Hold the edge loop of your weft firmly against the last warp, and draw the weft taut in the shed at an angle.

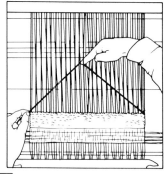

Hold the center peak of the weft as you draw the free end down to the fell.

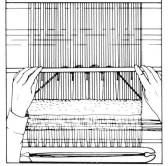

With closed shed, bring the bubbler forward to within 1″ or so of the fell.

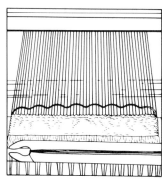

Change sheds before beating in the bubbled weft pick.

APPENDIX IV
Double Binding Technique

by Inga Krook

Threading

The double binding technique is a four-shaft block weave. The threading has a repeat of four threads: Block I – 3, 4, 3, 1 and Block II – 2, 1, 2, 4. These four threads are repeated as many times as the width of the block requires. When changing from one block to the next, the fourth thread is left out to make the border line between the blocks sharper. This leaves the tabby with a double thread in the same place, but it is of minor importance as the tabby is used only in the beginning and at the end.

Treadling

The tabby treadles are used only for the heading, either for a few wefts in the same material as the warp to "stop" the rag wefts (used in the rugs mostly), or for a wider hem also in the same material as the warp (in table mats, runners or similar). The tabby wefts should be woven very generously in little arches to prevent the weave from drawing in.

The treadles of the pattern, the double binding, are used in sequence: 1, 2, 3, 4, 1, 2, 3, 4, etc. Two colors of rags, single strips, are alternated. For example: for the first weft pick use a dark color; for the second, a light color. Continue to alternate the colors until the block is of desired height. Then change the order of the colors and begin with the light color, preferably on treadle 1 or 3 (but always following the treadling sequence), then the dark color and keep alternating. If the same height as width of a block is desired, weave the block a tiny bit higher to accommodate for shrinkage.

Weave with a good tension on the warp and beat hard so the blocks pack together properly. The weft should cover the underlying warp threads completely so the construction of the weave is hidden. If it is not, the weft strips are probably too wide or the beat is not hard enough. Be generous with the rags in each weft.

This appendix first appeared as part of an article by Inga in the May/June 1983 issue of Handwoven, *under the title "From Rags To Riches".*

A Selected Bibliography

Barrett, Clotilde. *Boundeweave*. Boulder, Colorado: Colorado Fiber Center, Inc., 1983.

Barrett, Clotilde. *Summer & Winter & Beyond*. Boulder, Colorado: Colorado Fiber Center, Inc., 1976.

Bevlin, Marjorie E. *Design Through Discovery*, second edition. New York: Holt, Reinhart and Winston, Inc., 1970.

Black, Mary E. *New Key to Weaving*. New York: Macmillan Publishing Co., 1957.

Collingwood, Peter. *The Techniques of Rug Weaving*. New York: Watson-Guptill, 1968.

Davison, M.P., ed. *A Handweaver's Source Book*. Chester, Pennsylvania: John Spencer, Inc., 1953.

De Sausmarez. *Basic Design: The dynamics of visual form*. New York: Van Nostrand Reinhold Company.

Evans, Helen Marie. *Man the Designer*. New York: Macmillan Publishing Company.

Frey, Berta. *Designing and Drafting For Handweavers*. New York: Macmillan Publishing Company, 1958.

Held, Shirley. *Weaving, A Handbook for Fiber Craftsmen*. New York: Holt, Reinhart and Winston, Inc., 1973.

Mattera, Joanne. *Rugweaving: Techniques for Two-Harness*. New York: Watson-Guptill, 1979.

Reed, Stanley. *Oriental Rugs and Carpets*. London: Octopus Books Limited, 1972.

Tidball, Harriet. *The Weaver's Book*. New York: Collier Books, 1976.

Tovey, John. *The Techniques of Weaving*. New York: Van Nostrand Reinhold, 1965.

The Weaver's Journal. Boulder, Colorado: Colorado Fiber Center, Inc., April 1977, October 1977, July 1978, January 1979, April 1980, Fall 1981.

Wilson, Jean. *The Pile Weaves*. New York: Charles Scribner's Sons, 1979.

Wong, Wucius. *Principles of Two-Dimensional Design*. New York: Van Nostrand Reinhold Co., 1972.

Page of *Two-Block Rug Designs* courtesy of Lyn Pflueger and Crys Harse.

Index